COUNTRY SOUL

COUNTRY
Soul

Making Music and Making Race

IN THE AMERICAN SOUTH

Charles L. Hughes

The University of North Carolina Press   Chapel Hill

4/27/19

To Dan,

Great to meet you in Madison,
an amazing weekend that I hope we'll
Continue to honor and build on in the
future!

All best,

This book was published with the assistance of the Fred W. Morrison Fund for Southern Studies of the University of North Carolina Press.

© 2015 The University of North Carolina Press
All rights reserved
Manufactured in the United States of America
Set in Miller by codeMantra, Inc.
The paper in this book meets the guidelines for permanence and durability of the Committee on Production Guidelines for Book Longevity of the Council on Library Resources. The University of North Carolina Press has been a member of the Green Press Initiative since 2003.

Cover photograph: © Bill Carrier, API Photographers Inc., The Stax Collection, Memphis

Library of Congress Cataloging-in-Publication Data
Hughes, Charles L., 1982–
Country soul : making music and making race in the American South / Charles L. Hughes.
pages cm
Includes bibliographical references and index.
ISBN 978-1-4696-2243-9 (cloth : alk. paper)
ISBN 978-1-4696-3342-8 (pbk.: alk. paper)
ISBN 978-1-4696-2244-6 (ebook)
1. Popular music—Alabama—Muscle Shoals—1961–1970—History and criticism.
2. Popular music—Tennessee—Memphis—1961–1970—History and criticism.
3. Popular music—Tennessee—Nashville—1961–1970—History and criticism.
4. Popular music—Alabama—Muscle Shoals—1971–1980—History and criticism.
5. Popular music—Tennessee—Memphis—1971–1980—History and criticism.
6. Popular music—Tennessee—Nashville—1971–1980—History and criticism.
7. Soul music—Alabama—Muscle Shoals—History and criticism. 8. Soul music—Tennessee—Memphis—History and criticism. 9. Country music—Tennessee—Nashville—History and criticism. 10. Popular music—Southern states—History and criticism. 11. Music and race—Southern states. I. Title.
ML3477.H84 2015
781.642089'00976—dc23
2014028957

For my mother,
LEE ANN HUGHES,
1948–1997

Contents

Illustrations

COUNTRY SOUL

INTRODUCTION

There's a Red-Neck in the Soul Band

In 1975 a black singer named Latimore released a single called "There's a Red-Neck in the Soul Band." Over a propulsive groove, Latimore tells the story of a visit to a "club in the ghetto" where a large audience of African American fans have gathered. Latimore's protagonist asks one clubgoer why the crowd is so big and receives a simple answer: "There's a red-neck in the soul band [and] he's gettin' down." When the protagonist finally gets inside the crowded club, he is surprised to see "a tall, skinny white boy" playing guitar with the otherwise all-black ensemble. Latimore adopts a twangy country accent when relating the white guitarist's words to the audience: "Every time I start to playing this ol' guitar, I get a funny feelin' and—by God—I start wonderin' about my own family tree." As the record fades, Latimore offers a simple moral to his story: "It makes no difference what color you are, when the spirit hits you, you've got to move!"[1] It was only a minor hit, but "There's a Red-Neck in the Soul Band" illuminates one of the most important chapters in U.S. cultural history.[2]

Latimore had good reason to think that listeners would understand the racial surprise at the core of his song. In the 1960s and 1970s, nothing symbolized the rift between white and black in the United States more than the musical genres of country and soul. Journalists and scholars presented country as the authentic voice of working-class whites and celebrated soul as the aesthetic and economic property of African Americans. Politicians and activists described country as the soundtrack of white conservative backlash to the civil rights and Black Power movements heralded by soul. Record labels, radio stations, and retailers used this language as a central part of their promotional strategies, tailoring country and soul releases to racially specific market segments. Listeners also embraced the dichotomy, and the supposed divide between the two genres became the basis for activism and even violent conflict from Mississippi to Vietnam. To this day, whether in the pages of political journalism or on the stages of *American Idol*, country and soul remain ubiquitous markers of racial difference.

Despite these perceptions, the two genres have shared roots. Not only did each draw from the same musical lineage, but they were intimately connected throughout the southern recording industry in this period. Country and soul records were made by the same people, recorded in the same places, and released by the same record companies. Indeed, even as the genres became opposites in the national consciousness, they were inextricably linked on the production level.

The key players in this process were the integrated cadre of studio players, songwriters, record producers, and executives who built the southern recording industry. This book tells their stories. It specifically explores the activities of musicians in Memphis and Nashville, Tennessee, and Muscle Shoals, Alabama, an interconnected recording economy that I term the "country-soul triangle."[3] In the 1960s and 1970s, the musicians who worked in this triangle produced a vast catalog of popular and acclaimed recordings that brought international renown to studios like Stax and FAME and made each city's signature "sound" a marker of quality and authenticity. The musicians won accolades from the national music industry, which heralded them as exemplars of professionalism and versatility, and from local leaders who championed them as crucial to their respective communities. Triangle musicians created hits for everyone from Bob Dylan to Bob Marley, but they were most identified with country, soul, and their musical hybrids. The styles and the people who created them traveled between the recording studios of Memphis, Muscle Shoals, and Nashville, making the region a center for this renaissance in U.S. popular culture. Backing up everyone from Aretha Franklin to Hank Williams Jr., the musicians of the country-soul triangle produced much of the period's most enduring and relevant music.[4]

They also became a favorite metaphor for the contested state of the South in this turbulent era. Politicians, writers, and the business community pointed to the triangle's commercial boom, cross-racial sound, and integrated studios as a sign of southern economic renaissance and social progress. But they also exploited the boundaries between country and soul by heralding them as oppositional expressions of racial authenticity and political purity. This seeming paradox defined a broader societal uncertainty about the continuing tension between interracial cooperation and racial division, which became the dominant debate in U.S. racial politics in the era of civil rights, Black Power, and white backlash. The relationship between country and soul was the South—and the United States—in microcosm.

The triangle's musicians stood at the center of this potent symbolism. They were the first to promote their recordings as symbols of integration by championing the interracialism of the "Memphis sound" or the transgressive potential of black country artists like Charley Pride and white soul singers like the Box Tops. Conversely, they capitalized on polarization by making and marketing records that appealed to a racially divided audience, whether that meant the Black Power soul of the Staple Singers or the backlash country of Merle Haggard. Throughout the 1960s and 1970s, triangle musicians both challenged and reinforced the racial perceptions surrounding their music and made little attempt to reconcile the contradiction. Maintaining that contradiction, in fact, was the most important part of their job.

Through their work, the musicians of the country-soul triangle became pivotal actors in the larger trajectory of U.S. racial politics in the twentieth century. Both literally and figuratively, they produced the cultural markers of race that defined this watershed moment and thus reshaped the ways people in the United States (and internationally) understood and articulated the supposed similarities and differences between white and black. "There's a Red-Neck in the Soul Band" is a singular encapsulation of how the musicians who created country and soul both reflected and directed the era's cultural narratives.

Soul's popularization in the 1960s and 1970s depended on the music's simultaneous promotion as the expression of both the ideals of integration and an assertively black identity. Triangle musicians promoted the soul music that emerged from southern studios as a symbol of interracial goodwill. At the same time, soul's importance to civil rights and Black Power activism and conceptions of modern blackness led the musicians to claim their work as a forceful demonstration of racial advancement.[5] This was particularly true in the second half of the 1960s, when "soul" became an accepted synonym (or even replacement) for the earlier "R&B" genre designation and a broader signifier for politicized blackness. Some nationalists dismissed soul music as the compromised commercialization of authentic black traditions, but a larger group claimed the genre as the apex of black culture's longer journey from cultural marginalization and economic appropriation to social acceptance and commercial prominence. To this day, "soul" remains an important keyword for discussions of historical and contemporary blackness as an aesthetic philosophy and sociopolitical identity.[6]

A large part of soul's cultural resonance in these years derived from its positioning in opposition to country.[7] Country music had long been considered a symbol of whiteness, but the association became particularly poignant in the late 1960s. This largely resulted from what Diane Pecknold describes as country's emergence as "a dominant metaphor for . . . the collapse of the New Deal order" and as the soundtrack for "New Right" conservatism, which took much of its language and constituency from the backlash to the civil rights movement.[8] But despite the powerful association between country music and white conservatism, triangle musicians demonstrated that the rhetoric around country was just as racially complicated as the one surrounding soul. As they asserted country as the voice of traditional southern whiteness, they also promoted it as the forward-thinking soundtrack of the modern South. Central to this assertion of country's progressivism was its overlaps with soul.[9] Even as artists and executives foregrounded the music's race-specific appeal, they used soul sounds—even disco—and personnel to suggest that country was the culturally progressive soundtrack for a reinvigorated "New South." Musicians, politicians, writers, and many fans continue to use country music and the concept of "country" to denote a brand of white southernness that toggles between tradition and redefinition.[10]

The musicians of the country-soul triangle played a complex and significant role in the rise of country and soul as musical genres and cultural symbols, but—despite their centrality—no scholar has fully analyzed their experiences. Most discussions of the relationship between black and white musicians in the 1960s and 1970s South have focused on soul music and presented integrated soul studios as an analogy for the national civil rights movement. Numerous writers—most influentially Peter Guralnick, in his compelling 1986 book *Sweet Soul Music*—have celebrated these studios as embodiments of what Guralnick calls a "Southern dream of freedom" that paralleled the national push for integration and countered the region's ugly legacy of white supremacy.[11] According to Guralnick and his followers, the harmony ended in the late 1960s when the rise of Black Power and the assassination of Martin Luther King Jr. in Memphis intruded on the studios and destroyed the earlier spirit of cooperation, just as those events ruptured the interracialism of the early civil rights movement. This led to the commercial and cultural decline of southern soul, which was finally destroyed by the rise of disco and other northern-associated forms in the late 1970s.

This story is usually buttressed by two connected assertions. The first is that southern soul helped redeem the white South from its racist past. Barney Hoskyns claims that southern soul "turned young whites against their own backgrounds of bigotry and prejudice," and white musicians like Steve Cropper and Dan Penn have become the most commonly cited embodiments of the "Southern dream of freedom."[12] (Guralnick even calls Dan Penn "the secret hero" of the southern soul story.)[13] The second is that southern studios were a transcendent space in which racial conflict or even identity did not exist, what Vron Ware and Les Back call "a kind of innocent non-racialized world [that] was lived and realized in sound."[14] The musical hybrids produced in these studios—which Brian Ward provocatively calls "mulatto" music—affirm their status as prophetic sites of interracial collaboration in an otherwise hostile environment.[15] At least, that is, until everything supposedly collapsed in the late 1960s.

This narrative remains the standard interpretation of integrated southern music and has become a crucial element to larger appreciations of the South in the 1960s and 1970s. Unfortunately, it is both inaccurate and misleading. Interracial ensembles continued to have great success in the country-soul triangle through the 1970s, and some studios—like Stax, FAME, and Muscle Shoals Sound—had their greatest success after 1968. Additionally, while southern soul declined in popularity by the end of the 1970s, it never disappeared. Finally, this narrative pays little attention to the complex role that country music and the Nashville recording industry played in this history, despite the fact that triangle soul musicians—both black and white—played a crucial part in developing country's sound and significance in the 1960s and 1970s.

These deficiencies are closely linked to a more troubling problem: the "Southern dream of freedom" fundamentally misrepresents how race worked in the country-soul triangle. Despite the utopian claims, African American musicians consistently objected to mistreatment from whites and worked to equalize the racial dynamics of southern studios from the very beginning. It was never an "innocent non-racialized world," at least not for the black musicians. This fiction is made more harmful by the fact that it implicitly credits whites with the racial breakthrough and blames African Americans for destroying the integrated magic. White players are congratulated for having the courage and vision to play soul music with black people, while African Americans get scolded for abandoning these sympathetic whites in favor of divisive racialist politics. A full examination of the country-soul triangle reveals a richer and more complicated story.[16]

Such an examination requires a new approach, so I analyze triangle musicians as workers and their studios as working environments. I choose this labor-based analysis—still relatively uncommon in studies of popular music and essentially unprecedented in studies of country and soul—because it significantly demystifies a story that has been routinely romanticized.[17] Many writers describe triangle musicians as vessels for authentic racial identity and the "Southern dream of freedom," but the musicians defined themselves as versatile professionals whose extensive training and hard work allowed them to play a wide variety of music, and to work across racial lines. They were craftspeople, not conduits; or, as Elijah Wald describes early blues performers, "pros, not primitives."[18] Over their careers, the triangle's musicians literally and figuratively "performed" whatever music and racial symbolism were economically and politically advantageous at the moment.[19]

Contrary to ill-fitting civil rights movement analogies, the experience of race in the country-soul triangle was inextricably linked to the work of making records. Labor historians have shown how other types of integrated workplaces possess a site-specific set of racial expectations and opportunities that do not necessarily correspond to broader societal codes or political trends. Writing of an integrated auto plant, for example, Kevin Boyle describes a "volatile mix" of "social groups battling over the boundaries of proper behavior" and "individual workers [carving] out places for themselves." These contests led to "negotiations" that "overlapped, crisscrossed, and collided" and produced moments of both collaboration and conflict.[20] The recording studios of the country-soul triangle exhibited just such complexity, and exploring them through this lens helps release them from the limitations of the traditional civil rights narrative.[21]

At the same time, though, triangle studios differed from most other integrated workplaces in one key respect. They were interracial work environments that helped produce the era's racial divide. Country and soul became internationally recognized shorthand for the distance between white and black, so the "negotiations" between the white and black musicians who made them offer a crucial addition to our understanding of integrated laboring in the United States. This work follows the example of "There's a Red-Neck in the Soul Band," in which Latimore explores the complexities of racial identity in the United States by telling a story about musicians at work.

Perhaps the most important benefit of a labor-based approach is that it illustrates that the racial partnership at the heart of the country-soul triangle was fundamentally unequal. There is an assumption in much of the scholarship on the 1960s and 1970s that the integration of southern studios was synonymous with racial equality, or even that the fact that black and white musicians worked together in the South must have meant that racial divisions did not exist in musical spaces. Still, as Brian Ward notes, "power relationships within the recording and broadcasting industries in the South were still defined along essentially racial lines."[22] The triangle's musicians understood that records could be made in an interracial context and still represent a society that was separate and unequal.[23]

It had been this way since the beginning of the U.S. recording business in the early 1900s, when—as Karl Hagstrom Miller describes—industry leaders created and policed a "musical color line." This "musical color line" paralleled the rise of Jim Crow segregation and established a "firm correlation between racialized music and racialized bodies" that structured the subsequent recording industry.[24] During this period white southerners were labeled "hillbilly" or "old-time" regardless of their musical influences, while black southerners of all stylistic stripes got clumped together under the category of "race music." Country and soul were the direct descendants of those two genres, and they became the latest chapter in a commercial environment where—as Miller puts it—"black people performed black music and white people performed white music."[25] Triangle musicians, even (or perhaps particularly) those who worked in integrated studios and pursued musical crossover, structured their work around their recognition of this "musical color line."

Of course, it was far easier to transcend the "musical color line" if you were white. In the 1960s and 1970s, as in earlier eras, white musicians had greater opportunities to move into black-identified styles like soul than their African American colleagues did with white-identified genres, especially country. Additionally, even though they defied segregation in important ways, some black musicians in Memphis, Muscle Shoals, and Nashville questioned or even resisted the entry of whites into black-identified musical spaces. African Americans did not have the same access to white-controlled environments; and, even in nominally "black" musical spaces, they often lost professional opportunities to their white counterparts. This disparity fueled the racial tensions that existed throughout southern studios. Indeed, the apparent interracialism of the country-soul triangle became an ironic illustration of racial privilege.

This privilege ultimately defined the triangle's larger historical trajectory. By the 1970s, musicians in Memphis, Muscle Shoals, and Nashville used soul music to enrich—both creatively and financially—white people, white-owned businesses, and white-identified genres. Nashville musicians incorporated soul into country as a means of maintaining relevance and expanding profitability. And, although the "Memphis sound" and "Muscle Shoals sound" had roots with black artists, white performers became increasingly important sources of revenue and notoriety for studios in the two cities. As Muscle Shoals producer Rick Hall said, the triangle's musicians became famous for "[taking] the white music, and [making] it sound black," and an astonishing number of white performers came to the area to add some soul to their recordings.[26] This process provoked controversies over racial appropriation and accompanied a larger departure of black performers from triangle studios. Ultimately, this transition provoked the decline in southern soul as much as the popularization of disco and had a far greater effect than the rise of Black Power.

The marginalization of African American musicians has been reiterated in much of the historical appreciation of Memphis, Muscle Shoals, and Nashville in the 1960s and 1970s. Particularly in post-Guralnick discussions of integrated southern soul, but also in much of the country literature, the focus has been on white musicians. This has rendered many of their black colleagues passive or secondary participants in the broader story of musical innovation and cultural progress. Whites like Steve Cropper, Rick Hall, Willie Nelson, Dan Penn, and others (almost always male) are credited with developing innovative musical blends that demonstrated their racial open-mindedness and thus ultimately helped to liberate the South and nation. On the flipside, black southerners are mischaracterized as the authentic voices who helped whites to become better people in the 1960s and then conveniently faded into the background by the end of the next decade.

Latimore's "There's a Red-Neck in the Soul Band" again provides a perfect encapsulation. In the late 1970s, country musicians used the sounds and symbols of soul music to achieve unprecedented levels of national success while soul artists like Latimore faced a shrinking audience and a growing association with the past. And, just as the black band offers the white guitarist a shot at liberation in the song, the complexity of the larger history has been rewritten as a story of white accomplishment through black assistance. Latimore presents his story as a celebratory moment of musical integration, but it actually reflects the racial ambivalence that lay at the core of the country-soul triangle.

I centralize this ambivalence throughout this work. I begin in chapter 1 by tracing the triangle's development through the experiences of Arthur Alexander, a black singer-songwriter who launched the Muscle Shoals recording scene and became one of the earliest southern soul stars.

Alexander and the white musicians at FAME—most notably producer and studio owner Rick Hall—understood that their success required them to literally perform a racial contradiction. They created a cross-racial blend of styles that reflected the many sounds they learned from years of listening and live performance, but they also understood that these genres—particularly country and soul—remained separated by the "musical color line" that structured the South's recording industry. In other words, Alexander and the FAME musicians made records that appealed to a diverse audience but marketed them in ways that affirmed the ideology of racial division. Additionally, though they were integrated in the studio, Alexander faced racial discrimination both in Muscle Shoals and later in Nashville, while Rick Hall and the white musicians at FAME used their success with Alexander to attract other black artists to Muscle Shoals. The creation and consequences of Arthur Alexander's "You Better Move On" offer a potent crystallization of the country-soul triangle's central dynamics.

Southern soul owed much of its popularity to the mid-1960s emergence of the "Memphis sound," a phenomenon that I discuss in chapter 2. From the beginning, the Memphis sound was a seeming incongruity. Writers and fans heralded it as the era's "blackest" pop music even as they also credited it to the interracial mix of black and white musicians (and of country and soul) in Memphis and other southern cities. By the end of the decade, the Memphis sound became an internationally recognized symbol of racial progress and reconciliation. In fact, despite its black roots, the larger appreciation of the Memphis sound as both sound and ideology was increasingly framed around its redemptive effect on white people. This erasure of African Americans paralleled a broader distortion in which southern recording studios became known as colorless utopias that were free from racial conflict. This notion remains central to the historical presentation of southern soul and denies a more complex history that can only be revealed by understanding how the Memphis sound developed as both music and mythology.[27]

Many of the deeper racial tensions obscured by the idea of the Memphis sound came to a boil in the late 1960s, when southern soul became both a symbol and an instrument of the Black Power movement. Chapter 3 charts this process, focusing specifically on the activities of Stax Records in Memphis. During this period, Stax—under the leadership of new chairman Al Bell—amplified the musical and lyrical "blackness" of its recordings, used nationalist rhetoric in its advertisements and public statements, and allied with African American political organizations in order to force the issue of racial disparity in the music business. This led to substantive changes in the label's musical approach and internal hierarchy. It also angered some of the label's white staff members and challenged Stax's long-standing image as a site of integration. Even as they promoted Black Power, though, Bell and others at Stax never abandoned the integrationist discourse of the Memphis sound, nor did they stop using white musicians. In fact, under Bell's leadership, many of Stax's biggest sessions took place with an all-white band in Muscle Shoals. The story of Stax Records in these years reveals the multifaceted role of Black Power politics in soul music, the country-soul triangle, and the U.S. recording industry.

Black Power had a similarly complex effect on Muscle Shoals, a story that I take up in chapter 4. After a decade of successes that began with Arthur Alexander, the late 1960s saw an explosion in soul recordings at both of the city's major studios, FAME and the newly opened Muscle Shoals Sound. The name of the latter studio coincided with the development of a "Muscle Shoals sound" as a corollary to its famed Memphis counterpart. The Muscle Shoals sound was similarly based on the ostensible enigma of authentically black soul recordings made by an integrated workforce. In the contentious Black Power years, the Muscle Shoals sound allowed white musicians in Muscle Shoals to assert their legitimacy within (and control of) the area's soul scene. This not only structured their relationships with the numerous labels—including Atlantic, Capitol, and Stax— that sent black artists to record in Muscle Shoals in these years but also attracted a growing number of white pop, rock, and country artists, who came to FAME and Muscle Shoals Sound to make soul-influenced records. The most notable and infamous example of this is the white pop group the Osmonds, who recorded their controversial smash "One Bad Apple" at FAME in 1971. By the mid-1970s, the primary beneficiaries of the Shoals' soulful style were white.

As soul became the soundtrack of Black Power, a related phenomenon took place in country music. In chapter 5, I examine the tight association between country and the racial backlash of the New Right. The Nashville-based industry allied with conservative politicians and causes in the hopes of making their music the soundtrack to the post–civil rights backlash that propelled Richard Nixon to the White House in 1968 and transformed U.S. politics. At the same time, Nashville's musicians continued using black-identified sounds and (occasionally) black personnel to craft their increasingly white-associated music. This tension played out vividly in the career of African American country superstar Charley Pride. Country's establishment as an expression of white identity took place in explicit opposition to soul's reputation as the voice of assertive blackness, which created a series of fascinating juxtapositions from the studios of Nashville and Muscle Shoals to the battlefields of Vietnam. These juxtapositions and their consequences form the basis of my analysis.

Country's association with racial backlash provoked a significant reaction among some white musicians and audience members. In chapter 6, I explore the development of three insurgent genres—"swamp music," "Outlaw country," and "southern rock"—that asserted their racial tolerance and cultural progressivism as an explicit alternative to country's conservatism and racial exclusivity. All three genres took creative inspiration (and sometimes had literal origins) in the studios of the country-soul triangle, and their artists foregrounded their love of soul music as part of their larger critique of the restrictions of Nashville. They became symbols of a musical New South renaissance that accompanied an economic boom and political resurgence. Still, the artists and audiences for the new southern genres were no more integrated than those of mainstream country; increasingly, the musical demonstration of post–civil rights southern progress had a white face. This had dual effects on African American musicians in the country-soul triangle: it resulted in a further loss of employment opportunities and framed their work as the nostalgic voice of the past. By the end of the 1970s, southern soul lost its cultural and economic cachet even as country stood at a period of unprecedented crossover. This moment is the topic of the final chapter.

As the Reagan era dawned, country and soul remained creatively and commercially connected throughout the triangle even as they diverged in cultural meaning in the larger United States. Chapter 7 completes the story. Country interpolated disco, the newest sound in black-identified music, to affirm the genre as the soundtrack of the modern South and changing nation. Southern soul, meanwhile, ended the decade as a primarily regional and heavily nostalgic music, with the visionary politics of the late 1960s and early 1970s replaced by a backward-looking focus on cultural tradition. Facing commercial decline and cultural irrelevance in the wake of disco, soul musicians turned to the past, celebrating—in the words of the period's most popular southern soul song—the "Down Home Blues" of the black South's roots. Many of these recordings (including "Down Home Blues") were produced at Malaco Records, a Mississippi-based label that recruited many triangle soul veterans to join its personnel and marketed itself as the "last soul company." These diverging paths signaled broader shifts in southern lives and livelihoods in the 1980s, reflected changes in the cultural positions of black and white southerners, and demonstrated the continuing importance of the country-soul triangle in the U.S. cultural landscape. It thus offers a fitting place to close.

In "There's a Red-Neck in the Soul Band," Latimore and his collaborators needed just five minutes to illuminate this rich and complicated history. Unfortunately, I am neither as precise nor as concise, so it will take me a few hundred pages. To make matters worse, you surely cannot dance to mine. Despite these flaws, I hope the reader will bear with me.

One

WE ONLY HAD THIS ONE THING IN

COMMON: WE LIKED ALL TYPES OF MUSIC

The Birth of the Country-Soul Triangle

Arthur Alexander loved country music. So when he stepped up to the microphone in a fledgling recording studio in Muscle Shoals, Alabama, in 1961 to record his composition "You Better Move On," it made sense that the young singer brought a noticeable country flavor to his performance. He delivered the aching lyrics with a graceful and resonant twang that was complemented perfectly by the tasteful accompaniment of the young studio musicians who backed him. Along with the country influence, Alexander incorporated the current sounds coming from R&B, bringing the stately phrasing and subtly Latin rhythms of that era's black pop artists into seamless dialogue with his more countrified influences. The studio players were awed by Alexander's marriage of the two genres, as was Rick Hall, the session's producer and owner of the small studio that bore the audacious name of FAME. Hall saw Alexander as a potential hit artist, and not just because of his prodigious talent and unique sound. Arthur Alexander was the first African American to work in the studio.

Hall and the white musicians at FAME saw Alexander's blackness as a significant opportunity. For one thing, they were excited by the fact that after years of being influenced by black singers on radio and records, they would finally get to work with an actual African American. (The fact that he shared their broad tastes, incorporating country and pop sounds into his music, made him all the more interesting.) But they also recognized the commercial possibility represented by Alexander's race. Hall and the FAME musicians believed that the singer's hybrid sound and dark skin might simultaneously break him on the pop charts and resonate with the R&B audience that FAME's all-white roster had not been able to access. Of course, they also knew that his blackness would make country stardom almost impossible, but they hoped that his country-influenced songwriting might win the favor of Nashville executives and lead to a profitable series of covers by (white) country artists. Their hopes were confirmed upon the record's release. "You Better Move On" reached the pop Top 25, launching the Muscle Shoals recording scene and making Alexander into a prototype for the southern R&B and soul stars of the 1960s.

The creation of "You Better Move On" appears to affirm the historical presentation of southern soul as a space of interracial collaboration. Alexander's work with the white musicians at FAME Studios demonstrates the cross-racial blending of music and personnel that has led many to use southern soul as a triumphant example of black-white collaboration in the 1960s. The record has frequently been cited as a key example of the way that the South's recording studios became an oasis of friendship in the turbulent civil rights era. Alexander's biographer, Richard Younger, even suggests that "if skin color was an issue on the streets, it never came into play" during Alexander's work in Muscle Shoals.[1] At the core of these presentations is the record's seamless musical blend of country and R&B.

But the hybrid sound of "You Better Move On" actually reveals that skin color was the *central* issue for Arthur Alexander and his colleagues at FAME. Even as the musicians synthesized country and R&B on record, the making and marketing of "You Better Move On" also reinforced these genres' importance to what Karl Hagstrom Miller calls "the musical color line." Developed in the early 1900s, this division erected both economic and ideological barriers between racially identified genres like country and R&B. Not only did black and white musicians work in separate and unequal music economies, but their music was presented as racially exclusive even when its origins or sound troubled that essentialism. The success of this musical color line in establishing the contours for the southern recording industry meant that country and R&B were ubiquitous icons of racial difference by the 1950s. Then, in the middle of that decade, the simultaneous rise of the civil rights movement and racially hybrid rock 'n' roll made the relationship between country and R&B into both metaphor and battleground for the nation's racial politics. With "You Better Move On," Alexander and his FAME colleagues entered this conversation.

They were prepared for this critical role by the balancing act they performed on a daily basis as working musicians. They demonstrated the fallacy of racially exclusive musical genres in their playing even as they marketed their recordings in a manner that confirmed their separation. And even as they worked interracially, Alexander's interactions with his white colleagues displayed many of the same inequities that characterized the rest of U.S. society. He played an uncomfortable role as the literal and figurative embodiment of blackness for the white musicians in Muscle Shoals, and his career stalled in the aftermath of "You Better Move On" in large part because he was unable to overcome the limitations of the "musical color line." Meanwhile, Rick Hall used Alexander's success to promote FAME Studios and its musicians as an integrated and country-influenced source of black R&B. Hall got rich while Alexander was left marginalized.

The racial complexity at the core of "You Better Move On" established the template for recording in Muscle Shoals and predicted the larger history of the country-soul triangle. In the coming years, the triangle's musicians mapped out the shared and divergent spaces between country and R&B (and later soul), negotiating the abstract politics of racialized sound and the tangible politics of a racialized workspace and marketplace. This forced them to engage the contradictions and manipulate the contours of the interracial spaces shared by black and white music and musicians. The story of "You Better Move On" illuminates the ways they succeeded and failed.

Like their counterparts throughout the country-soul triangle, Arthur Alexander, Rick Hall, and the FAME musicians were born into a world where southern music symbolized the nation's larger racial divisions. As they matured, they witnessed and ultimately contributed to a series of changes in musical practice that forever altered the U.S. cultural landscape and provoked a vast expansion in the southern recording industry. In the mid-twentieth century, the expansion of radio and records transformed the way individuals in the South and elsewhere heard, bought, and made music. These transformations revolved around the relationship between racially identified musical genres, and they established the ideological and practical foundations for the country-soul triangle.

The person who provoked the first transformation is not a musician or writer but President Franklin D. Roosevelt. In the early 1930s, the Roosevelt administration chose the Muscle Shoals area—specifically the hydroelectric plant at the Wilson Dam—as a major site for the ambitious Rural Electrification Administration (REA), through which it hoped to bring electric power to the 90 percent of rural Americans (many living in the South) who had none as of 1930.[2] Resources poured into the region, and its population increased significantly. One new resident was Arthur

Alexander's father, who moved to the Shoals in 1935 to work for the Tennessee Valley Authority (TVA), a hydroelectric project that became a primary REA engine. His son Arthur was born five years later, one of several TVA children who became contributors to the city's recording scene.[3]

But rural electrification's influence on Muscle Shoals music went far deeper than the employment provided by the TVA. In the 1930s and 1940s, the REA was a key part of a massive expansion of radio listenership throughout the southern United States. This led to new work for southern musicians and affirmed the importance of southern-identified genres like country and R&B on the national soundscape. In the 1930s and 1940s, a growing body of listeners heard an expanding variety of musical programming that simultaneously defied the supposed separations between musical categories, including "black" versus "white," and also reinforced them.[4]

Many in the national radio industry assumed that southern listeners like Arthur Alexander, Rick Hall, and their families would want to hear programs tailored to them, so they rushed to create programs that spotlighted the South. The primary beneficiaries were what were then called "hillbilly" and "race music," which had earlier been the twin catalysts of a record boom in the 1920s and now stood at the center of a second revolution in music consumption. Hillbilly—later renamed "country" in an effort to distance the genre from its culturally derided roots and identify it more broadly with rural America—received the greatest immediate boost thanks to the growth of "barn dance" programs like Nashville's Grand Ole Opry. Race music—which, as evidenced by its name, denoted less a specific set of musical characteristics than a general grouping of any style associated with African Americans—did not get anywhere near the boost of hillbilly/country, but black-identified styles also received greater exposure over the airwaves. At the same time, rural listeners blended these sounds with the various national pop styles of the day, enjoying a wide variety of programming that defied the racially or regionally determined expectations of the national music industry.

These eclectic tastes and the exponential growth in radio listenership led to a vast expansion in professional opportunities for southern musicians. In the 1920s, during the initial hillbilly and race-music boom, the music industry was based almost entirely in the North. Record labels brought artists to record in northern cities or sent remote teams to record southerners in their home locales, while many musicians born in the South relocated to New York or Chicago to launch recording careers. Once there, they promoted themselves as authentic exponents of southern identity (as well as black or white identity) even as they used northern songwriters, musicians, and producers.[5] By the 1940s, though, southern musicians could make money and reach a large audience in the South. In this new economy, eclecticism became a primary mark of professionalism. Musicians gained familiarity with a variety of different styles, and audiences expected live performers to perform a cross-generational, cross-regional, and cross-racial mixture of music. Arthur Alexander, Rick Hall, and others in the country-soul triangle grew up with this alchemical approach at the center of their musical consciousness.[6]

Still, this heterogeneous musical work—like the radio landscape itself—was structured by racial disparity. For one thing, most stations in the South and elsewhere kept black and white music segregated in their programming day. Programmers scheduled black-oriented shows in small segments of the broadcasting week, if at all, so many listeners had only one or two chances a week to hear gospel, jazz, or R&B. There were, of course, important exceptions to this, like Memphis's WDIA, which in 1949 became the first station in the United States to devote all of its programming to African American listeners.[7] But the majority of radio stations gave black musicians a much smaller space than their white counterparts.

This disparity meant that many southern listeners gained far greater familiarity with country music than with black-identified styles, which helps explain how both black and white triangle musicians reacted to country music. African American musicians' love for country on the radio is often invoked as a sign of southern soul's uniquely cross-racial origins, but many black musicians admitted that this deep affinity was partly due to country's disproportionate presence on southern radio. "Growing up in the country," recalled southern soul singer Millie Jackson, "we didn't have black radio, so I've always been a country-rocker at heart."[8] Conversely, the lack of black-identified musical programming helps explain the memories of southern whites who describe their introduction to black music as a wondrous epiphany that contrasted with or even cancelled out the country music and racial segregation of their childhoods. In this respect, even radio's liberatory aspects were themselves defined by racial exclusion.

The same tension between integration and segregation occurred on jukeboxes, which became increasingly common in the South during the 1930s and 1940s. Even though some jukeboxes stocked both black and white records, many cleaved firmly along racial lines.[9] In the wake of the Great Depression, when home phonograph and record sales dwindled to almost nothing, jukeboxes became the very lifeblood of the record business and the only way that many individuals—in the South and across the country—consistently heard recorded music. During World War II, a vinyl shortage halted most record production and further reinforced radio's dominance. As the Depression subsided and the war ended, phonograph sales increased and ultimately surpassed the heights of the 1920s.

The ubiquitous presence of radio stations, coupled with increasing demand for home phonographs and records, led to the development of a new record industry in the South. In the 1940s and early 1950s, a linked network of studios, mail-order retailers, and independent labels opened across the southern states. Like radio, this new economy followed a paradoxical path when it came to the segregation of genre. Musicians created and sold records that combined their many interests into new and exciting syntheses that disrupted many of Jim Crow's underlying assumptions about racial mixing. Moreover, they sometimes recorded this music in a racially integrated setting. But the most popular and significant products of the southern recording industry in these years—country and R&B—retained their broader resonance as symbols of racial difference.[10]

In the 1940s and 1950s, country music affirmed its close association with whiteness. Abandoning the hillbilly trappings of the early period, both in terms of image and sound, country artists updated their music and iconography to reflect newly popular versions of white southern "tradition" or myths of the "Old West." New country variants like honky-tonk and Western swing offered a remixed version of these tropes, featuring singers with twangy voices and cowboy clothes delivering material that called back to the string-band traditions of hillbilly while also appealing to a modern national audience. Both honky-tonk and Western swing bore the clear influence of black (and Mexican) music, but country's close association with whiteness only intensified in the postwar period.[11]

At the same time, R&B (abbreviated from "rhythm and blues") emerged in the late 1940s as a contemporary version of race music. The term, coined by *Billboard* writer Jerry Wexler, was specifically designed to provide a more dignified title for black-oriented records, and—like race music—R&B encompassed most of the secular music that was made and purchased by black people. It quickly became the dominant identifier for African American popular music in this period and a point of racial identification and pride. As rock 'n' roll artist Little Richard put it, "R&B stood for 'real black.'"[12] Of course, the R&B business was dominated by institutions controlled by white people, many of whom had initially been interested in marketing music by white artists. One of the most important of these institutions was the Nashville radio station WLAC.

WLAC had broadcast country and pop since the 1930s but took a new direction in 1946 thanks to a group of local black college students. They called deejay Gene Nobles during his regular late-night show and asked him to play "some boogie, or some blues." He agreed and asked them to bring some records down to the station, since WLAC did not have any. The response to these records was overwhelming and the station manager agreed to Nobles's request to change the show's format.[13] The only catch was that Nobles had to find his own sponsorship, so he partnered with Randy Wood, the white owner of a small Tennessee mail-order record retailer.

Like WLAC, Randy Wood started with white artists. He had not intended to be in the music business when he returned to his hometown of Gallatin, Tennessee, after serving in World War II. He opened an electronics store and put a few records in the back as an accessory to his selection of phonograph equipment, but the music soon outsold his more expensive items.[14] Wood initially sold pop and classical recordings, but he observed that a growing number of customers came into the shop looking for the R&B records they heard on WLAC. These records were not widely available in rural areas, so Wood started a mail-order retailer that he advertised on Nobles's program, cohosting a regular segment that featured the latest R&B hits available through his catalog. Soon, listeners from around the mid-South and eventually the whole country were inundating Wood with requests for records by black artists. Randy's Record Shop became a major force in the national popularization of R&B, especially after Wood began releasing his own records in partnership with several small independent labels.[15]

Neither Nobles nor Wood had a particularly keen ear for R&B, so Wood asked another young white deejay, Richard "Hoss" Allen, to select the records for his WLAC segment. Allen eventually replaced Nobles on WLAC, and he grew more popular than Nobles thanks to his unique delivery. Allen "sounded black," notes historian William Barlow, and—while he sometimes lapsed into racial caricature—Allen's loose, slang-filled patois made him a favorite among both black and white listeners.[16] He was replaced by a third white man, John Richbourg, who went by the on-air handle "John R." Even more than his predecessors, "John R." became a national R&B celebrity. Artists and producers flocked to his show to pay their respects and promote their current projects, while labels courted his approval and involved him in creative decisions; he even released a few records himself in the late 1960s. His skills gained him a wide and admiring audience. "He had so much soul that people in the black community thought he was black!," remembered soul star James Brown, whose early records were championed by Richbourg.[17]

The confusion caused by Allen's and Richbourg's on-air vocal style suggests that WLAC was a site of racial liberation. But this should not be overstated. Black-oriented programs remained a small and segregated part of WLAC's schedule; the station did not hire a black on-air personality until 1968; and—unlike some other southern stations—it never embraced the civil rights movement.[18] Ultimately, WLAC's greatest contribution to the struggle for black cultural advancement, and the development of the country-soul triangle, was demonstrating R&B's sizable economic potential. "Probably the biggest thing we did was to prove that black music was commercial and that a black radio station could be commercial," Hoss Allen remembered.[19] Arthur Alexander, Rick Hall, and the FAME musicians all listened to WLAC, and its deejays taught them a lot about how to make and sell R&B records.

They also learned from Randy's Record Shop, which became the South's most successful mail-order record retailer in these years. Randy Wood got rich by selling otherwise unavailable records to isolated listeners and jukebox operators across the South, and by far his biggest business was in R&B. Hoss Allen remembered that "guys that were in the record business began to cut black artists just so they could get on" Wood's segment on WLAC, and Allen estimated that at one point 85 percent of all sales of R&B in the Nashville area came through mail order.[20]

Randy's Record Shop and other mail orders allowed listeners to consume music in a way that bypassed segregated bodies and genre categories. As one mail-order employee observed, R&B "was not available at every little country town," and the brick-and-mortar stores that carried it often treated the recordings and customers with disrespect.[21] The catalogs made it easier for both African Americans and whites to purchase R&B records. Also, although the pages of Randy's catalog remained segregated by race and musical style, all that was required to get around that segregation was to flip through a few pages. Thus, even though the mail orders reconfirmed the underlying ideology of the "musical color line," they allowed listeners to transgress its practical applications. Nearly every major record label of the period—whether based in the North or South—followed this path in shaping the audiences it sought and the records it made.[22]

Nowhere was this more apparent than in Memphis and Nashville. Randy's Record Shop and WLAC made Nashville a center for R&B, but the city became synonymous with country in the years after World War II. Building on the rapid expansion of country's audience through radio and records, Nashville's music business exploded in the late 1940s, when local music professionals turned the once marginalized hillbilly genre into a nationally relevant commodity and made record production into one of Nashville's biggest industries. By 1950, when Capitol Records became the first national label to open an office there, Nashville's country releases attracted national attention as a prosperous part of the record business and an example of the cultural and economic vibrancy of the South—or at least the white South.

The ascent of country music had ambivalent consequences for the city's black musicians. "Nashville changed," recalled Ted Jarrett, a cornerstone of the city's R&B community and a crossover songwriter who wrote hits for country stars like Webb Pierce. "It became equated by the rest of the world with just one kind of music—country—even though so much else was happening," he remembered. "[As] early as the mid-1950s, changes were happening that would shorten the life of the R&B action in Nashville." Jarrett linked the consolidation of the country industry to other attempts to restrict black life in Nashville, including a "federally funded urban renewal project [that] did away with most of the black commercial district on Fourth Avenue North."[23] Indeed, even as Nashville maintained its national reputation as a modern and moderate southern city, the growth of the country industry both provoked and accompanied a broader limiting of African American opportunity.

The Memphis record business matured concurrently with Nashville's industry and shared many of its historical roots. But the music also made them commercial and political rivals. Memphis and Nashville became shorthand for the racial differences that listeners identified in R&B and country and for the political tensions that shook the South in the civil rights era. Musicians in both cities exploited this symbolism and helped shape the broader cultural understanding of what blackness and whiteness meant and how they sounded. Also, despite their differences, both Memphis and Nashville came to symbolize the ways white musicians used their adoption of R&B to demonstrate their position on the commercial and cultural vanguard.

The man who transformed the Memphis recording industry was originally from Muscle Shoals. Born in 1923, Sam Phillips worked at a Shoals-area radio station before leaving for jobs in Nashville—including a brief stint at WLAC—and Memphis. In 1949, he left radio to open a small studio called the Memphis Recording Service. Phillips initially recorded weddings and other social functions before he was hired in 1950 to produce a series of shows for the Arkansas Rural Electrification Program. The shows featured a white country singer, but Phillips subsequently decided to devote his attention primarily to local African American artists.

He originally leased tracks to Chicago's Chess Records, one of the nation's largest black-oriented labels, but a dispute with Chess led Phillips to start Sun Records in 1952.[24]

The impact of Sun Records on the country-soul triangle is immeasurable. "What really set us off was when Sam Phillips hit," remembered a cofounder of Muscle Shoals' first recording studio, and Sun's success provided an impetus for many entrepreneurs who started their own recording houses in the ensuing years.[25] But Phillips also presaged and provoked the triangle's central racial tension. In the mid-1950s, he shifted Sun away from African Americans in favor of white artists—most famously Elvis Presley—who synthesized R&B with country. He thus became a key and controversial player in the ongoing question of who would police the boundaries between country and R&B and who would benefit from their synthesis.

Before Sun's emergence, Memphis music was synonymous with blackness. In the early 1900s, African American musicians like W. C. Handy (who, like Phillips, was originally from Muscle Shoals) made the city and its Beale Street entertainment district internationally famous. "Memphis was the Blues," argued soul singer Carla Thomas, claiming that the success of Memphis's African American musicians in an unjust, segregated system was "what Memphis was all about."[26] The city also was also home to rich gospel, jazz, and R&B scenes, and Memphis became so well known that even some black musicians with no direct connection to the city—like a New York ensemble called the Memphis Students—used it as a musical authenticator.[27]

Sam Phillips surmised that recording Memphis's African American musicians would secure him a foothold in the national R&B market. Rather than mimicking the pop or country singers of the day, Phillips instructed his African American artists to play up what he called their "native type of influences" that originated from their experiences as black southerners.[28] Of course, as a veteran radio broadcaster and broadminded music fan, Phillips knew that music made from these "native type of influences" would be a product of conscious artistic choice and careful development in the recording studio. But he also concluded that a market existed for a gritty southern sound that he could promote as more authentically black than the slicker sounds of northern performers.

In the mid-1950s, Phillips abruptly changed his strategy and began recording white artists. Unlike with the R&B performers, Phillips now *insisted* on cross-racial stylistic synthesis. He had little use for straight country, especially because it was not worth competing with Nashville's established industry, so instead he sought white performers who blended country with R&B to create a cross-racial mélange that retained the uniquely southern sound he craved. Famously, if apocryphally, Phillips even said that he wanted to find "a white man with the Negro feel" with whom he believed he could make "a billion dollars."[29] Phillips did not believe in the creative superiority of white performers—he repeatedly said that he thought black music was better. But he nonetheless understood that, despite the growing profitability of R&B in the postwar years, a successful white artist still received far greater support and made more money than most African Americans. Most specifically, whites could become pop stars—and, crucially, country stars—much more easily than blacks could. Phillips bemoaned the inequities of this system but nonetheless jumped at the chance to improve his status and bank account balance by breaking a white hit-maker. He mostly stopped working with black artists and devoted his attention to the young whites known as "rockabillies," most famously Elvis Presley.

Presley, Phillips, and the Sun rockabillies were crucial to the rock 'n' roll explosion of the late 1950s, which was routinely presented as an interracial marriage. The music's stylistic blending of country and R&B, and its integrated cadre of creators and fans, led many to identify it as a racially insurgent—or even "mongrel"—music that would transform the rigidly defined contours of the "musical color line" as well as the racial mores of a nation on the doorstep of the civil rights movement. The music press debated the implications of the musical mixtures on the genres of country, R&B, and pop, while both supporters and detractors saw the music as an explicit challenge to Jim Crow. Much of this discourse surrounded Presley who—as the genre's most popular figure and embodiment of its effect on young whites—became a controversial symbol for the racial revolution.[30]

Phillips urged Presley and others to merge country and R&B, even when it was not their initial creative approach, and later used this cross-racial blend to assert Sun as a site of racial progress and himself as a vehicle for interracial cooperation.[31] But several of Sun's black artists have rejected this interpretation; Rufus Thomas, a WDIA deejay who recorded Sun's first big hit, said that Phillips simply "discarded all of his black talent . . . when Elvis came along."[32] Thomas and other African Americans have claimed that Phillips was not committed to black music or musicians in either ideological or economic terms, a notion at which Phillips unsurprisingly bristled. Asked about the complaints of blacks like Thomas, Phillips claimed that he had "knocked down a lot of barriers" in the 1950s by promoting the marriage of country and R&B. He also asserted that—even as he encouraged

white artists to incorporate black influences—he did not allow them to steal from African Americans. He "tried also to make sure that whites especially stay[ed] out of the black man's territory when it comes to trying to sound exactly like him . . . When we borrowed, we didn't steal, okay? And when we borrowed, we gave back." Musicians like Rufus Thomas, who had been "discarded" by Sun Records, found this argument unconvincing.[33]

Ironically, the musical "territory" that Phillips most obviously threatened in the 1950s was that occupied by his white neighbors in Nashville. Elvis Presley and other Sun artists scored big hits on the country charts in the late 1950s, making many established stars sound hopelessly old-fashioned by comparison and leading many longtime country fans to bemoan the increasing R&B influence on their music. In response, Nashville executives developed a new musical and promotional strategy called the "Nashville sound." On the most basic level, this was an advertising campaign for the city's studios and musicians. In 1964 *Time* magazine described it as a sign of a southern cultural and economic renaissance that originated with "a small, seasoned corps [of sidemen] whose musical prowess," the writer romantically and inaccurately claimed, "is more heart than art."[34]

Underneath this sunny boosterism was a barely subsumed critique of the Memphis rockabillies. Proponents implied that rockabilly was disreputable and low-class while the Nashville sound was the respectable voice of forward-looking southern whiteness. In keeping with this rhetoric, Nashville musicians rejected the regionalist strategy of Sam Phillips and instead developed recordings that they hoped would cross over to the national pop mainstream. They downplayed the most obvious sonic markers of country's roots and encouraged artists like Eddy Arnold or Patsy Cline to model their performances and presentations after the day's pop stars.

Their most obvious sonic signifier for this was the use of musical textures from black-identified genres like jazz and R&B. A few African Americans made it into the inner circles of Nashville's otherwise lily-white corps of songwriters and studio players. More significant, white Nashville sound architects like guitarist and producer Chet Atkins made black-identified music a key part of their hit-making formula. Some popular country artists—like Red Foley—even had major chart success with R&B covers. Most of these covers featured near-identical arrangements to those of their black counterparts (complete with handclaps, shuffling rhythms, and doo-wop-style background vocals) but did not caricature African Americans as minstrelsy or many early hillbilly versions of black-identified material had done. Earlier generations of white musicians lampooned African Americans through blackface and dialect, but the creators of the Nashville sound offered more respectful interpretations as part of their suave and sophisticated presentation.[35]

The successful interpolation of black-identified music into the Nashville sound ironically solidified the notion that country music—and Nashville itself—was a white space. In this respect, and despite their obvious differences, the Nashville sound and Memphis rockabilly actually had a similar effect. Memphis and Nashville each became famous in the 1950s as places where white musicians married country and R&B to create something new and exciting while African American performers took a backseat. Both Memphis rockabilly and the Nashville sound perpetuated the notion that the most innovative and forward-thinking southern music was made by whites who been inspired by black R&B, rather than by African Americans whether they had been influenced by country music or not.[36]

One such white musician was Buddy Killen, a bass player and songwriter from Muscle Shoals who came to Nashville in 1950. Killen liked the pop, R&B, and rock 'n' roll recordings that he heard on regional radio and later played as a teenager, but he chose to focus on country upon arriving in the city.[37] There, he quickly earned an enviable position in Nashville's booming music industry; by 1961 Killen was president and co-owner of Tree Music, the city's largest song-publishing firm. As he climbed the country ladder, Killen found time to record an R&B-influenced pop hit in 1960 called "Forever," released under the name the Little Dippers. Still a young man, Killen became one of the most powerful men in Nashville and a living representative of its bright, crossover-minded musical future. His accomplishments were not forgotten back home, where a newspaper columnist heralded him as a Shoals "native who has been making good in the music business."[38] The next year, Arthur Alexander and Rick Hall followed Killen's path with "You Better Move On."

Although "You Better Move On" was the Shoals' breakthrough, it followed nearly a decade of recording in the city. In 1951 a former TVA turbine operator named Dexter Johnson opened the area's first recording studio, a humble and short-lived effort that inspired James Joiner to start Tune Records, the first record label in Alabama, in 1957. Joiner envisioned Tune as a way for local country musicians and songwriters to impress Nashville executives, and he quickly fulfilled that mission when Tune released a syrupy ballad called "A Fallen Star" by local singer Bobby Denton.[39] Denton's record flopped, but a dozen country stars covered the song and turned the attention of Nashville executives toward this small town. Joiner had no interest in recording black performers, though, despite the growing market for R&B and the presence of local singers like future star Percy Sledge, whose music Joiner admitted he "couldn't hear." Joiner's limited ambitions soon clashed with the broader vision of Rick Hall and Billy Sherrill, who arrived in 1958.[40]

Born to Mississippi farmers in 1932, Rick Hall remembered that "my early life was spent in country music."[41] Seeing music as a viable alternative to agricultural work, he started playing fiddle in local talent contests and—after moving to Alabama in 1957—he toured with a popular country band. On the road, Hall met an electric saxophone player named Billy Sherrill, then a member of an R&B combo. While the two bands shared few gigs, Hall and Sherrill became friends and triangulated their musical interests by forming a rock 'n' roll band called the Fairlanes in 1958. Tired of touring, Hall and Sherrill hatched a plan to break into the recording business. They started writing songs and soon came to Muscle Shoals, where they met Joiner and local businessman Tom Stafford, with whom Joiner started Spar Publishing in 1958. Joiner and Stafford outfitted a two-room studio with equipment purchased in Nashville, and Hall and Sherrill became cornerstones of the new company.[42]

As in their live performances, Hall and Sherrill pursued an eclectic blend of music in the recording studio. They wrote a country ballad called "Sweet and Innocent" that excited Tom Stafford to such a degree that he arranged for Nashville saxophonist Boots Randolph to drive down to the Shoals for the session.[43] But they also made inroads in R&B, doing sessions in Memphis and releasing a single as the Fairlanes on a subsidiary of Chess Records.[44] But the duo's ideas outgrew Joiner's narrow taste, so—with Tom Stafford—Hall and Sherrill split to form FAME, or "Florence Alabama Music Enterprises," in 1959.[45]

The musicians who assembled at the new FAME provided the Muscle Shoals recording industry with its literal and figurative foundations. Most were new in town, having come to the area because of Tune's success. Each was highly skilled in country, rock 'n' roll, and R&B. All of them were white. Hall and Sherrill were particularly excited about a young singer/songwriter who they hoped would help them break into the country, pop, and R&B markets all at once. The reedy young Alabamian was named Dan Penn.

Penn was born in 1941. He was raised on Nashville country and loved the rock 'n' roll from Memphis, but his biggest passion was R&B. "Even before I heard Presley," he remarked, "I was already listening to WLAC."[46] By the time he met Hall and Sherrill, Penn was an R&B fundamentalist who claimed that it possessed demonstrable superiority in rhythm—"country never does hit a groove"—and vocality—"I just knew [black singers] were better. I don't know [why]"—over other genres.[47] Penn fully credits black singers with his vocal and performance style. "I was just imitating every one of them," he admitted.[48] He impressed crowds with versions of country, pop, and rock 'n' roll hits in his early performances, but R&B became his calling card.

He was joined in this devotion by a group of white musicians called the Mark V who hired Penn as their singer in the early 1960s. Although similarly versatile, they shared Penn's primary musical interest. "They asked me what I wanted to play," Penn recalled, "and I said, 'everything black.' And they pretty well liked it. Their heads were swinging that way too."[49] The members of the Mark V were not the only young whites who emulated the style and sound of African American performers, but their performances became legendary for their intensity. Stories circulated of Penn convulsing onstage in imitation of soul star James Brown, and the band ran through skillful, high-energy versions of hits by black artists like Bobby "Blue" Bland and Ray Charles. Led by their charismatic lead singer, the Mark V quickly became one of the most prominent young groups in northern Alabama. When Sherrill convinced Penn to come to FAME, Penn brought his group with him. They became the studio's house band.

The Mark V's early performances troubled both the musical and social manifestations of Jim Crow segregation. Drummer Jerry Carrigan remembered a recurring gig in rural Mississippi that ended when Penn refused to tone down his performance at the behest of the white club owner, who did not appreciate the attendance of the group's growing number of black fans.[50] Perhaps even more impressively, Penn and company were convincing enough to even impress the zealous fans on the southern "frat circuit," the segregated universities like Auburn or Mississippi that hired R&B bands to perform at campus gatherings and parties. On the frat circuit, white audiences demanded black entertainers—even as they prevented the entry of African American students to the same universities—and they did not take kindly to imitators. Dan Penn's talents made him one of the few white performers whom these crowds found acceptable, and his experiences negotiating the frat circuit's racial politics provided him with training and awareness that became crucial to his studio work.[51]

Penn's new employers at FAME relished the chance to work with such a talented R&B enthusiast. "[Penn] was the real thing," Rick Hall remembered. "He wasn't a rip-off or a fake. He knew more about black music than the rest of us put together."[52] Both Hall and Sherrill admired Penn's ability to convincingly sing and write R&B material and his attention to what was currently popular among African American listeners. But they also hoped to exploit Penn's talents in composing and performing other types of material. In fact, despite Penn's reputation, his first hit song was recorded by Nashville country star (and former Memphis rockabilly) Conway Twitty, who took Penn's "Is a Bluebird Blue?" into the country Top 40 in 1960. Flush with success, Penn followed up by making his own record, an R&B-flavored Billy Sherrill composition called "Crazy Over You." Hall and Sherrill thought the record was perfect for the pop charts, while Penn felt so confident in the record's R&B potential that he drove to WLAC to pitch it to his idol, John Richbourg. Unfortunately, "Crazy Over You" was nowhere near as successful as Penn's country hit.[53]

Despite this eclecticism, Dan Penn's early career has usually been presented as representative of the southerners who abandoned the sounds and politics of whiteness in order to embrace black music and African Americans. Richard Younger extends this notion to include all the young white musicians at FAME, suggesting they were "hungry for 'the beat,' which emanated from black music."[54] But this, too, is a misrepresentation. Penn and his cohorts certainly embraced R&B as a meaningful alternative (or

Dan Penn and Rick Hall at FAME Studios in the early 1960s. Penn's talents as a singer, songwriter, and producer made him a crucial contributor to FAME's emergence as a site of R&B recording. Courtesy of Rodney Hall. FAME Studio Records, Library and Archives, Rock and Roll Hall of Fame and Museum.

perhaps supplement) to country or white pop, but they never renounced these white-identified genres either as influences or commodities. Country was particularly crucial to FAME's early development, and the studio's personnel utilized their extensive Nashville connections to gain exposure before they ever had success in R&B. Ultimately, Penn and the others had no interest in abandoning their musical whiteness if it meant they could garner success on the country charts. Not everyone had the same privilege.

One such individual was a tall black man from Muscle Shoals who grew up singing country and eventually composed his own country-influenced material. Arthur Alexander's arrival at FAME Studios in 1959 made the musicians' dreams of R&B success and pop crossover into a tangible reality. But Alexander's greatest impact at FAME may have occurred before he ever recorded a note, because he brought—in Dan Penn's words—"the

Arthur Alexander promotional photo, 1962. Alexander's sessions at FAME Studios in the early 1960s represented both the promise and the limitations of interracial recording in the South. Photograph by Gilles Pétard. Getty Images.

actuality of a black person in the studio with us."[55] His initial experiences at FAME Studios demonstrated just how complicated this process of integration would be.

Alexander later recalled that, soon after he arrived, a white guitarist named Terry Thompson—whom Alexander called "the biggest racist there ever was"—made an unfriendly remark concerning "niggers," before quickly adding that his definition of "niggers" did not include Alexander. Alexander was not impressed. Ultimately, the two men reached what Alexander called "an understanding," an apparent truce that in no way signaled a breakthrough moment of racial healing.[56] Alexander and Thompson did not interact much outside the studio, and no evidence suggests that either man changed his beliefs. As Alexander's phrasing implies, the two men reached an agreement to behave professionally—as musicians, they were able to set aside personal animosity in the service of doing their job.

This tense incident is one reason why it is difficult to believe Dan Penn's subsequent claim that he and the others "didn't really think of Arthur as black," or another musician's suggestion that "the concept of blacks that existed [throughout the South] did not exist" at FAME Studios.[57] This persistent myth is most obviously challenged by Thompson's racial slur, but it is actually contradicted more profoundly by the excitement that greeted Alexander's arrival at the studio. Musicians like Penn were thrilled at the idea of working with an African American because they aesthetically romanticized his race—Peter Guralnick says they referred to themselves proudly as "a bunch of niggers"—and hoped that Alexander would expand FAME's recording interests into the untapped R&B market.[58] In both respects, Alexander's blackness—and his white colleagues' "concept" of it—was absolutely crucial to his time at FAME. As Penn also suggested, it took "someone big, black and shiny" to break Muscle Shoals to a larger audience.[59] Alexander always maintained that he was greeted warmly at the studio, but he noted that this spirit of friendship resulted from, and thus was limited by, the nature of musical collaboration. "We only had this one thing in common," he remarked. "We liked all types of music."[60]

This versatility first brought Alexander to FAME and led the studio players to imagine that he might have limitless potential. "Arthur was the very reason all the pop things happened in Muscle Shoals," Dan Penn attested, because his material came "not from a pure white or pure black standpoint." Penn was awed by the way that Alexander's songs were not "like Nashville or [R&B singer] Ray Charles." He instead located Alexander "somewhere in the middle" of a pop spectrum that ranged "from Ray Charles to [white teen idol] Frankie Avalon."[61] Even the musicians who were not particularly fond of him understood that his sound could reap larger rewards. "He wasn't a great singer," remarked FAME pianist David Briggs. "He just had this little style and it was commercial."[62]

Alexander developed this eclectic and commercial sound from his earliest days as a music fan. He was a voracious radio listener and admitted that "when I grew up, I heard white singers before I heard black singers" on the radio. He sincerely enjoyed country and considered it part of a mix that also included pop and R&B.[63] He formed several doo-wop groups as a young man, including one that was good enough to make it on a local TV show, but he left when he determined that his fellow members were not committed to making it in the music business. When Alexander started writing songs, he tried to emulate the era's popular music and admitted that "what got me into writing songs was wanting to [make] records."[64]

Because of both his sound and skin color, Alexander believed that he would be best suited for success in the R&B field, but his first breakthrough came when Tom Stafford sold his song "She Wanta Rock" to a Nashville country artist in 1959. Stafford got a sizable cut of the song's publishing royalties, and he, Hall, and Sherrill became Alexander's managers. The trio who founded FAME considered Alexander a friend, and Alexander remembered all three men fondly. But they were primarily interested in him as an employee or even commodity who could make them money as both a recording artist and songwriter. In fact, as evidenced by Stafford's decision, they were probably more excited by the songwriting. Song publishing was big business, especially in Nashville, where it made millionaires out of Buddy Killen and others. Stafford, Hall, and Sherrill believed that Alexander's material would fit perfectly with the R&B-inflected crossover push of the Nashville sound. Even though Alexander's race precluded him from country stardom, his hybrid songs could make a lot of money for whoever controlled them. And, from the very beginning, this was the white men at FAME Studios.

Rick Hall argued with his partners over their commercial ambitions, including Alexander's prospects, and he left Spar Publishing in 1960.[65] He took the FAME name and built a new studio, while Alexander stayed with Stafford and soon released his debut single as a performer, "Sally Sue Brown." Local reporter Bill Jobe heralded the record as a major moment in Shoals musical history, specifically because Alexander "is the first Negro from this area to be recorded professionally, and he does a fine job of singing on his first release." Jobe further noted (with apparent surprise) that Alexander's "voice is commercial and he has the ability to sing most any type of selection."[66] Despite the fanfare, the single was not a success.

Frustrated, Alexander soon returned with "You Better Move On," which both he and Tom Stafford recognized as a masterpiece. Fearing that his small studio could not capture the song's potential, Stafford contacted Rick Hall, who recorded "You Better Move On" with the core group of FAME musicians and two background singers who had worked in Memphis and Nashville. Hall described this process as "work and rehearse and work and rehearse," and Alexander remembered, "I must have sung that song a hundred thousand times, or more, before we got a take that we were satisfied [with]." If Sam Phillips wanted his records to sound unproduced, and the Nashville sound announced its prefabrication with its lush arrangements, Alexander and Hall split the difference—they wanted "You Better Move On" to sound composed but not contrived, professional but not overwrought. This process took a lot of labor. "Unlike what most . . . people conjure up in their minds," Hall pointed out, "in those days and in that particular instance and most of my instances, no record was cut live. . . . Most of 'em drug on and you cut 'em and recut 'em and you fixed this and you started all over."[67] Their efforts paid off. "You Better Move On" was by far the most accomplished recording to emerge from Muscle Shoals.

It was also a near-perfect example of how popular music sounded at the beginning of the 1960s, seamlessly combining the textures of the era's country, pop, and R&B. Alexander's idiosyncratic talent was perfectly complemented by the versatility of the FAME players, while Hall made the finished product sound as sophisticated and marketable as possible. On musical terms, the record symbolized the possibilities inherent in the cross-racial interactions of the country-soul triangle. Here was a black man who loved country music singing a pop ballad with a group of R&B-loving white men in a studio that was heavily supported by Nashville's country industry. It was both a product of the southern music industry and a new chapter in it. But Alexander, Hall, and the others knew this meant nothing if nobody got to hear the finished work, and they understood that selling "You Better Move On" required them to negotiate the tricky commercial boundaries between country, pop, and R&B. These borders were determined by race and limited the music's transcendent potential.

Rick Hall was both enthusiastic and cautious about the record's prospects. "It's a hit," he recalled thinking at the time, "but there's no way I can get it on the market.'"[68] Despite Alexander's race, Hall decided to focus primarily on companies that specialized in country, a decision that seems less surprising given that Hall's first interest was in publishing firms. Hall sensed that he could sell "You Better Move On" to a Nashville sound artist, even if it meant that Alexander's might go unreleased or underappreciated. These firms had purchased FAME's songs before (including one of Alexander's), but they passed on "You Better Move On."

Hall moved on to record labels and he again directed his attention at companies that primarily serviced white artists. The country labels had no interest in releasing Alexander's record. As Richard Younger writes, they "expressed an interest in having their own singers cut the song [but were not] impressed by a vocalist who sounded 'too black . . . wobbly and all over the place.'" Even those who liked Alexander's performance worried about trying to sell a record to an African American audience. Chet Atkins said he was "sure it's a good record, but I don't know anything about black music," and Sam Phillips's Nashville office also passed.[69] Apparently, these labels did not consider marketing Alexander as a country or pop artist, even though one of the few R&B labels that Hall approached told him that the song sounded "too white" for black listeners.[70] When it came to marketing himself, Alexander found himself trapped by the very racial ambiguity that made him so creatively interesting to Hall and the musicians at FAME.

Hall had almost given up when he took "You Better Move On" to Dot Records, where he met with the label's founder, Randy Wood. Wood had started the company with the money he earned from the success of Randy's Record Shop, and his greatest success came with the release of white crooner Pat Boone's infamous covers of rock 'n' roll hits by black artists like Little Richard.[71] But Wood also owed much of his success to R&B. He began recording local black acts on small labels back in the late 1940s, often in collaboration with Gene Nobles and other WLAC personalities, and launched Dot in 1950. As with Randy's Record Shop, the Dot catalog included country, gospel, pop, R&B, and rock 'n' roll, and Wood marketed this eclectic mix to an audience that wanted musical diversity but still represented racially distinct market segments.[72]

Wood chose white Nashville deejay and song publisher Noel Ball to run Dot, and it was Ball who recommended that Dot release "You Better Move On." While Alexander maintained sole songwriting credit, and thus earned songwriting royalties, he did not receive any of the lucrative publishing income: Ball split those with Hall and Stafford. Ball got a cool reception when he came to Muscle Shoals to meet his new client. Alexander said that he had "no understanding of music," while Hall suspected that Ball wanted to get Alexander out of FAME—which Ball supposedly derided as a "funky little bathroom"—and into Nashville's more professional studios.[73] Hall was likely further nonplussed by Ball's insistence that FAME's musicians join the American Federation of Musicians, which ensured their future as session players but also guaranteed (at least in theory) that Hall would have to pay them union wages.[74] Still, Ball was well known and well liked in Nashville's music industry, so FAME's leadership grudgingly advised Alexander to follow his lead. "Work with this guy," Alexander remembered hearing from Tom Stafford. "He's got all the things that you need."[75]

Dot released "You Better Move On" in January 1962 alongside a new Pat Boone single. *Billboard* gave it a tepid review, but two weeks later ran a front-page story called "Nashville Sees Hot 'Move On'" noting that "three out of four retailers" in the city reported that Alexander's "record was breaking wide open."[76] In the coming months, "You Better Move On" reached number twenty-four on the pop charts, a huge success by any standard and one of the first such milestones for a southern R&B record. It got there in large part because of Alexander's tireless promotion of the record at radio stations and live shows throughout the South. He usually rode with some of the FAME musicians who supported him on early performances, and this interracial group of young men provoked some unwanted attention as they drove across Alabama, Mississippi, and Tennessee during the height of the civil rights movement. "I remember going with Arthur to places like Birmingham, and we'd be worried about being seen in the car with him," remembered David Briggs. Alexander recalled that when "driving on those country roads, because the freeways wasn't [*sic*] in, and we'd get stopped in these little country towns and get gas, get ridiculed, you know."[77]

Sometimes they were saved by the very racial beliefs they challenged on record. One night, a group of Klansmen approached the group and began asking threatening questions. Just when it appeared that Alexander and company would be physically attacked, the Klan members became star-struck when they realized that they were accosting the man behind "You Better Move On." They assumed that the country-influenced singer was white. "Same guys who wanted to kick my ass were buying my records," Alexander recalled.[78] Here, one kind of segregation protected a different kind of integration, but Alexander nonetheless faced significant indignities on the road. "They'd play Arthur's records," musician Donnie Fritts remembered, speaking of radio stations, "but Arthur couldn't take a shit."[79]

As the FAME musicians feared, Noel Ball had no intention of recording Alexander in Muscle Shoals and brought him to Nashville. This initially seemed fortuitous for the young singer-songwriter. He had the backing of one of the nation's largest record labels, the guidance of a seasoned promotional mind, the support of top-flight studio musicians, and a hit that was still spinning on radios and jukeboxes. Unfortunately, his time in Nashville was a disappointment, and Alexander came to believe that this was because he was black.

Dot did not initially market Arthur Alexander to a specifically African American audience. Alexander's onetime manager Phil Walden chalked this up to the fact that "being saddled with Dot"—the home of Pat Boone— "was akin to having [segregationist governor] George Wallace as your manager, if you were an R&B singer."[80] Walden's statement is hyperbolic, especially since Dot had a history of recording black artists, but the label seemed neither interested nor capable of a full-scale push into the R&B market. Instead, Dot marketed Alexander alongside pop and country performers, while reviews promoted him as an artist who transcended stylistic boundaries.[81]

The advertisements and reviews reflected a broader interest in the increasingly blurry lines between country, R&B, and pop in the early 1960s. The simultaneous growth of country and R&B, combined with the rise of rock 'n' roll, led many to believe that artists who crossed stylistic lines would transform the mainstream and even cause old genre lines to disappear. Record companies foregrounded the multigenre potential of their new releases—Conway Twitty's version of Dan Penn's "Is a Bluebird Blue?"

was lauded as a "Swingin' New Rockin' Pop, Rhythm & Blues, Country Hit!"—while journalists shared their exuberance.[82] At one point in the early 1960s, both *Billboard* and *Cashbox* got rid of their separate R&B singles chart to reflect what *Cashbox* called the lack of "any dividing line between R&B and pop."[83] They kept the country charts, but noted that "'the Nashville sound' has become . . . synonymous in our industry with 'a commercial sound,'" and that "country music is the hit sound of today."[84] But these same journalists also worried that this would result in a tainting of both country and R&B. "Only six or seven years ago," one editorial claimed, "singles were in sharply defined pop, rhythm & blues and country categories." But, in the intervening years, "both rhythm & blues and country began to lose their clearly defined identity" by crossing over into pop.[85]

These worries reflected a broader debate over racial coexistence in the age of integration. The "absorption" of country and R&B into the pop market seemed to signal the promise of a desegregated and color blind America that motivated much early integrationist rhetoric. But the concern over the loss of "identity" in country and R&B reflected both segregationist fears over the denigration of the white race and some African Americans' worries about racial assimilation in the push for access to white-controlled institutions. When Arthur Alexander released "You Better Move On," his musical blending of country, pop, and R&B became a metaphor for the contested trajectory of U.S. racial politics. This tension shaped his early career.

Noel Ball tried to position Alexander within this crossover matrix. This made sense, since he seemed to embody the vanishing "dividing line" between R&B and pop and the groundbreaking success of Ray Charles's 1962 album *Modern Sounds in Country & Western Music* made it possible that Alexander might even hit the country charts.[86] Ball filled Alexander's first Dot album with a mishmash of cover versions of current country, pop, and R&B hits. Despite earning warm reviews, the LP flopped, as did a subsequent single where Alexander covered a pair of country and pop hits.[87] Returning to Alabama, Alexander was frustrated with his stalled career and the teasing that he got from his friends for what Richard Younger describes as "the [country] flavor of some of his records."[88]

Much of Alexander's frustration stemmed from Noel Ball's insistence on releasing cover songs as singles, despite the fact that Alexander's initial success came with an original and style-blending composition. "I started getting all these bad songs [that] Noel Ball was pushing . . . on me," Alexander remembered. "I said 'I've got to write!'"[89] After the failure of his second single, Alexander convinced Ball to release his song "Anna (Go to Him)" and he was rewarded with the biggest hit of his career. Alexander wrote and demoed the Latin-inflected ballad while still in Muscle Shoals, and—like "You Better Move On"—the gracefully twangy tune offered a far better demonstration of Alexander's genre-crossing ability than the grab bag of his debut album. Unfortunately, Alexander did not duplicate the success of "Anna" with an original follow-up, and Ball again insisted that Alexander release covers on his subsequent singles.[90]

Ball's decision can be partly attributed to the fact that many singers (in country, pop, and R&B) did not write their own material in this era. But Alexander saw Ball's decision as part of a systemic problem in the country industry that belied its rhetoric of crossover. Alexander said that they "never do nothing excepting white songs" in Nashville, and—while inaccurate— this complaint was compounded by the fact that Ball, who owned the publishing rights to Alexander's material, made sure that plenty of white artists covered Alexander's songs even as his own recordings went unreleased.[91] The first hit came in 1963 when pop artist Steve Alaimo recorded "Every Day I Have to Cry" at a Nashville session and reached the pop Top 40.[92] As demonstrated by the Alaimo hit, Alexander's songs were tailor-made for Nashville's push toward greater stylistic crossover. Still, he did not benefit as a performing artist, nor did he receive any publishing royalties. He grew disillusioned at what he perceived as a hypocritical and greed-driven example of music-business racism.

Alexander ultimately recorded "Every Day I Have to Cry," and—as he suspected—it became a hit. Unfortunately, the hit came in 1975, long after Alexander left Dot Records, split with Noel Ball, and become a marginal figure on the national music scene. He cut the record as part of a comeback effort launched in Muscle Shoals, which flourished in the wake of his departure. Beyond the increased business that FAME enjoyed after the release of "You Better Move On," Alexander became central to the mythology that Shoals musicians, especially Rick Hall, used to attract other black artists to the area.

Hall—who used the money he made from "You Better Move On" to build a new and improved FAME Studios—later claimed that he knew exactly why Arthur Alexander had not lived up to his potential. "They took [him] to Nashville and used country musicians [and] didn't use black people," he explained. Ball "was going to make it convenient for him[self] . . . and not take Arthur where he needed to be, which was with black musicians and somebody whose knack was producing hit records on black artists."[93] Hall neglected to mention that he was not using black musicians at FAME. And he did not explain why Nashville's versatile, country-trained musicians were less qualified to work with Alexander than the versatile, country-trained musicians in Muscle Shoals. Despite these inconsistencies, Hall offered Alexander's lack of commercial success as a symbol of the supposedly impermeable racial divide between R&B and country, Muscle Shoals and Nashville, and the musicians in both places.

Hall made this story central to his larger claim that he turned Muscle Shoals away from restrictive white country and toward a liberating focus on black R&B. "I didn't want anything to do at that time with Nashville. I considered [country] degrading music, [Nashville] a degrading town, a bunch of rednecks. It was ignorant," so he instead decided to try "the R&B approach."[94] This mischaracterizes every element of FAME's early development, but perhaps its most egregious distortion is that it reduces Alexander—whose musical eclecticism and professional ambitions fueled FAME's interest in him—to a passive and essentialized symbol of R&B, blackness, and Rick Hall's visionary heroism. In Hall's telling, he was so horrified by Alexander's lack of success that he decided to strike a blow against the "degrading" and "redneck" culture of Nashville country by establishing an integrated home for black music in Muscle Shoals.[95]

Rick Hall was unquestionably central to the development of R&B and soul in Muscle Shoals. He is a masterful producer, an underrated songwriter, and an exceptional judge of talent. But he was neither a civil rights pioneer nor a particularly passionate R&B fan. He had no direct role in bringing Arthur Alexander to FAME and showed little interest in hiring African Americans to be a part of the studio band. Even after the success of "You Better Move On," he did not seek out African American acts; Linda Hall, Rick's wife and longtime studio secretary, recalled that it was actually the opposite. "When word got out that there was this white guy working with black people," she said, "they infiltrated in."[96] Leaving aside the fact that "infiltrated" evokes the language of segregationism, FAME's ascendance as a center for R&B was a product of African American musicians seizing the opportunity to achieve professional success. Dan Penn, who played a much more direct role than Hall in pushing FAME toward black artists, admitted that their success resulted from "the black people walking into the studio wanting to record."[97]

One of those people was Jimmy Hughes, who became FAME's second homegrown R&B star. Hughes was a factory worker whose gospel group regularly performed on the radio and who auditioned at FAME in 1962 because "Arthur Alexander had a hit, and I wanted one, too." Hughes was particularly proud of his smoldering gospel-style ballad "Steal Away," but Rick Hall supposedly did not feel it was commercial enough to release as a single. He pushed instead for "Lollipops, Lace and Lipstick," a sugary pop tune that, conveniently, Hall cowrote and for which he owned publishing rights. It took Hughes and Dan Penn together to persuade Hall that "Steal Away" was a better choice for the topside of the single.[98] Hughes and Hall signed a distribution deal with Vee-Jay Records, one of the largest black-oriented labels in the country, and Vee-Jay's promotional push propelled Hughes's record into the Top 10.

The spare, gritty gospel of "Steal Away" did much more to establish the musical characteristics that came to define southern R&B and soul than did the delicate country-influenced pop of "You Better Move On." This distinctive sound and the record's commercial success led another important client, one of FAME's first supporters in Nashville, to return to the studio. But Buddy Killen had a different reason to come back to the Shoals this time. Sitting atop his publishing empire in Nashville, Killen started a small R&B label to capitalize on the genre's popularity and provide a home for the recordings of a talented black singer/songwriter named Joe Tex, who Killen felt would benefit from FAME's racially integrated blend of country and R&B. They came to the studio in 1964.

Tex—born Joseph Arrington Jr. in 1935—was a minor R&B star when he met Killen backstage at the Grand Ole Opry in the late 1950s.[99] "He wore a purple cowboy outfit with a ten-gallon hat," Killen wrote in his autobiography, and this unusual getup piqued Killen's curiosity. "He once told me a funny story about how he got started. Since he loved the songs of Hank Williams and some of the early country singers, he decided he'd become a country singer as well, and he bought a western outfit and guitar. Somehow, he got booked into a Texas honky-tonk." The club's white owner grew incensed at the flamboyant black man singing country music in a cowboy suit. In Killen's telling, the owner demanded that Tex leave the stage because "he ain't country, he ain't white, he can't be country."[100]

Killen recounted this story as a humorous racial mix-up, but the belief in country's whiteness structured his own dealings with the singer. Tex loved country music and was good at it, but he found that his country flavor made it difficult for him to get a record deal in Nashville. In a parallel to Arthur Alexander, the city's record labels passed on Tex because—in Killen's recollection—"they didn't know what he was either, 'cause they didn't know anything about rhythm and blues [and] were really more interested in country music."[101] After Killen opened Dial Records in 1961, he cautioned Tex that having too much country influence on his R&B releases would create racial confusion that would make them difficult to sell.[102]

Killen furthered this separation in the bodies of the musicians themselves. At Tex's first Nashville sessions, Killen only hired white country players and refused Tex's repeated requests to use members of his African American road band. Killen finally agreed to use Tex's musicians only after failing to cut a hit with his players. In each case, the producer claimed to be unimpressed. "When I put Tex with the Nashville musicians," he wrote, "they used clean, country techniques that didn't fit with his soulful style. When I acquiesced to Tex's wishes and used his band, I had to endure their sloppy musical techniques. They were road musicians and had more capacity to feel a song than they had skills to play it."[103]

Killen's comments reflected his acceptance of the racial ideology articulated through the categories of country and R&B. He felt that white musicians had "technique" and "skills to play," while black musicians had inherent musicality and "more capacity to feel a song"; in other words, white musicians had style and black musicians had soul. This essentialist belief had long characterized musical practice in the United States, and it now limited the career of an artist who defied the supposed artistic boundaries between black and white music. Tex remained hitless for the first three years of his Dial career. Fed up with the lack of success, Tex asked Killen to release him from his contract, but Killen convinced him to work one last session. This time, they went to FAME Studios.

Killen felt that FAME's increasingly well-known mix of black and white offered a chance to successfully harness Tex's idiosyncratic talent. Where he earlier insisted on racial separation in the studio, Killen now combined white studio regulars with the black rhythm section from Tex's road band to create an integrated ensemble that offered an embodied illustration of Tex's country-R&B mash-up. The result of that experiment, "Hold What You've Got," deftly combined the genres through Tex's powerful vocals and the musicians' spare, pulsing arrangement. "In the early 1960s," Killen wrote later, "no one would have dared to use the country sound of an open string acoustic guitar on a funky R&B record." While this is not necessarily true, the hybrid sound of "Hold What You've Got" reflected a musical marketplace that was at once rigidly segregated and hungry for cross-racial overlaps. Killen said that he "knew they would get limited rhythm-and-blues airplay [without using country players], but I was looking for something bigger," and the interracial group of musicians served as much to reinforce racial norms as to challenge them.[104]

"Hold What You've Got" went Top 10 on both the pop and R&B charts in early 1965, further cementing Muscle Shoals' reputation as a site of cross-racial R&B. In his autobiography and elsewhere, Killen aligned himself with this ascendant narrative, writing that he brought together country and R&B and thus struck a larger blow for racial progress.[105] But

Joe Tex promotional photo, 1966. After recording "Hold What You've Got" at FAME Studios, Tex began a run of success that lasted fifteen years and brought him to all three cities of the country-soul triangle. *Memphis Press-Scimitar* Collection, Preservation and Special Collections, University of Memphis Libraries.

Joe Tex was by no means a passive participant in these sessions or the direction of his career. The musicians who worked with Tex remember him as a powerful presence who provided as much input as Killen in the creation of individual tracks. He also asserted himself against his white patron, pushing back against Killen's refusal to employ black musicians in the studio and resisting Killen's attempts to control his recording career. And Tex was just as interested in the possibilities of the country-R&B blend as Killen.[106]

In fact, he may have been even more interested in these hybrids. Given his early career, Tex likely understood that the mix would appeal to several demographics, perhaps even the country audience to which he had been denied access. He later echoed Killen in crediting his successful career—with twelve years of hits following "Hold What You've Got"—to his use of "half soul musicians, half country musicians" on his recordings.[107] Killen occasionally admitted that he and Tex were equal and sometimes combative creative partners. "The thing we understood most," he wrote, "was that we didn't understand each other's creative process."[108]

Killen's remark is the inverse of Arthur Alexander's admission that he and the FAME musicians "only had this one thing in common: we liked all types of music," but the two observations are equally illustrative of the racial terrain that musicians reflected and reshaped in the early days of the country-soul triangle. This terrain was best symbolized by the relationship between country and R&B, the two genres with which the triangle became the most strongly identified. By 1960 they were cornerstones of the music industry and well-known symbols of racial division in the South and the rest of the United States. Interactions between the two genres represented both the possibility of desegregation and the tenacity of segregated racial categories. The emergence of the country-soul triangle—crystallized by "You Better Move On"—represented both the pinnacle of this historical relationship and a transformational moment within it.

But, as evidenced by the divergent career trajectories of Arthur Alexander and Rick Hall, and by the experiences of Buddy Killen and Joe Tex, this cross-racial blending did not have equal consequences for black and white musicians. While African Americans struggled to incorporate country into their professional identities, whites used their familiarity with R&B to achieve greater success in a diversifying music business. Conversely, black artists—even those with eclectic musical influences—were artistically and commercially pigeonholed because of their race. This disparity reveals that, contrary to any utopian ideas of racial tran-scendence, the day-to-day experiences of triangle musicians were defined by complex and sometimes uneasy interactions between black and white. From its beginnings, the triangle was built on a fundamentally unequal relationship that simultaneously created and restricted the possibility of interracial collaboration.

The development of the early Muscle Shoals recording scene—like the stylistic marriage of country and R&B—has been rewritten as primarily a story of racial progress and white redemption in a divided South. Whites like Rick Hall and Buddy Killen (and Sam Phillips before them) have suc-cessfully positioned themselves as visionaries who made the courageous choice to abandon the music and politics of the South's racist past in favor of a liberating alliance with black musicians and R&B. Meanwhile, African American artists like Arthur Alexander and Joe Tex have been relegated to a secondary role as the beneficiaries of the tolerance and innovations of white men. In a sense, this historical misrepresentation is the final step in the marginalization that defined the triangle's earliest days.

This was put on vivid display at the University of North Alabama in 1999, when a panel titled "The Men Who Made the Music" sought to explain and celebrate Muscle Shoals' rich history. Rick Hall, Buddy Killen, and Sam Phillips were all there to discuss their roles as musical innovators and cultural liberators. They spoke of the transformative effect that R&B had on them and discussed their roles in bridging the musical and societal gaps between black and white. Additionally, they heralded the interracial friendships among musicians and dismissed the idea of racial conflict or discrimination. No African Americans spoke at the event.[109]

The fourth man on the panel was Jerry Wexler, the white Atlantic Records executive with whom Buddy Killen signed a deal to distribute Joe Tex's "Hold What You've Got" in the spring of 1965. Wexler, the former *Billboard* writer who coined the term "R&B," was one of the most powerful men in the black-music business in the mid-1960s, and he recognized how significant Muscle Shoals could be to the pop-music landscape and to Atlantic's bottom line. But he had a deeper interest in the music made at FAME. Wexler saw the studio's success as confirmation of a personal philosophy that fueled his initial interest in R&B and had recently drawn him to the records made in the integrated studios of another southern city. He believed that the interracial music of the country-soul triangle represented more than an important new style; to Wexler, it was the soundtrack of racial healing. He and others called it "the Memphis sound."

Two

I GOT WHAT I GOT THE HARD WAY

The Music and Mythology of the Memphis Sound

In 1947 a recent college graduate named Jerry Wexler published a short story called "The Lost Summer." Set in Wexler's hometown of New York City, the story portrays a black elevator operator named George, a recent transplant from Memphis who introduces a white teenager named Danny to the blues. Wexler presents Danny as a troubled kid whose friendship with George and exposure to "those lovely hopeless chords" of Memphis's black musical heritage help him to accept his impending adulthood. The young author's moral was clear: the music of black southerners has healing powers for white people.[1]

Fifteen years later, Wexler was one of the most powerful men in the music business. After writing for *Billboard*, where he coined the term "rhythm and blues," Wexler became a partner and producer at New York's Atlantic Records in 1953 and helped Atlantic become the nation's most powerful R&B label for the rest of that decade. But Atlantic was in decline in the early 1960s, losing ground to upstart labels like Motown. Wexler blamed this "rigor mortis" on the label's adherence to the New York–based musicians who he felt were recycling their previous successes rather than staying current. Looking to restore Atlantic's commercial footing and rekindle his creative fire, Wexler turned to the black South in the hope it would inspire him just as it had the protagonist of his short story.[2]

Over the next few years, Wexler signed production and distribution deals with Buddy Killen's Dial Records in Nashville, Rick Hall's FAME Studios in Muscle Shoals, and—most profitably—Stax Records in Memphis. The country-soul triangle made Atlantic bigger and more profitable than ever before, and other national companies began sending their own black artists (along with an increasing number of whites) to record in Memphis, Muscle Shoals, and Nashville.[3] Wexler's investment brought an economic boom to the triangle's recording studios.[4]

Wexler's appreciation for the musicians of the country-soul triangle went beyond their commercial success. He quickly grew infatuated with what Peter Guralnick called "the southern studio approach," the way that studios like Stax used small interracial ensembles to record material that blended country, R&B, and other styles.[5] For Wexler, this was more than just a fresh musical style—it was a sign of social progress. "The musical integration was a joy to hear and to behold," he wrote later, and he was particularly interested in the effect on the white players. "Despite the ugly legacy of Jim Crow, their white hearts and minds were gripped, it would seem, forevermore."[6] In southern studios, Wexler saw his short story coming to life; just as George the elevator operator helped Danny by exposing him to Memphis blues, the interracial R&B of the country-soul triangle represented a larger process of white redemption.

Wexler made this belief central to his Atlantic promotional strategy. He became crucial to the popularization of the "Memphis sound," the central motif around which southern R&B and soul recordings—even those not recorded in Memphis—were promoted and understood in the 1960s and beyond. Labels like Atlantic used the concept to distinguish southern-based records in the crowded marketplace, and both journalists and fans embraced the term to convey the music's quality and cultural authenticity. The success of the Memphis sound led to a recording boom in the city that surpassed even the success of Sun Records in the 1950s and gave Memphis a new, and distinctly black-identified, musical identity. Its popularity reshaped the strategy employed by musicians in Nashville, who reacted by asserting their own commitment to cross-racial, soul-influenced music. By the end of the 1960s, "the Memphis sound" transcended its roots as a musical slogan to become a nationally recognized symbol of the era's broader push for integration. To this day, it structures both scholarly and popular understandings of this music and its historical significance.[7]

The Memphis sound was based on a seemingly irreconcilable racial contradiction. Writers, activists, and fans heralded it as the "blackest" popular music of the era, most reflective of African American musical traditions and most expressive of the black experience in the civil rights era. But, at the same time, they claimed that the Memphis sound owed its distinctiveness to the interracial group of musicians who blended the South's musical traditions into a unique and transformative mixture. One Memphis reporter referred to this alchemy as a "white overlay on blackish music."[8] In this era, the Memphis sound was widely understood as authentically black music produced by racially integrated groups of authentically southern musicians.

The musicians of the country-soul triangle were at the center of Memphis sound discourse, playing a key role in the sound's initial popularization as a musical style and its broader acceptance as a symbol of racial change. Through packaging, advertisements, public statements, and the recordings themselves, triangle musicians—particularly in Memphis—exploited the Memphis sound as a means to get more and better work. Many of them believed in the sound's social value, but this political resonance only added to its value as a promotional tool. The integrationist politics of the Memphis sound paid huge dividends.

Ironically, though, the promotion of the Memphis sound also quickly and fundamentally distorted the larger appreciation of these musicians. For one, it misrepresented their accomplishments by framing them less as the result of hard work—the painstaking production of popular music—and more as the expression of a cultural or even natural essence that one record executive said "cannot be duplicated anywhere else . . . [and] cannot be taught."[9] It ignored the musicians' extensive training, denied their musical versatility, obscured their desire for commercial success, and erased their role in helping to construct this very mythology of musical naturalness. In other words, the Memphis sound turned the triangle's musicians from skilled professionals into cultural conduits.

By naturalizing the production of the music, the promoters of the Memphis sound—both within and outside the recording industry—also oversimplified its racial politics. They presented southern studios as racially harmonious sites of collaboration that confirmed the success of the national civil rights movement and offered a redemptive vision of white southernness that contrasted with contemporaneous stories of regional hostility. "Everybody who knows . . . the real South knows that, despite the Klan and the lynchings and the brutality, the liberated Southern white is a hell of a lot closer to the Negro soul than the Northern white liberal," Jerry Wexler told *Cosmopolitan* in 1968, adding that the "Memphis sound" reflected "something about the *good* there is in the South."[10] This narrative of healing contributed to an astonishing turn by the end of the 1960s, in which the Memphis sound was increasingly framed around the innovation and redemption of white people. This white-centered story of racial progressivism retains its primacy in the historical memory of the South and the 1960s.[11]

There is no question that southern studio musicians defied white supremacy in significant ways. This included everything from traveling and working in integrated groups to smaller, yet no less significant, subversions like the ability of African Americans to refer to their white colleagues by their first names without titles like "Mister" that blacks were expected to use when addressing whites but rarely received themselves.[12] Still, their experiences of race were far more complex than the happy imagery of the Memphis sound and were inextricably linked to the musicians' roles as workers in a racially unequal marketplace. Southern musicians credited their ability to collaborate across racial lines not to the broader push for integration or the push to show "the *good* there is in the South" but to their professional abilities and their desire to work with the most talented people. Conversely, there were numerous racial conflicts in triangle studios in the 1960s, most of which specifically concerned professional conduct and few of which ever received significant attention from those who publicized the Memphis sound. Triangle musicians juggled these precarious racial politics throughout their studio work, which makes their accomplishments all the more astounding. To paraphrase a Stax hit, they got what they got the hard way.[13]

The Memphis sound originated in the city's live-music scene, which—despite the success of Sun Records in the 1950s—was still the center of the Memphis music economy. As pianist Bobby Wood remembered, recording in Memphis was "pretty much dead" by 1960, but musicians still "could make a decent living just playing clubs."[14] Particularly important were the city's many venues specializing in R&B, some of which catered to an African American audience, while others were exclusively for white customers. Evocatively named clubs like the Plantation Inn and Lil Abner's Rebel Room became well known for the large African American ensembles, led by bandleaders like Ben Branch and Willie Mitchell, who performed the most popular sounds of the day for a lively audience of paying, dancing customers. Sam Phillips's shift to white artists at Sun Records shut many of Memphis's biggest stars and best musicians out of the chance to make records, but these multigenerational black groups remained the core of the city's live scene and formed the backbone of its recording boom in the 1960s.[15]

Besides playing for African American audiences, the most popular groups also performed at whites-only nightspots, where they faced a unique kind of segregation. In one sense, black musicians occupied a place of prestige that was denied to most other African American workers. They were hired to entertain white patrons, many of whom—like the frat circuit audiences that Dan Penn wowed in Alabama—demanded to

Willie Mitchell, live on stage in 1969. Mitchell was one of Memphis's preeminent bandleaders and later became in-house producer at Hi Records, where he made significant contributions to the city's soul boom in the 1960s and 1970s. Photographed by Barney Hudson. *Memphis Press-Scimitar* Collection, Preservation and Special Collections, University of Memphis Libraries.

be entertained by African Americans because of their supposed musical gifts. Onstage, black performers held sway over a white crowd that viewed them with a certain degree of respect and even adoration. But this had obvious limitations. Black musicians were not allowed to mingle with white patrons before the show and during breaks; instead, they left the premises and huddled together on the back steps. Even as they provided white customers with top-quality entertainment, they still had to rest and refresh themselves in the barest of accommodations and faced severe con-sequences for any perceived violation of the Jim Crow order. The segre-gated experiences of black musicians in Memphis left deep and painful impressions that they brought with them into the recording studio.[16]

Though they were mistreated, African American musicians were hailed as heroes by a small but growing number of white players who collabo-rated with the black bands in the late 1950s. These teenage musicians heard R&B on radio stations like Memphis's WDIA and Nashville's WLAC and acquired a library of records by black artists through mail order and the few record stores that carried them. Many of them also had gigs with country groups, and their familiarity with the genre allowed them to attain the versatility that being a successful live musician required. They were both products and progenitors of the musical crossovers that built the country-soul triangle and defined the Memphis sound.

These young white musicians came to the clubs to learn R&B from seasoned African American professionals. As Peter Guralnick describes, they saw black players as "the pinnacle of cool [with] a level of musicianship and formal elegance to which they could scarcely aspire."[17] The most prominent of these whites were a group of Memphis high schoolers called the Royal Spades. The teenagers bonded over their love of the music being made at venues like Club Handy, a Beale Street spot that they attended before they were of legal age. The group's guitarist, Steve Cropper, recalled that Club Handy's African American owners let the white kids listen from just outside the doors but told them to leave quickly if any trouble should start, lest the police find underage white patrons in a blacks-only club. At the clubs (or just outside them), Cropper and his friends took in the sounds of Memphis's prominent black bands, which they eventually emulated in their own group.[18]

The presence of white musicians like the Royal Spades became a common element in the promotion of the Memphis sound.[19] But the early interactions between black and white musicians in Memphis—like those of their contemporaries in Muscle Shoals—were not immune from the discomforting dynamics of American racial politics. For one thing, Memphis's black musicians did not view white R&B players as freedom fighters. They saw them as potential collaborators but also as competition whose whiteness afforded them opportunities unavailable to African Americans. This might mean using the bathroom in a whites-only club or being able to supplement their R&B income by playing country shows. White guitarist Bobby Manuel summed up this attitude as "not another little white boy over here, we're sick of this."[20] Black musicians had long used stereotypes of inherent musicality as a kind of racial capital, and their concern about the presence of whites in the Memphis R&B scene can be understood as a desire to police this boundary and protect their professional turf.[21]

Additionally, while white musicians felt kinship with the black players, they sometimes romanticized and even fetishized them. For example, band member Don Nix says that they called themselves the Royal Spades because "that was a great black name."[22] As Robert Gordon notes, "The name's racist overtone smacks of teens believing they're getting away with something," and Nix and his friends used their affection for black culture as a symbol of their distance from the cultural mainstream.[23] Nix

The Royal Spades in 1960. The group represented the growing
number of young whites who became interested in performing
R&B in Memphis in the late 1950s. Later, the group worked at Stax
Records as the Mar-Keys. Left to right: Don Nix, Steve Cropper, Charles
"Packy" Axton, Donald "Duck" Dunn, Terry Johnson, Ronnie Stoots,
and Wayne Jackson. Stax Museum of American Soul Music.

described the black musicians' lack of mobility as a reflection of his own
sense of alienation. "They'd all sit . . . on the back of the stage where they
were playing and I always thought that was cool, I always wanted to do
that."[24] It is doubtful that Nix felt segregation was "cool," but his sense of
shared outsiderhood conflates the discrimination faced by African Americans with the authentic expression of musical realness. Nix and his friends
were hardly the first whites to do this—in fact, from antebellum slave owners to the Harlem "slummers" of the 1920s to the beat generation in the
1950s, young whites had long presented their contact with black music
as part of a larger cultural transgression.[25] This philosophy was crucial to
how they undertook their careers as professional musicians.

Even more troubling is Royal Spade horn player Wayne Jackson's recollection that his bandmate Charles "Packy" Axton sought to immerse himself in black culture as a means of rebelling against his own race and class

privilege. Jackson called Axton the "blackest white man" he knew, someone "who hung out with blacks when it wasn't cool," dated black women, and had a black roommate. Jackson claimed that this love of African Americans came from Axton's impulse to "embarrass his mother or his father."[26] This characterization strains credibility, especially since Packy Axton's mother, Estelle, cofounded Stax Records and (as discussed below) worked enthusiastically with black musicians. Still, other accounts confirm Jackson's observation that Packy Axton's zeal for black culture arose in part from the racial masquerade that underpinned blackface minstrelsy and has characterized the historical relationship of whites to black music and musicians.[27] Axton's attitude, like that expressed by Don Nix about the hipness of the black players or the name the Royal Spades, shows that the racial transgression of white musicians working with African Americans in the Memphis R&B scene drew from murky wells of racial desire.

It is important to note that, with the possible exception of Packy Axton, there is little evidence that any of the Royal Spades sneaked into R&B clubs primarily because they wanted to transgress Jim Crow. Instead, they wanted to learn the music they loved in order to develop their professional craft. The only way to achieve this education was through direct exposure to the African American players whom they revered. The city's black musicians sometimes accepted and sometimes resisted this move. Both sides recognized that the Memphis R&B scene required them to negotiate both the restrictions of segregation and the cross-racial collaborations that possessed their own set of dangers.

One overriding reality unified the experiences of club musicians regardless of race: versatility equaled success. This was true both for scuffling youngsters and established players like black saxophonist Fred Ford, who said that if "you weren't able to play a polka . . . you couldn't get any gigs. So . . . we didn't get tied up with this type of music or that type of music. We just tried to make whatever we played sound good."[28] African American bandleader Willie Mitchell further recognized that this versatility needed to be directed toward what was currently popular: "If you're going to work the clubs you've got to play what's on the radio," he noted. "We usually opened with a jazz set [to] warm the musicians up, [then] we'd play pop music, we'd play R&B music, we'd play hillbilly music, anything. The bigger variety you had . . . the [more] popular your band was."[29] For Mitchell, Ford, and others, the ability to play numerous styles—including those not identified with blacks—was a job requirement.

The Memphis sound emerged from this fertile ground of professional training and collaboration, not from any racial or regional essence.

A group of young musicians perform at Memphis nightclub Hernando's Hideaway in 1965. This ensemble featured several studio mainstays who trained on the club circuit and supplemented their studio income by performing for live audiences. Left to right: Charles Chalmers (saxophone), Donald "Duck" Dunn (bass), Bill Strom (organ), Gene Chrisman (drums), Wayne Jackson (trumpet), Bobby Wood (piano), and Lee Adkins (guitar). *Memphis Press-Scimitar* Collection, Preservation and Special Collections, University of Memphis Libraries.

Musicians trained in a variety of settings, became experts at a wide range of styles, and deployed these skills to please their paying customers. Additionally, they did not seek cross-racial brotherhood but instead nurtured a professional respect that did not always avoid the pitfalls of working across racial lines. They brought these dynamics with them to a new record label that opened in 1959. Stax Records became the most successful and influential studio of the Memphis recording boom, the home of some of the era's most acclaimed R&B and soul, and the primary vehicle for the dissemination of the Memphis sound as musical trademark and cultural symbol. But the Stax story begins with a white country musician who wanted to follow in the footsteps of Sam Phillips.[30]

A banker by day, Jim Stewart played fiddle in country bands around Memphis after returning from the Army in 1953.[31] One night, he got a glimpse into the future when "a kid by the name of Elvis Presley came in and started doing the intermissions." Stewart's love of country—which he credited to his childhood exposure to the Grand Ole Opry—kept him from fully embracing the new rockabilly sound, but he did try to cash in on the success of Sun Records by cutting a couple of unsuccessful singles.[32] Stewart turned to his sister, Estelle Axton, a fellow banker who mortgaged her house in order to help Stewart purchase a studio-quality tape recorder and in exchange became a partner in her brother's fledgling Satellite Records. Looking to protect her investment, Axton insisted that Satellite also open a small record-retail business. Although Axton initially sold records only to her friends, she expanded this surprisingly profitable enterprise after Satellite moved into a former movie theater. As Rob Bowman notes, "By 1960 [the theater] had been relegated to little more than the occasional country-and-western performance . . . and as the neighborhood began to shift from white to black, even the country rentals had begun to fall off."[33] The studio was in the rear, run by Stewart and a white guitarist named Chips Moman, and the Axton-run record store was out front. After a legal dispute, Satellite was rechristened Stax to reflect the last names of its two founding partners.

Jim Stewart was Stax's titular head, but Estelle Axton supported him both financially and creatively, pushing Stewart to let the listening tastes of the local black community determine Stax's artistic and commercial strategy. "Jim Stewart really wanted to record country music," Wayne Jackson recalled, "and Estelle said, listen, I'm out here working with these black kids all the time, let's make music for them. We can sell the records to them."[34] Deanie Parker, an African American who worked in the record store as a teenager before becoming a key member of Stax's front-office staff, called Satellite "the research and development division" for the label and remembered Axton holding late-night listening sessions so Stax's musicians could listen to the latest hits from Motown or Atlantic to learn the secrets of commercial success.[35] By drawing on the talents and tastes of the local black community, Estelle Axton crafted a distinctly pop-minded and black-focused strategy for Stax.

The musicians who attended Axton's listening sessions and worked in the studio represented a cross-section of the Memphis music community. There were older veterans of local black bands, younger African Americans who hungered to make records with the more experienced musicians, and the white members of the Royal Spades. All played in a variety of

Estelle Axton, cofounder of Stax Records, late 1970s. Axton convinced her brother Jim Stewart to shift Stax's productions toward the music favored by young African Americans. Photograph by William Leaptrott. *Memphis Press-Scimitar* Collection, Preservation and Special Collections, University of Memphis Libraries.

ensembles and each knew that versatility was the key to success. They wanted to make records and were ready to work hard. Stax's early roster of artists exhibited the same dynamics.

The label's first hits came from Rufus Thomas, the WDIA deejay who—after his moment of success at Sun Records and abandonment by Sam Phillips—left recording in favor of his radio show and live appearances, not to mention his day job at a textile mill. Still, when word of a new company recording black artists in Memphis reached Thomas, he raced to the studio with demos in hand, including some by his teenage daughter. Carla Thomas was no novice. As a child, she absorbed her parents' vast record collection and listened to the Grand Ole Opry with her mother. She and her brother Marvell even learned how to yodel. They "could yodel in harmony," Carla remembered, and Marvell showed off his solo skills at talent shows: "It was so odd to see a little black kid yodeling that I always won," he recalled.[36] Both children also received formal voice and piano lessons. As they grew, the Thomas children joined WDIA's Teen Town Singers, which featured many future professional musicians and appeared on a weekly radio show and at community functions. "We did a lot of jazz things," Marvell attested. "And, we actually sang big band arrangements, as though we were the instruments and not singers. So we learned a lot of things."[37]

Both Thomas children continued performing through their adolescence. Marvell played with high-school ensembles and worked with bandleader Ben Branch when he was sixteen years old. "I knew all of the radio stuff," he remembered.[38] The Thomases also worked on their songwriting. "I use[d] to sit around just like daddy and write songs," Carla remembered, and her compositions blended the many sounds she heard on radio and records.[39] Her father helped her record them and brought the tapes to Stax.

Excited by the material, and no doubt emboldened by Rufus Thomas's celebrity and access to the WDIA audience, Axton and Stewart immediately recorded several cuts by Rufus and Carla Thomas both as solo artists and as a duo. Rufus and Carla's single "'Cause I Love You" became Stax's first hit in 1959 and Carla's composition "Gee Whiz" soon repeated the success. It reached Top 10 on the national R&B charts in 1961. Although the Memphis sound came to be defined by spare, funky arrangements and gospel-influenced singing, the swooning "Gee Whiz" bore greater resemblance to the lushly orchestrated pop and Nashville sound country of the late 1950s. In fact, although she eventually became known as the "Queen of the Memphis sound," Thomas's taste gravitated toward what she called "sweet pop," and she said that it was only later that she moved toward a more identifiably "southern soul" sound in the hopes of scoring more hits.[40]

The national success of "Gee Whiz" showed that the Stax crew possessed the creative chops and commercial wherewithal to compete in the pop market. Rufus Thomas lauded the success as another example of his family's importance to the Memphis music industry. "We launched both companies. I launched the first one [Sun Records], and my daughter and I launched the second."[41]

The band backing Carla Thomas at her early live shows was the Royal Spades, now rechristened the Mar-Keys. (Robert Gordon writes that Estelle Axton made them change their name because "all-white kids playing black music and calling themselves the Royal Spades just wasn't going to play.")[42] It was not hard for them to get work at Stax, since Packy Axton was Estelle's son—Jim Stewart's nephew—and he was one of the earliest to encourage his mother to push Stax toward R&B. The Mar-Keys became Stax artists as well, recording the hot-and-heavy grooves they played around Memphis; one song, "Last Night," became a breakout hit. Some of the musicians who played on the record were not part of the Mar-Keys' road ensemble, including several black players who worked regularly at Stax in the early period. When the Mar-Keys returned to the road as an all-white ensemble, the African Americans were not pleased. "It was an all-white band. And, they made some money out there," recalled horn player Floyd Newman. Newman, along with black bassist Lewie Steinberg, interpreted this loss of income as a professional slight and a thinly veiled display of racial favoritism.[43]

It is important to remember that the session players who created hit singles were often not the musicians whose names got listed on the record sleeve, regardless of race. Moreover, the Mar-Keys had already established themselves as a performing entity, so it made sense that their known personnel would promote their hit single. But the choice to send the all-white Mar-Keys to perform in front of black audiences was resented by some of Stax's African American personnel, especially after the black studio musicians also created a *second* Mar-Keys single, "The Morning After," while the white group was on the road.[44]

Many audiences were surprised by the disconnect between the visual and musical components of the Mar-Keys' live presentation. "It was pretty weird," admitted Wayne Jackson, remembering a Texas tour where "we played the chitlin joints out in the cotton field. . . . The people—the club owner, the bartender, the guy barbecuing and everybody else would say, 'Where's the Mar-Keys?'"[45] Don Nix recalled that urban crowds were just as surprised. When the group played Chicago, "it was shock . . . because there was [*sic*] no white acts on any of those shows."[46] The combination of the group's R&B sound, promotion on black-oriented radio stations, and lack of photographs on records or promotional materials led audiences of both races to be astonished by the fact that the group was white. Of course, the Mar-Keys' whiteness also brought them the privileges of segregation. When they backed up Carla or Rufus Thomas, they had access to white hotels and restaurants, while the stars settled for inferior accommodations or none at all.[47]

Although the success of "Last Night" gave the Mar-Keys steady live business throughout the South, guitarist Steve Cropper tired of the endless grind and decided to come home to Stax. "I was just missing being in the studio," he recalled. "I missed being in that creative element."[48] Cropper became the studio's primary session guitarist and producer. He was soon joined by three musicians who—working together as Booker T. and the MGs—represented the backbone of Stax's ascendancy, the laboring heartbeat of the studio's releases, and the best-known symbol of the Memphis sound's interracial partnership. But, as with the rest of Stax's origins, the story is more complicated.

Booker T. and the MGs came together for the first time in 1962 when Jim Stewart booked a session featuring former Sun rockabilly artist Billy Lee Riley and looked to hire musicians with a variety of musical skills. Steve Cropper's ubiquity at Stax made him an obvious choice. To join him, Stewart hired three black veterans of the Memphis live-music scene.

Bassist Lewie Steinberg's father played piano at a Beale Street club for decades, and Lewie was an experienced musician by the time he was a teenager. He even backed his brother Luther on an R&B recording, but Lewie recalled that "he had to use the name Lou Sergeant. He didn't use Luther Steinberg because, back in them days, what would it look like— here's a man with a Jew name out there playing rhythm and blues, you know? It just wouldn't work."[49] The Steinbergs' light skin and surname led some to assume they were white, but Lewie recalled that their ambiguous features actually restricted their opportunities when it came to working as musicians in a racialized genre like R&B. Steinberg's understanding of these politics marked his early days at Stax. He played bass on the Mar-Keys' "Last Night," and he was among those who felt cheated by the decision to send an all-white band on the road. "You see, every time Stax would get a hit record," he explained, "I would be the one that would put the bass to it, put the bottom in it. . . . And every time it comes out, somebody else is reaping the benefits."[50] Steinberg's anger foreshadowed subsequent events.

Helping Steinberg put "the bottom" in the MGs was drummer Al Jackson Jr., whom Steinberg knew from the club circuit. Jackson's father led a big band that was among the most popular of its day, and Al Jr. was well known by his early twenties. For the young Stax musicians, he was the gold standard. Marvell Thomas called Jackson the "human metronome," and horn player Andrew Love echoed a widespread opinion that he was "the greatest drummer I ever saw and the greatest drummer I had ever been around."[51] Jackson's influence did not end with his musicianship; he also did more than anyone to establish a stable working environment for Stax session players. Given the steady paycheck provided by his club gigs, Jackson was reluctant to devote much time to this unproven studio. He agreed to come to Stax only when they promised him a guaranteed salary. "We weren't used to that," Steve Cropper recalled. "We got paid for work but nobody was salaried."[52] Jackson's moves to professionalize the Stax musicians reached fruition when each member of the MGs became Stax executives as the company expanded, achieving an unprecedented amount of worker control at a southern studio.

The person who convinced Al Jackson to come to Stax, Booker T. Jones, made up the final member of the quartet. Jones was also the youngest, having just graduated from Booker T. Washington High School, but he too had a wide array of experiences on the Memphis club circuit. A formally trained musician and arranger, Jones knew how to play more than a dozen instruments and was experimenting with his own compositions when he started working sessions at Stax.[53]

Given the talents of the assembled musicians, Jim Stewart had high hopes for the session with Billy Lee Riley, but it fizzled out. Once it ended, however, Cropper, Jackson, Jones, and Steinberg started jamming on a blues riff that sounded just like the slow-dragging songs they played late at night in the clubs. Intrigued, Stewart decided to record it for release as a single. After laying down the first song, called "Behave Yourself," Stewart asked the foursome if they could come up with anything that Stewart could put on the flipside, so Cropper asked Jones to play a riff that he and the young keyboardist picked up from the radio a few weeks earlier. The musicians quickly fell in behind a pulsing groove that became "Green Onions."[54]

"Green Onions" became one of the definitive Memphis sound recordings, heralded as a perfect encapsulation of the raw sound that made southern R&B so distinctive. As Cropper explained it, however, the song was not an attempt to unearth the authentic sounds of the South but rather an explicitly pop-oriented record that the MGs hoped would resonate with the young dancers who made up Stax's target audience. "We knew what we liked to dance to and we liked to dance to songs that had a great beat to it," he said. "So, consequently, when we were creating and writing, obviously, those influences took over." This love of dancing led the MGs to create consciously "commercial music" that Cropper hoped would work "to get people's emotions going, to get their body moving, to get them into a rhythm."[55] The MGs wanted to ensure their continued success as working musicians by playing the popular trends of the day. (Cropper's words echo those of keyboardist Bobby Wood, who asserted that "Memphis was primarily a pop market" in the 1960s.)[56] Just as Carla Thomas's "Gee Whiz" represented a crystallization of contemporary pop, the first sessions by the MGs symbolized a similar consumer-minded synthesis.

"Green Onions" reached the R&B Top 10. For the next several years, Booker T. and the MGs released a string of hits under their own name, worked as backing musicians on nearly every Stax release, and—in their capacity as worker-managers—helped guide the company in its period of expansion.[57] They also became the literal and figurative faces of Memphis sound interracialism.

Nonetheless, the rise of the MGs included a significant moment of conflict. In 1964, after two successful years, the group fired Lewie Steinberg and replaced him with Donald "Duck" Dunn, Cropper's high school friend and bassist for the Mar-Keys. Steinberg again believed that his ouster was racially motivated. The presence of Al Jackson and Booker T. Jones makes it difficult to believe that race was entirely to blame for Steinberg's departure—Cropper had several talented friends in the all-white Mar-Keys, but there is no evidence that he tried to replace the group's other black members. (For their part, Jackson and Jones remained silent on the matter.) Instead, Cropper said that Dunn was simply a better fit for the job. He claimed that Steinberg's older, jazz-influenced style did not fit the Stax sound, while Dunn had a greater acuity for the "commercial music" that young folks wanted to hear.[58] But it is difficult to believe that a seasoned pro like Steinberg could not adapt his sound to the new musical model, particularly after he helped establish it through his playing on "Last Night" and "Green Onions." Versatility, after all, was a point of pride for Memphis musicians.

In all likelihood, it was some combination of Dunn's expertise, his long friendship with Cropper, and his race that provoked Steinberg's firing. (According to Robert Gordon, Steinberg's drinking was also a factor.)[59] But Steinberg's complaint was not isolated. It was the culmination of a feeling among black musicians at Stax that racial preferences played an important role in company decisions, especially when it came to who would benefit professionally from Stax's successes. Even if Steinberg and the others are wrong about the racial undertone of these decisions (and they most likely are not), their memories of Stax are stained by what they saw as discrimination within a company that became an internationally recognized symbol of racial progress and cooperation.

Their anger has been compounded by the fact that Steinberg is one of several Stax studio players who have been marginalized in the memory of the company's 1960s accomplishments. These individuals, like Howard Grimes, Bob Talley, or Marvell Thomas, were usually African American and played a crucial role in the company's success but have not achieved the fame of the MGs.[60] This process was not necessarily race-based, but some black musicians have argued that the absence of these players from the Stax story has reinforced the false notion that white musicians played a greater role in the label's development and the larger story of the Memphis sound than they actually did.[61] The firing of Lewie Steinberg is perhaps the most obvious symbol of this larger silencing, especially since many appreciations of Stax do not even mention that he was the MGs original bassist.

Of course, none of the controversy meant that Duck Dunn was a slouch. He grew up in Memphis and worked in country, pop, and R&B bands, including an enviable gig with bandleader Ben Branch. But Dunn's time in Branch's group gave him insight into one of the risks of playing in an interracial combo. "I think [Mar-Keys guitarist] Charlie Freeman and I were the first ones to integrate, but we got a lot of hell from the union," Dunn recalled.[62] The union to which he referred, the American Federation of Musicians (AFM), had long wrestled with the issue of race. Its national leadership embraced integration in the mid-1940s but many local branches resisted racial unification into the late-1960s. The biggest objections came from black locals who worried that their autonomy would be challenged—and their treasuries plundered—by white members; by the spring of 1966, twenty-five cities still had segregated AFM locals.[63] Even beyond race, AFM locals were notoriously protective and criticized fellow chapters for employing too many musicians from another branch.[64] With the question of integration added in, it is quite possible that Dunn and Freeman's involvement in a black band raised the ire of members of both races, offering an institutionalized parallel to Bobby Manuel's memories that black musicians were "sick" of all the "white boys" working in Memphis R&B.

Duck Dunn heard that other authorities also did not approve of this racial mixing. "My brother-in-law was a captain on the police department and [told me that] they're really watching this band up there and wondering because they didn't like the integration thing. . . . They didn't just like [having] an integrated band playing for a bunch of white people." Musicians also resisted presenting integrated ensembles at gigs, and their fears were not limited to the potential reactions of white audiences. Dunn observed that Branch did not call him for gigs in blacks-only nightclubs. "They just didn't ask me and I probably understand why. . . . [I] didn't feel slighted."[65]

Indeed, although studios were not the interracial utopias of Memphis-sound mythology, places like Stax offered a much freer environment than club gigs. Live performances were public affairs and thus subject to the laws and expectations dictating racial decorum. The image of an interracial band onstage in an officially or unofficially segregated venue challenged Jim Crow in a way that an all-black band performing in an all-white club did not. Reggie Young, a white guitarist who became a member of two integrated Memphis studio ensembles, played a wide variety of music with both black and white musicians, but whenever he played with African American bands at the all-white Plantation Inn he sat behind a curtain so that the audience would not see that the musicians were mixed. "We couldn't be on the stage with them or we'd all got killed, you know," Young recalled.[66] The carefully maintained segregation ensured that musicians remained separated onstage and gave the illusion that white audiences were being entertained exclusively by black players. Of course, Reggie Young and Duck Dunn could always unplug their instruments and sit in the audience, whereas their African American collaborators and mentors could not. Studios like Stax gave musicians of both races greater mobility to interact with each other as colleagues.

Given Jerry Wexler's long fascination with Memphis music and interest in reviving Atlantic, it made sense that Stax's unique sound and interracial personnel piqued his interest. He first heard of the label in 1960 when a Memphis retailer told him about the local success of Rufus and Carla Thomas. Wexler distributed their debut single on Atlantic and signed Stax to a long-term agreement. The agreement established Stax in the national market and convinced Wexler to bring Atlantic artists to record at the Memphis studio. These included gospel shouter Wilson Pickett and high-energy duo Sam & Dave, both of whom had languished at Atlantic but found major success working with the MGs. Pickett and Sam & Dave, along with homegrown Stax stars like Otis Redding, specialized in a distinctive brand of R&B defined by gospel-influenced vocals and the spare funk of the MGs. Promotional staff at Atlantic and Stax began calling this blend the Memphis sound.

First and foremost, the Memphis sound was a musical distinction designed to separate Stax's recordings—and others produced in the South—from their counterparts at northern-based labels like Motown. Generally, the Memphis sound employed a smaller group of musicians (using one guitarist instead of Motown's standard group of three) and eschewed the lush, string-heavy arrangements that characterized northern-based R&B in the late 1950s and early 1960s, the sound that Stax mimicked on Carla Thomas's "Gee Whiz." Instead, Stax developed an approach that foregrounded the interplay between rhythm instruments, a warm bed of piano or organ, and sharp stabs from a horn section in response to the vocalist. Generally funkier and grittier than most northern offerings, the Memphis sound echoed its roots in the blues and gospel of southern tradition and offered an accurate reflection of its origins in the city's club scene. The success of "Green Onions" and other Stax recordings established this approach as a commercially viable and creatively exciting alternative.

Stax became synonymous with the Memphis sound, but it modeled its approach, at least in part, on that of another local company. Hi Records was the first label to use "the Memphis sound" as a slogan to market a series of instrumental R&B hits recorded by an interracial roster recruited from local clubs.[67] The parallels extend to the company's history. Like Stax, Hi initially recorded country music, but its derivative early releases made no dent in the market. Stymied, Hi's owners asked local black bandleader Willie Mitchell to reorient the label's sound toward R&B. Mitchell responded by bringing his talented players to Hi and becoming the label's in-house producer. Hi's first hit—"Smokie, Part 2" by the white Bill Black Combo, featuring guitarist Reggie Young, who had played behind the curtain at the Plantation Inn—was a bluesy shuffle that came straight from the dance halls, with a unique skittering guitar sound that Young adapted from jazz drummers.[68]

The creation of "Smokie, Part 2," also demonstrates that, like Stax, Hi weathered incidents of racial conflict. The Bill Black Combo, as constituted on the record and its aftermath, was composed entirely of whites, but both Willie Mitchell and Reggie Young recalled that black musicians were present at the recording, including a pianist named Joe Hall, who abruptly left the session after a white engineer made what Young called "a racial statement." Hall was replaced by a white player, but Young insists that "Joe should have gotten credit for it because [on the recording the white player] played the same thing . . . Joe played."[69] In many ways, it was Hi—not Stax—that most clearly established the parameters of the Memphis sound.

Hi made it into a recognizable tagline, but Jim Stewart says that Jerry Wexler imposed the idea of the Memphis sound on Stax. "That title . . . came from outside," he told Rob Bowman. "We really weren't thinking about it. We came to work each day, we did what we had to do, and we went our separate ways." But Stax realized the slogan's value as a marketing tool in the mid-1960s and began actively deploying it. "We were promoting the Memphis sound as a whole and trying to give a definition of a Stax sound," remembered Stax publicity director Deanie Parker.[70] Stax leaders—most of all the company's ambitious promotions director, a black man named Al Bell—realized that the Memphis sound could improve their sales, and this decision made southern studios and their personnel

A Sam & Dave session at Stax in 1966. Images of interracial
sessions like this became central to the promotion of Stax and the
Memphis sound in the 1960s and 1970s, but the campaigns masked
a more complicated racial history. Photograph © Bill Carrier.
API Photographers, Inc., The Stax Collection, Memphis.

into well-known cultural symbols of racial change and cultural integrity
by the end of the decade.

From the beginning, those who sought to explain the Memphis sound
struggled to find a coherent definition, but everyone seemed to agree that
it was the meeting point between authentic blackness and real southernness.[71] In June 1965 several white Memphis executives explained it this
way to *Billboard* magazine. Sam Phillips chalked it up to the "spontane-
ity" and "off-the-cuff . . . intensity" of Memphis musicians and the music's
roots in "the uninhibited nature of the Negro in the South." Hi cofounder
Joe Cuoghi celebrated the "Southern musician" and said that the "Memphis sound" "cannot be duplicated anywhere else in the country," "cannot
be taught," and possessed a "raunchy . . . blues influence" and "rhythmic

quality" that clearly marked it as African American. And Stax's Jim Stewart asserted that the "Memphis sound" at their label "goes back to the colored influence in the early blues and folk lore music of the South."[72]

Musicians, too, struggled to find a simple description. "The Memphis Sound is unique, very versatile," Carla Thomas told a reporter in 1968. "Once there was a definite sound," she noted, citing the early dominance of guitars and horns. "Now you can't quite tell . . . it's whatever they are recording at that moment," she claimed, before abruptly declaring that "Stax is the Memphis Sound."[73] Indeed, Stax's success with the slogan further complicated an already confusing issue. Pianist Bob Talley went so far as to distinguish between "the sound of Memphis," which included all the artists who recorded in the city, and the "Memphis Sound," which Talley identified strictly with Stax.[74]

Despite these differences, though, all observers claimed that the Memphis sound was synonymous with R&B and soul. Stax declared in one press release that the Memphis sound had "propped up Soul music at a time when interest in it was flagging."[75] Local producer Marty Lacker declared that "Memphis isn't just a soul music city like the Memphis Sound is supposed to imply."[76] The press routinely used the term to describe southern soul records, celebrating them for their connection to African American traditions and current experiences. Even those outside the music world deployed the term. In 1969 advertising executive (and former disc jockey) Wilson Northcross stated that the "Memphis Sound is basically soul and this is now happening in commercials."[77]

The blackness of the Memphis sound had specific resonance in Memphis as a corrective to the way that—thanks to Sam Phillips and Sun Records—the city's music became identified with whites in the 1950s. The Memphis sound allowed Stax and other R&B/soul studios to reestablish the city as a center for African American artists and newly assert the city's musical identity as black. Looking back, David Porter—a black Memphian who worked as singer, songwriter, producer, and executive at Stax—made this clear: "Now there's reality, and then there's real reality. Reality is that the Memphis sound was all of the records that came out of Memphis." But, Porter continued, the "REAL reality is the Memphis sound was black music. . . . THAT'S the Memphis sound."[78]

The term also became a key component in the emergent cultural understandings of soul music. In the late 1960s, writers and scholars began seriously considering the aesthetics, poetics, and politics of the past decade in black popular music, and for them the Memphis sound was the repository of soul's authentic roots. In her 1969 book *The Sound of Soul*, the first extended history of the genre, *Ebony* journalist Phyl Garland claimed southern soul as the authentic musical expression of the black experience, the realer alternative to Motown's "slick, pop-oriented" music. Still, Garland's racial essentialism, like that of soul's other early chroniclers, did not preclude her from embracing the "Memphis sound's" interracialism. She declared that "soul's essence is indisputably black" but that its southern variants resulted from of the blending of black and white musicians.[79]

The centrality of racial integration became dominant in the discourse after the 1968 assassination of Martin Luther King in Memphis. In this turbulent context, writers used the Memphis sound as an example of the continuing promise of integration and racial progress in a political atmosphere that was increasingly polarized. In 1969 Memphis reporter Kay Morgan declared that the music possessed "the spirit of the New South," with a "universal" appeal that spoke across racial lines.[80] That same year, Burt Korall of the *New York Times* argued that the Memphis sound signaled "the increasing sense of democracy within pop music," a stylistic "melting pot" that represented "the very basic and real Southern heart and sound and sentiments [that] are potently honest and a true reflection of today below the Mason-Dixon line." Even if the South remained the most obvious site of American racial conflict, southern music—specifically the Memphis sound—offered its clearest hope of racial transcendence.[81]

All of the music industry figures Korall discussed were white. He congratulated Jerry Wexler for bringing black music to a wider (and whiter) audience and celebrated Steve Cropper as "an architect of the Memphis Sound who typifies the fusion of musical components from the Southern tradition." Korall described how Cropper loved country music as a youth but was soon "drawn to black rhythm and blues because of its stark realism in subject matter and sound," thus making this very simplified version of Cropper's musical development into a metaphor for the larger process of white redemption that occurred through the Memphis sound.[82]

For Korall and many others in this era, no one symbolized the racial promise of the Memphis sound better than Cropper's group, Booker T. and the MGs. The group's centrality to Stax and their picture-perfect image of integration—two black members and two white members—made them the go-to subjects when profiling the music and its implications. *Variety* said they represented the new trend of "breakthrough" interracial recordings, and *Rolling Stone* writers repeatedly lauded them for their musical and racial cross-pollination. "It is music that is universal and unafraid to borrow from sources black, white or brown," gushed reviewer Peter Guirado in 1968.[83]

The most striking use of the MGs, Stax, and the Memphis sound as symbols of racial integration came from *Coronet* magazine's Glenn Kittler, who profiled Stax Records in May 1970. In an essay bluntly titled "Can Integration Really Work?," Kittler poses a simple question: "Mix the country music of the white South with the rhythm-and-blues of the black South—and you get the Memphis Sound. Groovy. But what happens when you mix the people, too?" With an odd combination of wide-eyed optimism and post-King-assassination skepticism, Kittler used Stax and the MGs to argue that integration is still possible and desirable in the United States. He celebrated the group as "a combination of the white South and the black South" and detailed the ways Stax's black and white employees shared duties and responsibilities. Like the other writers, Kittler saw the MGs, Stax, and the Memphis Sound as representatives of racial equality in the midst of racial turmoil. And, like the other writers, Kittler did not discuss Lewie Steinberg.[84]

Stax publicity director Deanie Parker included the Kittler and Korall articles in press kits sent to reporters and fans, and she and other Stax leaders foregrounded the coming together of black and white southerners when promoting the label's releases. According to Parker, promotions director Al Bell—the black disc jockey and civil rights activist who joined Stax in 1965 and soon became the label's leader—even insisted that every document sent from the Stax offices include the phrase "the Memphis Sound."[85] But Stax leaders deemphasized the national civil rights movement and instead credited the blending to the musicians' professionalism. "Without our realizing," Jim Stewart told Glenn Kittler, "it has broken down racial barriers simply because we have all become so interdependent in our determination to turn out records we can all be proud of."[86] Al Bell told Phyl Garland that the musicians' versatility gave Stax the freedom "to move . . . through pop, R&B to a country tune. They can play anything they want to play and it comes off sounding like it should because they are accomplished musicians."[87] Stax promotional materials foregrounded the skills of its employees rather than political contexts. In a late-1960s press release, an uncredited writer (probably Deanie Parker) wrote that, while most associated Booker T. and the MGs with their own hits, the group members themselves were proudest of being the backbone of the Stax staff. "Many of their fans feel that the group should get out on the road more often, but they believe that 'first and foremost our job is to get the company's records to sell,'" the author wrote, detailing their long hours and extensive resumes as reasons why the MGs remained the best embodiment of Stax's identity.[88] In its promotion of artists like the

MGs, Stax leadership both helped construct the integrationist narrative surrounding the Memphis sound and grounded it in the working lives of the label's musicians.

The idea that the Memphis sound represented integration made it easy for many writers and promotions departments to focus on its effects on white people. They credited the progressive vision of whites like Steve Cropper, Jim Stewart, or Jerry Wexler with bringing black music to the forefront of U.S. popular culture, and suggested that the ultimate value of the Memphis sound was in liberating white musicians and listeners from racially restrictive practices. The headline of one 1970 article bluntly claimed that "Fate, Luck, [and Jim] Stewart Combined for Memphis Sound," and similar appraisals could be found throughout the era's press.[89] Some African American journalists participated in this process, too, as did record companies like Stax that made these discussions central to their advertising strategy. But most black observers framed their appreciation for white collaborators around the understanding that southern soul was primarily a black thing. Meanwhile, many white writers presented the Memphis sound as a chance for white performers and listeners to demonstrate their cultural and political broadmindedness. By the end of the 1960s, as the civil rights movement shifted away from interracial alliance and toward Black Power, the Memphis sound affirmed the notion that white people still had a role to play in the fight for racial progress.

But these reassuring political bromides also promised that southern soul would heal white people's psychological wounds. Just as he had in his 1947 short story, Jerry Wexler, in his 1960s comments about the Memphis sound, expressed his belief in the healing powers of the music of southern blacks. But a more striking example came from white rock star Janis Joplin, a Texan whose vocal and performance style was deeply influenced by blues and soul singers. In 1968 Joplin performed at Stax's Christmas show and claimed that "being black for a while will make me a better white."[90]

This increasingly white-centered rhetoric had significant practical effects on the country-soul triangle. As national audiences embraced the notion that whites could and should participate in the black-rooted Memphis sound, executives and producers responded by sending a number of prominent white artists to record soul-influenced tracks with the city's famed (and famously integrated) musicians. By the dawn of the 1970s, many of the most famous Memphis-sound sessions involved such visitors. It is fitting that the recording studio that cornered the market on these outsiders had the evocative name of American.

Stax cofounder Chips Moman opened American Studios after falling out with Jim Stewart in 1964. He hired the all-white studio band from Hi and quickly filled American's session calendar with a variety of pop and R&B sessions. (Future soul star Bobby Womack also worked at the studio in this period.) Even in the hectic world of recording sessions, Moman was famous for the length and intensity of his workdays. Dan Penn, who left FAME Studios in 1966 to work full-time with Moman, remembered that "when I got to Memphis it was this cut-all-night business. . . . When they start cuttin', they could go for about sixty-two hours! That gang of boys right there, they wanted to make better records than Stax."[91] Moman did work with local artists, but he focused on attracting outsiders who came to the studio expressly to work with the talented studio players. "They came to us because we would keep working until we came up with a sound on a particular song and artist," remembered pianist Bobby Wood.[92] Moman's wide-ranging ambitions, extensive list of contacts, and the ensemble's well-known versatility made American a popular site for sessions ranging from the soul of Joe Tex to the country-pop of a former FAME staff singer named Sandy Posey. In the late 1960s, American Studios was as successful and prolific as Stax.

Seeking a way to distinguish his studio, and aware of the increasing cultural salience of the Memphis sound, Moman decided to specialize in white artists who were influenced by southern R&B. The studio's most popular homegrown act, the Box Tops, were a group of Memphis-area teenagers whose gritty sound and guidance from producer Dan Penn made them one of the era's most popular exponents of the subgenre known as "blue-eyed soul." American also hosted prominent sessions by a series of white visitors who consciously sought to link their established musical personae with the soulful Memphis sound. The most famous of those visitors was well aware of the power of recording cross-racial music in Memphis.

Elvis Presley's session at American in 1969 represented his musical homecoming. After becoming the white hero of Memphis's 1950s recording boom, he returned to work there after several years spent making movies and soundtracks in Los Angeles and Nashville. Tired of these projects, and seeking a local recording environment that could revitalize his career, Presley and his management selected American for Presley's creative rebirth. He worked there for two weeks, and he and the musicians produced several of Presley's most enduring hits, all of which reflected the soul-influenced sounds being made at American.[93] Many critics and historians have pointed to these sessions—released on the album *From Elvis in Memphis*—as Presley's return to both artistic relevance and the interracial southern musical traditions that originally inspired him.[94]

Chips Moman in 1968. Moman was an early staff member at Stax before leaving to found American Studios. In the late 1960s, Moman presided over many of the biggest Memphis sessions, including visits from Elvis Presley and Dusty Springfield. *Memphis Commercial Appeal* Collection, Preservation and Special Collections, University of Memphis Libraries.

A similar mythology surrounds the sessions of Dusty Springfield, a successful pop singer from Britain who signed with Atlantic Records in 1968. Jerry Wexler's immediate instinct was to take her to American, and Springfield was excited at the prospect. She loved black singers and understood the "impact of my being an English lady signing with what is basically a soul label."[95] Springfield's understanding of the cultural narrative surrounding the Memphis sound was matched by her awareness of its musical characteristics. Writing to Wexler, she worried that one song that Wexler wanted her to record might not be "right for Memphis" because it was a "big, dramatic ballad," while noting that another was perfect because it "totters very successfully between black + white styles."[96] Ironically, Springfield never actually recorded at American, instead laying down her vocals in New York, and the album sounds little like the southern soul of the popular imagination and more like the "big, dramatic ballads" that Springfield worried would be inappropriate. The two exceptions are the only songs penned by triangle songwriters: the slinky "Breakfast in Bed" by Muscle Shoals–based writers Donnie Fritts and Eddie Hinton, and the gospel-drenched "Son of a Preacher Man" by American's Mark James. The album—titled *Dusty in Memphis*—was not a major hit at the time, but its impact has grown exponentially since its release. Many critics consider it one of the best albums of the pop era, and it remains an exemplar of the Memphis sound's blending of black and white influence.[97]

Dusty in Memphis inspired a series of imitation recordings by other white female singers that replicated its combination of a well-known pop voice with earthy southern players and material. In the late 1960s and early 1970s, Petula Clark, Jackie DeShannon, and Brenda Lee recorded albums with the American musicians, while Cher, Lulu, and Liza Minnelli cut LPs in Muscle Shoals. Springfield, Clark, and Lee all included the word "Memphis" in their album titles, and—like Presley and others—they intended it as more than a geographic locator.[98] It was a sign of the soulful sincerity that gave white artists and fans the opportunity to bathe in the authenticating, healing waters of black music produced in the integrated South. But, despite all the collaborative rhetoric, the Memphis sound also reinforced perhaps the best-known division in American musical culture: the perceived separation between country and R&B/soul, which was still most obviously encapsulated by the divide between Memphis and Nashville.

Nearly everyone who talked about the Memphis sound acknowledged that country was one of its stylistic roots. In fact, its promoters loved to note that white musicians and record executives in Memphis began their careers in country before shifting to R&B. Still, the mythology of the Memphis sound clouded the mechanics of this shift behind mystical language of cultural transformation and racial epiphany. Supposedly, executives like Jim Stewart rejected country—the musical representative of southern segregation—in favor of the cross-racial understanding embodied in R&B and soul. In reality, most Memphis executives did exactly what Rick Hall did in Muscle Shoals: they shifted to black-identified music because they thought they could make more money. Stewart is the highest-profile example, but there was also Quinton Claunch, who cofounded Hi before starting the soul label Goldwax in 1964. "I saw the success of Jim Stewart [and wanted to do something similar, with] anything that was good, mostly soul and rock and roll," he told Roben Jones. Claunch also claimed that his shift bespoke a fundamental reality. "You can't hardly cut country in Memphis," he said, because "the musicians don't understand it [and] neither do the engineers."[99]

Claunch's comments are inaccurate and unfair to the musicians—black and white—who played plenty of country in Memphis and elsewhere.

But they are consistent with the city's use of "the Memphis sound" as the primary means to distinguish its music industry from Nashville's in the 1960s. In this construction, nurtured by several decades of cultural narratives that culminated in the rock 'n' roll era, Memphis's music was organic while Nashville's was contrived. Memphis's recording industry was created by a ramshackle group of country folks and outsiders while Nashville's represented modern industry and streamlined efficiency. Most important, the Memphis sound was black and the Nashville sound was white. The resonance of "Memphis" and "Nashville" in larger debates over racial and cultural politics found its most obvious shorthand in the supposed separation between country and soul.

Memphis music entrepreneurs saw the Memphis sound as a competitive edge over the long commercial advantage held by Nashville, whose executives routinely dismissed the Memphis music industry as small change. One unnamed executive told the *Wall Street Journal* in 1970 that "Memphis music is peanuts, it's always been peanuts and it always will be peanuts."[100] The success of the Memphis sound offered a stiff rejoinder to that argument. The Recording Academy, which held the prestigious "Grammy" awards, opened an office in Memphis in 1973, making it only the fourth branch in the United States. (New York, Los Angeles, and Nashville had the first three.) The powerful Nashville-based songwriters' organization BMI held a huge party honoring the Memphis sound in 1968, and the Memphis Chamber of Commerce sent copies of *Billboard*'s special report on the city's music to all its members in early 1969.[101]

The industry and civic boosters who heralded the Memphis sound understood it in terms of competition with Nashville and between country and soul. "A lot of non-Tennesseans you meet tend to think all music produced in this state is like Nashville's," one Memphis reporter noted, "but on that point, all good Memphians must very quickly hush them up, shet [*sic*] their mouths or however you prefer to put it."[102] In 1971 local musicians and executives formed Memphis Music Inc., a booster group modeled after the Nashville-based Country Music Association that hoped to "promote 'the Memphis Sound,' which is noted for its r&b flavor."[103] Feeling threatened, a group of area country fans and performers formed the Tri-state Country Music Association in 1971, meant to promote the recording of country music in the city. The new organization hoped to reverse the trend that began when, in the words of a local reporter, "the Memphis Sound finally discovered its own soul a few years ago and headed off down another road."[104]

This separation occurred at the very moment that recording professionals in Nashville were working to expand the city's recording identity beyond country. The city boasted a flourishing R&B and soul scene in the 1960s. While Nashville soul never achieved the prominence of its counterparts in Memphis, Detroit, or other cities, the city produced hits by artists like Bobby Hebb, Esther Phillips, and Joe Tex. Many of these artists recorded with prominent country session players and released their records on labels—like Buddy Killen's Dial or Gene Autry's Champion—that were controlled by powerful members of the country industry. Nurtured by a bustling nightclub scene on Sixteenth Street, the center of Nashville's black entertainment district, and supported by John Richbourg and others at WLAC, black popular music remained a crucial part of Nashville's music industry in this boom period.

Additionally, Nashville's elite country musicians incorporated the sounds of southern soul into their repertoires. Just as in the 1950s, when they included jazz and R&B in the Nashville sound, the city's musicians now used the newest developments in black-identified popular music in the hopes of attracting a wider variety of session work. It helped that some of Nashville's most important musicians in the 1960s came directly from making R&B in Muscle Shoals. FAME cofounder Billy Sherrill moved to Nashville in 1963, and the original FAME band—who played on Arthur Alexander's "You Better Move On" and other recordings—followed a year later. The Muscle Shoals transplants quickly became some of the most sought-after professionals in the Nashville industry and key contributors to its assertion of musical diversity. David Cantwell describes the arrival of the Muscle Shoals rhythm section in Nashville as "the most important development in country music between Elvis and Garth [Brooks]."[105] Their prominence, like that of Billy Sherrill, made a simple argument: Nashville's recording personnel were both musically and racially forward-thinking.

In the wake of the Memphis sound, this argument became central to how Nashville musicians promoted themselves. In the *International Musician*, the national newsletter of the AFM, much of the writing on Nashville noted this versatile progressivism as a main reason for the city's increasingly prosperous recording scene.[106] Even more illustrative is "Nashville Cats," a 1971 article in *Rolling Stone* magazine. *Rolling Stone* rarely talked about country music at all, but here it devoted several pages to writer John Grissim's enthusiastic profile of the new generation of Nashville's studio musicians. Grissim described this new infusion of talent as "the vanguard of a small invasion" and argued that this "new blood . . . would make Nashville a primary center of pop as well as Country activity." Three of the profiled musicians had been in the original FAME band, and Grissim used country and soul as the binary points through which to articulate the musicians' skills. "So many of these boys are perfectly capable of walking into a [Stax] studio date in Memphis and getting it on with the best of the R&B pickers," he wrote, and—while he cautioned readers against assuming that this made them politically progressive—he suggested the change in Nashville's recording practices represented a broader transformation in the culture of the South.[107]

Unlike most other writers of the period, Grissim detailed just how hard the musicians worked to achieve their success. He again focused his discussion on their eclecticism. "I think the key to success of the Nashville musicians is that most of guys who play here do a lot of listening—country, rock and soul," bassist Norbert Putnam (formerly of Muscle Shoals) told Grissim. Putnam insisted that this versatility was a matter not of cultural broadmindedness or even personal interest but rather professional necessity. "If a guy is going to work dates in Nashville he's got to be able to work with [pop-jazz bandleader] Al Hirt and a full orchestra and cut corny tunes that were popular in the Forties, then he's got to turn around and work [rock star] Bob Dylan or [folksinger] Joan Baez or somebody, then he's gotta work [country singer] Kitty Wells—and it all happens on the same day."[108]

The emergence of the Memphis sound helped make these musicians famous, but it also obscured their skills behind romantic language of cultural authenticity and racial breakthrough. The naturalization of musicians' accomplishments structured a second unhelpful narrative: the idea that integrated southern studios were transcendent spaces of racial interaction. These stories of interracial friendship became the central lens through which the activities and accomplishments of southern musical laborers were presented to the public. The "Memphis music industry is the most integrated subculture in the city," declared *Memphis Press-Scimitar* reporter Mary Ann Lee, because the musicians "are all brothers under the skin, all from a more or less shared Memphis experience. And while I say 'brothers,' the same goes for 'sisters.'"[109] Just as the Memphis sound obscured the laboring lives of musical workers, so too did it greatly simplify the contours of their racial collaborations and conflicts.

Interracial friendships outside of work were rare among the musicians of the country-soul triangle. When musicians socialized, sharing meals or hanging out at places like Memphis' Lorraine Motel, it was usually while on a break from sessions, traveling between gigs, or at work-related functions. This does not deny the quality or significance of these interactions, of course, but the musicians' primary understanding of each other was as colleagues. "Musicians can get together regardless of *what* color they are," black Stax artist Albert King told Phyl Garland. "Now we might go

separate ways once we leave the bandstand, but when we're on the bandstand, we're together."[110] White Memphis pianist Jim Dickinson put it even
more bluntly when he dryly remarked that "Booker T. and the MGs played
music, not golf."[111] Moments of camaraderie were almost always structured
around musical work.

Even workplace collaborations were sometimes fraught with racial tension. African American musicians in the country-soul triangle repeatedly
objected to what they perceived as mistreatment by white coworkers and
management figures. Arthur Alexander was greeted with a racist epithet
by one of his FAME collaborators, and both Alexander and Joe Tex resisted attempts by their white producers to restrict their creative and commercial autonomy. In Memphis, Hi engineer Ray Harris slurred pianist
Joe Hall and then removed him from the session, while black musicians
at Stax resented their removal from the Mar-Keys touring lineup and
Lewie Steinberg's subsequent firing from Booker T. and the MGs. Also,
Stax stars Sam Moore and Rufus Thomas accused Steve Cropper of getting
too much credit (and accruing too many royalties) for the records made at
Stax. "Stevie [sic] didn't have that much love for blacks," Moore told Portia Maultsby, "but he saw that he could make money."[112] Black musicians
observed racial disparity on all levels of their profession, from the larger
trajectories of the business to the day-to-day operations of studios.

The most obvious example of this professional discontent, and the most
extreme example of racial conflict in southern studios, occurred when
Jerry Wexler took Aretha Franklin to record in Muscle Shoals in January
1967. Wexler thought this session would be the artistic height of southern
soul, the pinnacle of the integrated Memphis sound, and the culmination
of his belief in the transformative power of black music. Unfortunately, the
session actually became a brilliant illustration of its limitations.

Jerry Wexler signed the prodigiously talented Franklin away from
Columbia Records, where she had made a series of recordings that Wexler felt were too old-fashioned and poppy to accommodate her church-
trained voice. He thought that by recording Franklin—who, though raised
in Detroit, was born in Memphis—with northern musicians, the Columbia
executives were missing the true nature of her talent. Instead, he wanted
to combine her skills with those of the southern musicians with whom he
became infatuated and who had helped Atlantic reassert its place in the
national pop market. He immediately made plans to bring Aretha Franklin back to the region of her birth.

Unfortunately for Wexler, returning Franklin to the *city* of her birth
was not an option. Atlantic and Stax could not reach an agreement on the

terms of Franklin's visit, so Wexler—on the lookout for another integrated recording house that mixed soulful grit with skilled professionalism—turned to FAME Studios. "It was the boys in Muscle Shoals who taught me a new way of making records, spontaneously, synergistically," he noted.[113] In 1966, after Atlantic distributed local singer Percy Sledge's smash hit "When a Man Loves a Woman," Wexler decided that Wilson Pickett would be the label's first major star to record at FAME. Pickett was initially skeptical about recording in rural Alabama—"I see black folks pickin' cotton, and I say 'Shit, turn this motherfuckin' plane around, ain't no way I'm goin' back there'"—and about Rick Hall. "How did I know Jerry Wexler was gonna send me to some big white Southern cat?" Pickett remembered. "Woulda never got on that plane."[114] But the ensemble ultimately produced a set of hits (including "Land of 1,000 Dances" and "Mustang Sally") that defined the sound of southern soul and confirmed Wexler's belief that FAME was the perfect place to record his newest soul prodigy.

Wexler called Aretha Franklin "a natural for the Southern style of recording," and FAME's musicians agreed; Dan Penn even returned to Muscle Shoals to witness the event.[115] Despite the excitement, a noticeable racial tension underlaid the session even before it started. Franklin arrived in the company of then-husband Ted White, a northerner whose politics tilted toward black nationalism and who deeply mistrusted the studio and its surroundings. "Oh, there was serious tension because I was in Muscle Shoals, Alabama in 1967. It *wasn't* a relaxed situation," he recalled.[116] White's concern may seem unfounded in light of the Pickett sessions, but black musicians have echoed his concern. Stax's Marvell Thomas enjoyed working with the Shoals musicians but turned down a full-time position at FAME because the "atmosphere for black people in Muscle Shoals, Alabama, was not all that cool at that time."[117]

Ted White's concern was also shared by Jerry Wexler. As with the Pickett sessions, Wexler picked musicians from the American and FAME house bands but pleaded with Rick Hall to include at least one African American musician for the sake of what he called the "racial mix."[118] Since FAME and American both had lily-white rhythm sections, this meant hiring an integrated horn line. Accounts differ as to why no black horn players were hired to play the session. Some say Hall ignored Wexler's request, while at least one musician argues that Hall hired an integrated section that fell through at the last minute, leaving Hall to rely on white saxophonist Charles Chalmers to make the hires.[119] Both Chalmers and Hall certainly knew and worked with many talented African American horn players in the area, but the section remained entirely white. The final seat went to

Wilson Pickett recording at FAME Studios, 1966. The success of Pickett's visit to Muscle Shoals helped solidify its reputation as a source of successful recordings and interracial collaboration. In this image, Pickett is surrounded by several key members of FAME's house band. From left to right are guitarist Jimmy Johnson, keyboard player Spooner Oldham, drummer Roger Hawkins, and guitarist/bassist Junior Lowe. Courtesy of Rodney Hall. FAME Studio Records, Library and Archives, Rock and Roll Hall of Fame and Museum.

Ken Laxton, who had never worked a session in Muscle Shoals and whom most of the musicians did not know. Laxton's arrival provoked unease among some of the triangle regulars, including Chips Moman, who noted that the trumpeter "had kind of an arrogance about him" that led Moman to "keep his distance" during the session.[120]

Despite the consternation, the proceedings began smoothly with a bluesy cut called "I Never Loved a Man (the Way I Love You)" that came out so well that—according to Dan Penn—the musicians danced as the song played over the studio speakers.[121] The trouble started when it came time to record the B-side, a countrified ballad called "Do Right Woman (Do Right Man)." Franklin sang it a few times, but Wexler was unhappy with what he felt was her lack of engagement with the song. To motivate her, Wexler sent Dan Penn, the song's cowriter, out to the studio floor to demonstrate what Wexler felt was the properly "soulful" way of singing the song. This striking inversion was not unprecedented. White producers often told Penn (sometimes dressed in overalls) to sing a "blacker" version of the song to either encourage or embarrass black singers. Penn described this as putting on his "black throat," and—as the name suggests—Penn understood it as blatant racial one-upmanship. He described it with particular clarity and purposeful bluntness as being "sent out there to tempt the niggers."[122]

The gambit failed. Franklin still did not produce a result that pleased Jerry Wexler and the frustrated producer called for a break. During the downtime, Ken Laxton and Ted White began poking fun at each other. The exchange was initially good-natured, but both men's jibes became increasingly unfriendly. "A redneck patronizing a black man is dangerous camaraderie," Wexler observed, and it was made even more dangerous by the whiskey that made its way around the room.[123] The words between White and Laxton soon turned racial, leading to a heated argument and ultimately a physical confrontation.

There is no clear account of what happened next. Several in the room claim that Laxton pinched Franklin's rear end. (Dan Penn, not implicated in the actual fight, responded to this suggestion incredulously: "I always heard he patted her on the butt or somethin'," adding, "What would have been wrong with that anyway?")[124] Others say Laxton made an inappropriate sexual comment. Some remember that Laxton was fired after White complained to Rick Hall. What is clear is that the maelstrom continued back at the motel where the out-of-towners were staying. Here, in a misguided attempt to defuse the tension, Hall produced more whiskey and attempted to salvage his disintegrating session with further drinking. "He was trying to mediate," guitarist Jimmy Johnson told Roben Jones. "He meant well, but it went bad."[125] Now it was Hall who got into it with White, and the two men wound up screaming racial epithets at each other. Several accounts have the confrontation descending into physical violence. Regardless of the specifics, everyone knew that the session was over.

Franklin and White boarded a plane the next morning. Wexler was furious at Hall for stoking the fires of racial hostility and leaving the job uncompleted, so he devised a scheme to finish production on Franklin's debut Atlantic single and album. He knew that Hall would never let FAME's musicians travel to Atlantic's New York studio to work with Franklin and Wexler, so Wexler told Hall that he needed the group to come to New York to finish an album by well-liked black saxophone player King Curtis. After the musicians arrived, they realized that they would also be completing the Franklin project, cutting two full albums in just three days. This time,

Wexler ensured that some of the horn section and all the background singers were African American.

Franklin and White claimed no ill will toward the white musicians. Franklin asked to work with them again and White told journalist Charlie Gillett that he offered to fund their trip to New York with his own money. White became infamous for his abuse of Franklin during their marriage and his hot-tempered conduct in Muscle Shoals, but Jimmy Johnson confirmed that White had a good relationship with the FAME players. "He gave us gifts for playing on her sessions," he recalled. "He was always very nice and intelligent-acting." Unfortunately for the musicians, Rick Hall learned of Wexler's chicanery and immediately called the FAME musicians home before they could finish work on Franklin's album. He claimed they were needed for a session but Jimmy Johnson said this was untrue. "We got home and there was no work. It was pure political bullshit."[126] The fracture between Hall and his rhythm section eventually led to the musicians' departure from FAME in 1969.

The failure of the Aretha Franklin session in Muscle Shoals has assumed a specific and significant place in the writing on southern soul, with numerous writers using the session to symbolize an abandonment of integration in southern music production that directly reflected a larger shift in U.S. politics.[127] In short, they use it to mourn the death of the Memphis sound. But they do not examine how this incident challenges that mythology by revealing the centrality and fragility of the interracial musical workplace. Despite the differences in individual accounts of what happened that night, everyone involved attributes what happened to three things. First, the two individuals who were not familiar with the working mechanisms of the studio—Ken Laxton and Ted White—came to dominate and disrupt it. Second, the client—Aretha Franklin—was mistreated and let down by the lapse in professionalism. Finally, the management figures—Rick Hall and Jerry Wexler—failed to adequately address the problem. Indeed, in this *Rashomon*-like story, one common theme emerges: everybody failed to do their job.

Still, just as in the larger mythology of the Memphis sound, historians have eschewed the complex dynamics faced by Franklin, Wexler, and their collaborators and instead shoehorned them into broader narratives of civil rights conflict. This tendency both misses the nuance of the interactions and externalizes the racial discord. Laxton and White uniformly (and correctly) get blamed for the fight, but writers suggest that external forces of racial conflict somehow *intruded* on otherwise harmonious studio environments. The Franklin incident was undoubtedly an exceptionally severe incident and larger societal tensions certainly played a crucial role in producing and exacerbating it. But its root causes were by no means unprecedented or unacknowledged in integrated southern studios.

Despite its difficult production, Aretha Franklin's debut Atlantic single, "I Never Loved a Man (the Way I Love You)" backed by "Do Right Woman, Do Right Man," was a smash, making Franklin an immediate superstar and an icon of the ascendant Black Power movement. *Ebony* magazine declared 1967 the year of "'Retha, Rap [Brown] and Revolt," while poet Nikki Giovanni wrote a 1968 piece titled "Poem for Aretha" and later called her "the voice of the civil rights movement, the voice of black America."[128] Her coronation as the "Queen of Soul" culminated in June 1968 when an elegant portrait of Franklin appeared on the cover of *Time* magazine. Inside, writer Chris Porterfield profiled the singer as an embodiment of the quality that made soul music a "badge of black identity." "The closer a Negro gets to a 'white' sound nowadays," he wrote, "the less soulful he is considered to be, and the more he is regarded as having betrayed his heritage." But "Aretha will never go white, and that certainty is as gratifying to her white fans as to her Negro ones." Franklin's Atlantic recordings, made with what he described as "a funky Memphis rhythm section," made her the pinnacle of soul's expressive capacities and cultural meanings.[129]

Aretha Franklin's success represented the culmination of the Memphis sound as both a stylistic movement in U.S. popular music and an overarching ideology of cultural progress. The music's popularity vastly expanded the opportunities for music professionals in the country-soul triangle and created the language through which they identified and promoted themselves in the coming years. But the mythology also greatly oversimplified the way music like Aretha Franklin's was produced. Instead of foregrounding the long and tedious process of professionalization undertaken by southern musicians, the notion of the Memphis sound credited their accomplishments to vague conceptions of regional authenticity and musical miscegenation. Additionally, the promoters of this myth constructed an ill-fitting civil rights analogue that misinterpreted the racial collaborations and conflicts that produced it. Even as the Memphis sound created the national recognition of an interracial southern recording scene, it also became the primary obstacle to understanding its full complexity.

The Memphis sound also played a critical role in the rise of soul music as a symbol of black identity. In the turbulent late 1960s, soul became a political hot-button as an abstract symbol of African American assertion and a concrete site of civil rights activism. This had significant and complicated consequences for the interracial studios of the country-soul triangle. Appropriately, the story starts in Memphis.

Three

SELLING SOUL

Black Music and Black Power in Memphis

In July 1968, two weeks after *Time* magazine heralded Aretha Franklin as the embodiment of soul's blackness, a reader from Memphis named Charlie Freeman exposed a simple yet devastating flaw in the magazine's argument. Referencing reporter Chris Porterfield's description of the musicians that helped Franklin produce her soul recordings, Freeman wrote a pointed letter to the editor. "I would like to point out," Freeman noted, "that the 'funky Memphis rhythm section' that became the vehicle which made it possible for Aretha to do her thing is composed of all white musicians."[1] Freeman was not just a knowledgeable fan—he was a former Stax studio musician and Mar-Key who had worked on soul records since the early 1960s and helped craft the Memphis sound.

Freeman's comment about the whiteness of Aretha Franklin's "funky Memphis rhythm section" exposed a broader contradiction in the era's cultural politics. He revealed that the promotion of southern soul as a symbol of blackness—even the antithesis of whiteness—in the late 1960s failed to account for the complexities of record production in the country-soul triangle. It erased the creative contributions of white musicians like Freeman himself and ignored the fact that southern studios were interracial workplaces where African American and white musicians interacted as collaborators and colleagues. More profoundly, it obscured the complex ways that southern soul musicians of all races responded to the assertive and sometimes divisive racial politics of the Black Power era.

During the late 1960s, soul music became a key expression of the Black Power movement.[2] Soul artists like Aretha Franklin were presented as embodiments of an essential blackness rooted in racial tradition and blossoming in the transformative atmosphere of the 1960s. As William Van Deburg notes, "black culture *was* Black Power" to many activists, and they asserted soul's centrality to the larger struggle for liberation.[3] Culturally, they argued, soul music was the latest manifestation of a clear and observable black musical identity and thus the creative property of African Americans. This argument echoed the Afrocentric and Black Arts movement rhetoric that defined much of the era's Black Power ideology, in which influential theorists like Amiri Baraka presented music as central to the historical continuum of the African diaspora.[4] Soul was also an engine for economic empowerment. Black power advocates demanded greater opportunity for African Americans in the record industry and called for more black ownership of soul and other black-identified genres. This stance corresponded to a larger "black capitalist" ideology that called on African Americans to take control of the resources and markets that affected their communities.[5]

While cultural and economic strategies sometimes opposed each other in Black Power politics, soul music provided an obvious opportunity to link them.[6] Other cultural forms—from movies to cuisine—provoked similar discussions, but nothing surpassed soul as a demonstration of black expression that required black control. To be sure, some who pushed for greater economic opportunity refuted the musical essentialism and insisted that whites did indeed have soul. And some who believed most strongly in a black musical continuum criticized or even dismissed soul music as a white attempt to commercially exploit the African American community. Generally, though, these two arguments stood side-by-side throughout the late 1960s and early 1970s. As activist and radio host Booker Griffin wrote in 1971, "There is a certain type of music that is the folk music of the black experience. . . . If anyone should sell it, it should be black people."[7]

The music professionals of the country-soul triangle played a central role in securing and shaping soul's reputation as black music. They produced recordings that amplified the musical and linguistic cues that signified soul's supposedly inherent blackness. Their advertisements, press releases, and public statements employed Black Power rhetoric and connected soul releases to the larger struggle. And some of southern soul's creators embraced the cause of black advancement in the record business, working with organizations that fought for greater power for African Americans in the recording industry. Many musicians, black and white, sincerely supported those efforts, but their personal beliefs were ultimately less important than their recognition that embracing the language and imagery of Black Power was good for business. In short, soul's creators knew that—in the late 1960s—black meant green.[8]

Of course, they were not the first to draw this connection. Since the nineteenth-century development of the idea of "black music," the notion of a distinctly racialized set of musical characteristics had been both a severe hindrance to African American musicians—limiting their professional opportunities and fueling racist stereotypes—and an opportunity for them to assert their unique talents.[9] Even in the early 1960s, with the stylistic crossover embodied by Arthur Alexander and the integrationist rhetoric of the Memphis sound, the suggestion of black musical difference remained a crucial element to the successful promotion of southern R&B and soul singers. By the end of the decade, when the music became linked to the civil rights and Black Power movements, record companies increasingly spotlighted the supposedly uninhibited blackness of soul artists like Aretha Franklin as a main selling point. This commercial relationship—a shift from earlier periods—made soul music into what Mark Anthony Neal calls "the ideal artistic medium to foreground the largest mass social movement to emerge from within the African American experience." And it was the musicians' manipulation of this relationship that made soul into both the symbol and instrument of Black Power.[10]

Just as with the Memphis sound, southern soul musicians performed a skillful balancing act in response to the new racial politics. They appealed to the worldwide assertion of black essence while continuing to work in interracial contexts. They employed nationalist rhetoric and brought Black Power political campaigns into the recording industry even as they continued to market themselves and their products as the proof of integration's successes. For the producers of southern soul, these strategies were not irreconcilable. They were the day-to-day reality of their work as musicians.

Unfortunately, this complexity has been lost in subsequent discussions of southern soul and Black Power. The few scholars who have discussed the experiences of southern soul musicians in this period have presented a story of dissolution, what Peter Guralnick calls "fragmentation," of both the music and its cultural value.[11] Supposedly, the rise of Black Power—along with the 1968 assassination of Martin Luther King Jr.—destroyed the interracial partnerships that, for many, defined both southern soul and the civil rights movement. But the experiences of music professionals in the country-soul triangle reveal a more complicated story.

The racial politics of southern soul undoubtedly changed during the late 1960s and early 1970s. African Americans asserted a greater ownership over the creative and commercial direction of soul labels and some whites grew disillusioned in the new environment. But the suggestion that Black Power represented an outside intrusion that led to the downfall of racially harmonious southern studios is both inaccurate and oversimplified. It is inaccurate simply because no southern soul studio ever stopped working with white players. It is oversimplified because it both denies the history of racial tensions in the country-soul triangle and erases the critical role played by southern musicians in transforming the music business and shaping the cultural politics of this turbulent era. Reframing this story around the musicians' experiences offers a fresh perspective on the complex relationships linking the making, marketing, and meaning of southern soul.

Nowhere was this complexity more evident than at Stax Records. Stax embraced the politics of Black Power under the leadership of Al Bell, who became the label's co-owner and first African American leader in 1968. During his tenure, Bell—who was pivotal to the earlier popularization of the integrated Memphis sound—rebranded Stax as the cultural attaché for the larger struggle against racial injustice. Nonetheless, he continued working with white musicians, most notably the Muscle Shoals Rhythm Section, to craft his thoroughly black-identified recordings. Additionally, Bell instituted a policy of greater racial equality in Stax management and sought to make the label a model for greater African American control over the soul-music business. Bell's actions—including his hiring of two controversial activists—was greeted with hostility by some white members of the label's interracial workforce, like cofounder Estelle Axton and mainstay Steve Cropper. As an internationally popular purveyor of deep soul music, and one of only two prominent soul labels controlled by African Americans (the other being Motown), Stax had a unique opportunity to connect with Black Power's energies and demands. As an interracial work organization, the label's relationship to the era's racial militancy was more ambivalent. Taken together, these threads reveal the complex collision between Black Power and interracial soul.

Two months before the *Time* writer celebrated the "funky Memphis rhythm section" that backed Aretha Franklin, the killing of Martin Luther King Jr. sent shock waves through the Memphis music community. Sessions were canceled and postponed, nightclubs were closed, and both American and Stax Studios—integrated, white-owned businesses located in Memphis's poorest black neighborhoods—braced for the impact of riots that followed in the aftermath of King's assassination. Although the immediate unrest in Memphis was less cataclysmic than originally feared, the wounds did not heal quickly among African American musicians. Dan Penn remembered that a session with African American soul singers the Sweet Inspirations had to be scrapped over fears of racial violence.[12] Stax writer and producer Isaac Hayes described himself as unable to create music for a year.[13] The Masqueraders, one of the first African American clients at American Studios after the King killing, saw their session nearly collapse when lead singer Lee Jones became frustrated by white drummer and producer Gene Chrisman's requests to sing the same line over and over again. "Yassuh, massa," Jones angrily replied. "This was during a time when we were all tired," white arranger Mike Leech recalled later, "and Gene's question was taken the wrong way."[14] Duck Dunn and Al Jackson from the MGs argued in the Stax studio over accusations that Dunn used the "n-word."[15] Memphis-based musicians reeled in local turmoil, and black artists across the country grew skeptical of coming to the city.

But the King assassination did not signal the end of integrated recording sessions in Memphis, despite the claims made by Peter Guralnick and many others.[16] "It seemed no coincidence," Guralnick writes about the killing's aftermath, "the soul movement, too, should have fragmented [and] the good feeling clearly engendered by the music should have fled."[17] Musicians have reiterated this notion: Isaac Hayes described himself as "filled with bitterness and anguish" toward white people, while white guitarist Jimmy Johnson said that the King assassination "changed everything" and led to the decline of integrated sessions.[18] Jerry Wexler even suggested that the assassination was "the end of rhythm and blues in the south."[19] But, despite these recollections, no studio in Memphis stopped working interracial sessions in the aftermath King's death. In fact, the killing actually provided the integrated Memphis sound with a significant promotional boost, as the Memphis civic and business communities turned to it in the hopes that it could repair the city's tarnished image.

In a front-page *Wall Street Journal* article titled "Memphis Hopes Boom in Recordings Will Aid Local Racial Harmony," reporter Paul Bernish described a 1970 meeting of the Memphis Chamber of Commerce in which "five white Chamber executives" expressed their "hopes [that 'Memphis sound'] music may help produce a better racial atmosphere and a brighter image for this troubled city." Both Bernish and the Chamber members celebrated the Memphis sound as the "blend of white country music and black soul" and trumpeted the fact that the workforce was composed of both black and white personnel. In their minds, the Memphis recording scene was a profitable embodiment of integration that defied the city's racial divisions. As one "leading banker" put it, "The Memphis Sound can do a lot for this city from an image point of view. And let's face it, our image has suffered recently."[20]

This newfound attention struck some in the city's soul community as disingenuous. Bernish quoted one anonymous musician complaining that "those Johnny-come-lately backers probably never heard a soul record before a few months ago."[21] Looking back, Stax's head of publicity, Deanie Parker, saw a cynical agenda among Memphis leaders. "People in high places—especially in the political arena—really didn't think very much of what we were doing at [Stax], until they needed someone . . . whom [sic] they thought they could call to appeal to the people who they thought were going to burn this city down." After the racial trouble, "we were invited into the halls of the Mayor's office."[22] Indeed, Mayor Henry Loeb—a virulent enemy of the sanitation strike that brought King to Memphis—declared September 27, 1968, to be "Memphis Sound Day" in the city and publicly praised the music and its creators.[23] The musicians' complaints were certainly understandable, particularly given how desperate Memphis's white leaders were to publicize a feel-good racial story. But the interest of city fathers in promoting the Memphis sound was also a testament to Stax's success in promoting its records as a symbol of racial harmony and healing.

Indeed, despite their skepticism, the staff at Stax continued promoting the integrationist Memphis sound in the wake of the King assassination. In a contemporaneous *Stax Fax* promotional mailer, the label's publicity department reprinted a *Record World* article in which label cofounder Jim Stewart exclaimed that "if we've done nothing more, we've shown the world that people of different colors, origins and convictions can be as one, working together towards the same goal." Stewart suggested that Stax could be a beacon for understanding and cooperation in the current turmoil. "When hate and resentment break out all over the nation, we pull our blinds and display a sign that reads 'Look What We've Done—TOGETHER.' . . . I'd like to think that because of our philosophy as a record company, we've encouraged others in our city to take note and do likewise."[24] So, even though Stax's management may have privately resented the fact that Memphis's white leaders now turned to them as symbols of improved race relations, they nonetheless recognized that the interracial Memphis sound and integrated Stax workforce were still very good for business.

Stax deployed this rhetoric at the very moment that it embraced Black Power under new chairman Al Bell. A radio man, Bell worked with Stax in its earliest days before leaving for jobs at radio stations in Little Rock and Washington, D.C. During his time in radio, Bell became well-connected in

Deanie Parker in 1976. Parker was a crucial member of Stax's front-office staff from the early days. As its publicity director, she played a pivotal role in shaping public perceptions of the label. Photograph by Richard Gardner. *Memphis Press-Scimitar* Collection, Preservation and Special Collections, University of Memphis Libraries.

the worlds of black music and civil rights politics; he even quit one radio job to work with Martin Luther King Jr. His experiences shaped his vision for Stax, to which he returned as promotions director in 1965. "I had come to Washington realizing that most of the city's population is black, and that most had moved there from the South," he told *Cashbox* in 1972, and Bell made it his mission to increase the national presence of the distinctively southern music being made at Stax.[25] A large part of this required promoting the Memphis sound, and Bell played a key role in popularizing the music and affirming the integrationism it symbolized.

Bell's success and enthusiasm made him an immensely popular figure in his early days at Stax. "We weren't a professional company before Al," remembered Booker T. Jones. "We didn't have big business going on. We had big music going on, but not big business."[26] Atlantic Records' Jerry Wexler recognized a kindred spirit in the ambitious executive, and he worked closely with Bell during Stax and Atlantic's successful mid-1960s partnership. Meanwhile, the label's musicians appreciated the fact that Bell recognized them as skilled professionals and compensated them accordingly. MGs bassist Donald "Duck" Dunn recalled that Bell "got us a day job. He . . . got us out of the nightclubs and put us on salary where we could go in and work from ten in the morning and go home at five or six in the afternoon and didn't have to go to the nightclub [until] one in the morning."[27] Bell's popularity at all levels of the organization made him a perfect choice to lead Stax in 1968.

Bell inherited a label on the brink of collapse. In the previous year, Stax had lost its national distribution deal with Atlantic, its biggest star Otis Redding died in a plane crash, and Memphis was rocked by the King assassination. Bell quickly moved not only to ensure Stax's survival but also to make it the nation's premier outlet for black-identified music. Central to Bell's agenda was his plan to make Stax synonymous with Black Power. "We must keep up with changing attitudes," Bell demanded in a fiery 1971 press release titled "Black Record Companies Must Be a Part of the Black Community." "We must know where the Black community is at, where it's going and where it's going to be." Part of this involved putting African American faces, like Bell and publicist Deanie Parker, at the forefront of Stax's public identity. Industry leaders and everyday listeners were thus even more likely to associate Stax with black folks, black politics, and blackness itself. But Bell recognized that asserting Stax's black identity meant more than presenting strong and eloquent African Americans as the label's leaders. Stax would also have to prove that it "[knew] where the Black community [was] at" through musical choices and political alliance. In both respects, this required Stax to distance itself from some of the earlier connotations of the Memphis sound.[28]

Musically, Bell hoped to disprove conventional industry wisdom about African American artists and audiences, particularly the idea that "the only way r&b singles could reach the Top 40 was to have them completely diluted so they sounded like standard pop (pap)."[29] Bell's plan to avoid such "dilution" sometimes involved playing up the funky rhythms and gritty vocals that defined real black music, and southern soul, for many listeners and writers. But Bell also pushed to expand that definition—promoting what he called "diversification" and "cross-fertilization"—and encouraged Stax artists to incorporate other musical textures.[30] Black artists had long used string sections, sweet harmonies, and other sweetening approaches, of course, including some at Stax dating back to Carla Thomas's "Gee Whiz." But these sonic characteristics were still considered "white" in much of the era's cultural discourse, from the pages of black revolutionary scholarship to the *Time* magazine profile of Aretha Franklin. Some of the label's stars, most successfully Isaac Hayes, went even further by experimenting with song structures and

Stax billboard, early 1970s. During its second period of
national prominence, the label continued to utilize the idea of
the Memphis sound even as it expanded its musical parameters and
cultural connotations. Stax Museum of American Soul Music.

arrangements that were not designed for Top 40 success but still became hugely successful. Additionally, under Bell's leadership, Stax expanded its catalog to include, jazz, blues, gospel, soundtracks, comedy, spoken word, rock, and even country.

Stax's primary motivation was to sell more records. Bell and other leaders understood that stylistic expansion was the key to growing their bottom line, so they adopted this holistic approach to entrench the label in as many genres as possible. Although the label enjoyed only limited commercial success outside of soul, Stax's commercial fortunes skyrocketed in these years. Many of the label's most successful soul artists—such as Isaac Hayes and the Emotions—sounded very different from the gritty style that made Stax famous. For Al Bell and other company leaders, this was not irreconcilable with their campaign to make Stax the soundtrack for Black Power. If anything, the label's greater success and versatility demonstrated the possibilities of a black-controlled recording company.

This musical move corresponded directly with the more overtly political arm of Bell's rebranding of Stax. In that 1971 press release, Bell foregrounded Stax's "sincere commitment and social awareness" in the fight for black liberation, specifically mentioning the company's extensive work with Rev. Jesse Jackson's Operation Breadbasket. Bell met the young minister while they were both working with Martin Luther King Jr., and Jackson became perhaps Stax's most prominent Black Power ally. (Another key partner was Ben Branch, the Memphis bandleader who worked with both Jackson and Martin Luther King Jr.) The relationship was beneficial for both sides: Stax artists raised money for Operation Breadbasket and released recordings of Jackson's speeches, while Jackson championed Stax as both a musical treasure and force for positive change.[31] Bell's rhetoric of the period is almost interchangeable with that of Jackson and other Black Power leaders. In one address, given to graduating seniors at a black college in his native Arkansas and later distributed through the Stax mailing list, Bell asserted that African Americans "face continued subjection to a serious segment of society that has no intention of giving up willingly or easily its position of priority or authority."[32] Bell hoped that Stax Records would be an active element in the fight against this entrenchment.[33]

This push started inside the Stax offices as Bell began hiring more African Americans in front-office positions. Bell's move to alter the racial demographics of Stax's management—which remained largely white even into the late 1960s—directly challenged the utopian rhetoric of the integrated Memphis sound and exposed the racial discontent that simmered under the label's surface from the beginning. Isaac Hayes remembered this initiative picking up after the King assassination, when Stax began a greater effort to "beef up the hiring practices to include more blacks in the administrative part of the company."[34] Hayes's recollection echoes the memories of white Muscle Shoals guitarist Jimmy Johnson, who played numerous sessions for Stax in this period and recalled that the King assassination was when African Americans began to "take control of their music" in the studios of the South.[35]

The attempt to "take control" of soul music became an important part of the broader Black Power landscape. Nearly every important African American political leader and organization of the era organized around soul, arguing that its musical blackness required that African Americans have a greater say and larger stake in its production.[36] Jesse Jackson made the music industry a central focus of his Operation PUSH and a featured topic at his popular "Black Expo" events in the early 1970s. The Congress on Racial Equality floated the idea of starting its own record label in order to give African Americans greater opportunity.[37] The Southern Christian Leadership Conference (SCLC), the Student Nonviolent Coordinating Committee (SNCC), the National Association for the Advancement of Colored People (NAACP), and the Black Panther Party all spotlighted the inequities in the soul music business.[38] Soul thus became more than just a recognized symbol of black nationalist politics: it became a cause in itself, giving sympathetic record companies like Stax the opportunity to turn their ambitions into action. As Stax executive Larry Shaw said in 1971, speaking of the label's commitment to the black community in Memphis, "Stax believes in the creation of music *for the people*, it must be done *by the people* for whom it is designed to appeal."[39]

While the involvement of outside organizations was crucial, the most significant efforts for black control over soul music came from within the music industry. The biggest of these was launched by the National Association of Television and Radio Announcers (NATRA).[40] NATRA formed in the late 1950s as the National Association of Radio Announcers (NARA) and at first was essentially a fraternal organization of R&B deejays. Recognizing the genre's new commercial prominence and their role as its gatekeepers, NARA's founders hoped that a national organization would promote unity among radio personalities who specialized in black music. Although a few prominent whites joined NARA, including founding board member John "John R." Richbourg from Nashville's WLAC, it was essentially an all-black organization from the beginning. Al Bell was one of its earliest members. Local chapters appeared around the country, but for the first few years NARA did little more than hold an annual national convention, swapping tricks of the trade over cocktails and attending concerts and parties sponsored by record companies.

NARA changed its tune (and its name) in the mid-1960s when a group of members calling themselves the "New Breed" took over the organization. Led by New York jock Del Shields, the New Breed argued that NATRA, as the united voice of the nation's black broadcasters, should take a more active role in confronting racial disparities. New Breed candidates swept the elections for national offices at the organization's 1964 national convention, and NATRA greatly expanded its political reach under their leadership. At first, the New Breed worked with local and federal authorities and generally advocated that NATRA's members—in the best tradition of the Memphis sound—publicize their successful work with white collaborators. But, as the decade progressed, the organization and its members shifted their approach. In 1968 NATRA titled its annual convention "The New Breed's New Image Creates Self-Determination and Pride," which president Del Shields said showed the organization's commitment to the now synonymous projects of "Black Power and Soul Power."[41] Still, at this meeting in Miami, a group of young insurgents decided that NATRA was not going far enough.

These activists—a New York–based group calling itself the Fair Play Committee (FPC)—took over the proceedings and demanded that NATRA adopt a militant Black Power stance. The FPC was as old as NATRA, started in 1959 as an advocacy group for the rights of African American recording artists. Its members quickly became known for their aggressive tactics, their disdain for the racial hierarchies of the recording industry, and their connections to the criminal underworld. Cofounder Dino Woodard even admitted that the FPC hoped to establish a Mafia-esque "black 'family'" that could compete with other criminal "families" who influenced the music industry during this period.[42] But the FPC also shared goals and tactics with the civil rights movement, where many of the group's members cut their political teeth. Woodard said that the group was "ready to die for our rights," which included the promotion and protection of African Americans within the music business, while FPC member George Ware said the group offered "a fusion of that street feeling and experience with college educated militants" that "made it a kind of confrontative [sic] organization."[43] Despite this experience, many of the record executives whose companies came under the FPC's watchful eye did not see the group as legitimate activists. Jerry Wexler summed up the common view when he described them as "con men[,] . . . extortionists, and racketeers" who disrupted the friendly atmosphere between white executives like Wexler and their black employees.[44]

The FPC's primary goal was to combat inequality within the white-controlled recording industry, but it also directed fierce criticism at NATRA. "We thought NATRA was big for nothing, important for nothing," George Ware recalled. "So we started going to their conferences as critics, sort of like protesting them, saying you guys are not doing what you're suppose[d] to do."[45] In Miami in 1968, where convention speakers included Jesse Jackson and the recently widowed Coretta Scott King, the FPC demanded that NATRA insist on the immediate transfer of economic power in the soul-music business to African Americans.

It got ugly, and many of the harshest attacks were directed against leading figures in southern soul. Jerry Wexler was scheduled to get an award from NATRA but fled the meeting because of threats of violence; activists later burned Wexler—whom they accused of stealing from Aretha Franklin—in effigy outside the convention hall. Phil Walden, an Atlanta-based promoter who managed the careers of Otis Redding and other stars, was physically threatened. And white producer Marshall Sehorn, who worked with numerous black artists in his native New Orleans, was pistol-whipped. Sehorn remembers his attackers yelling,

"We don't want any more white niggers" and "You have robbed your last black man." Some even said that the FPC violently intimidated Al Bell into embracing the group's demands.[46] By the end of the convention, NATRA replaced its earlier emphasis on interracial collaboration with a call for Black Power.

Many of the whites who produced and distributed southern soul felt betrayed by NATRA and alienated by the new militancy. Jerry Wexler called it a "shakedown," and Phil Walden, who admitted that the confrontations were an inevitable consequence of tensions both inside and outside the recording industry, said that NATRA's turn "made it really hard for me to maintain a real interest [in black music], when I saw all the things I worked for being destroyed." Walden soon turned to promoting and recording white rock artists.[47] Dan Penn blamed the FPC for shattering the interracial harmony of recording sessions in the country-soul triangle. "Immediately after [the NATRA convention]," Penn claimed, "people quit signin' blacks. . . . That's when the whole Muscle Shoals era came to a screeching halt, when the NAACP told us we had to do this and that, and it very quickly began to disintegrate."[48]

His specific claim is inaccurate—no one "quit signin' blacks" after the NATRA convention—but Penn crystallizes a larger belief among many of southern soul's white creators that African Americans became unreasonable in their demands for control at the end of the 1960s. Additionally, Penn's conflation of the controversial FPC with the relatively mainstream NAACP (which had no direct role in the Miami meeting) illustrates that the 1968 NATRA convention was part of a larger shift in which black political organizations of all kinds took direct steps to end racial disparity in the production of black-identified music. To Penn and others, this project placed an unfair burden on the South's white music professionals and killed the interracial dreams of the Memphis sound.

To be fair, the 1968 NATRA convention was in some way exactly the "shakedown" that Jerry Wexler claimed it to be. But it was also part of a growing response by African American music professionals to the injustices of the white-controlled recording industry. Rather than recognizing the legitimacy or potential benefits of such an organization, many whites dismissed the FPC as a group of scheming and unreasonable blacks whose only goal was to cheat white folks and push them out of their rightful place in the business. Jerry Wexler even said that NATRA's 1968 convention was "one of those moments when the surge of Black Power infected the whole record business," a dismissiveness that echoes a larger rejection of nationalist politics as an intrusion or even a disease.[49]

Black music professionals had a more ambiguous take. Many criticized the FPC's tactics and intentions but admitted that it was a necessary contributor in fighting the persistent racial inequality in the music business. Jerry Williams—hired as the first African American staff producer at Atlantic Records in 1968 because of pressure from black political organizations—described the Miami incident as "a great idea that was rowdy and disorganized" and suggested that the FPC won an increase in money and opportunity for African American artists. Stax songwriter Homer Banks believed that the convention was merely an expression of already-existing tensions and provided a convenient reason for whites to abandon soul music. Capitol Records executive Logan Westbrooks—a Memphis native who later headed the black-music division at CBS Records—thought that the FPC and NATRA's activities had "a great impact" on the music business in subsequent years.[50] Most striking of all, Al Bell hired the group's two founders, Johnny Baylor and Dino Woodard, to front-office positions at Stax in the months after the NATRA convention.[51]

Bell's hiring of the FPC's cofounders, like his larger attempt to demonstrate Stax's commitment to black power, was rooted both in his political beliefs and his commercial ambitions. But it also likely stemmed from his desire to deflect the specific criticisms that some black nationalists directed at the soul industry. Much of this discourse initially surrounded radio. African Americans had long understood radio's importance and fought for greater representation both on the air and in the front office of stations around the country.[52] The rise of soul as both expression and commodity in the late 1960s gave fresh fuel to these debates. In demanding greater African American control of black-oriented stations, activists condemned the way the white-dominated radio industry used soul music and terminology to mislead or cheat the black community.[53] "If we live in a ripoff society, black radio stands as a prime illustration," argued Douglas O'Connor and Gayla Cook in a 1967 article bluntly titled "Black Radio: The Soul Sellout."[54]

One of the most prominent and provocative denunciations of the misuse of soul by white-owned companies came from within the country-soul triangle. In 1970 Bernard E. Garnett of the Race Relations Information Center in Nashville published a pamphlet called "How 'Soulful' Is Soul Radio?" Garnett acknowledged soul's importance as a cultural signifier, noting that the increased use of words like "soul" and even "black" transformed the broadcasting industry, "especially that sector geared primarily to the nation's Afro-American communities. . . . 'soul' radio ended the decade reflecting a 'blackness' that was taboo 10 years ago."

But he also argued that the embrace of "soul" by white radio consisted of only "the recognition of black power as a new commercial commodity" or "superficial sales slogan" and thus represented no real progress. Garnett slammed the white owners of "soul radio" for too narrowly casting the black experience within a commercial R&B framework instead of including either nonsoul music or public-affairs programming. Quoting a fellow activist, Garnett denounced "the 'soul music' mentality" created by the nonstop diet of soul on stations controlled by whites for black listeners.[55] Garnett's words were reprinted in newspapers and magazines throughout the country.

Unsurprisingly, Stax never denounced the "soul music mentality" or encouraged radio programmers to stop playing soul records, but Al Bell and publicity director Deanie Parker made this confrontational discourse a regular part of their promotional materials. They gave NATRA president Del Shields a regular column in their *Stax Fax* mailer: in one column, a tribute to white writer Bill Gavin, Shields praised Gavin for "recognizing the [radio] industry's lack of committment [*sic*] to equal opportunity and full participation by blacks."[56] They also included more militant voices. In that same *Stax Fax* issue, deejay Chris Turner of Memphis station WDIA blasted black-oriented radio and suggested that, despite some important gains, the relationship between white management and black employees and audiences remained unfair and disingenuous. "Today, some black radio stations try to compensate by giving charity to black people. The white capitalistic station owners realize that this does not help the dignity of the recipients, and it denies them of the respect of a self-supporting individual." Turner concluded that white station owners must hire African Americans and contribute to causes that would constructively help listeners, while black broadcasters must devote themselves to fostering "pride and self-identity" among their audience.[57] WDIA was the first station in the United States to devote all of its programming to black audiences, and it had a celebrated history of community involvement. It was thus fitting that such scathing criticism came from one of its representatives and was publicized through a record label closely associated with the cause of African American equality.

The appearance of these editorials in *Stax Fax* showed that Stax considered the support of NATRA and its ideological allies as crucial to the label's success. But Stax continued to promote the integrated Memphis sound alongside the Black Power rhetoric. Jim Stewart remained a prominent presence during this period, appearing in photos with Bell and speaking of Stax's continued commitment to integration. At the end of 1969, Stewart addressed the label's staff and condemned the "rumors" circulating among Stax's increasingly fractious staff. "The Blacks are taking over; the Whites are taking over," Stewart listed, "Al Bell is getting rid of Jim Stewart; Jim Stewart is taking power away from Al Bell." Stewart—who hired Bell and supported his rise to power—insisted that Stax's second phase would remain integrated even as African Americans asserted a new prominence in the company.[58] Although his day-to-day role at the label receded in the early 1970s, Stewart's continuing involvement demonstrates the balance between Black Power militancy and Memphis-sound interracialism that persisted into the Bell years.

This delicate political calculus also characterized Stax's role in the ongoing musical rivalry between Memphis and Nashville. In *Stax Fax*, Chris Turner's fiery editorial decrying the white appropriation of black radio appeared next to a tribute to Nashville's powerful and mostly white chapter of the National Academy of Recording Arts & Sciences (NARAS). Here, Stax thanked the Nashville NARAS chapter for recognizing the contributions of Memphis's interracial cadre and heralded the growth of Memphis-Nashville unity. "The combined strength of the two Tennessee centers of the recording industry will have a telling effect on the world wide music industry," proclaimed NARAS vice president Bill Williams, and the accompanying photos offered an image of black-and-white togetherness.[59] Amid the paeans to interracialism, though, the writer noted that it was the black artists and executives at Stax who bridged the divide between Memphis and Nashville (and country and soul) to create a new music-industry powerhouse. Propelled by Stax's success, Memphis formed its own NARAS chapter in 1973. Particularly in contrast to the perceived whiteness of Nashville, Stax ensured that Memphis's success was associated with African Americans.

Stax's embrace of Black Power politics became an explicit part of the creative and commercial strategy that Bell and others hoped would make Stax the vanguard of black culture. Rebuilding the label's catalog and brand name after the losses of 1967 and 1968, Bell bargained that Stax's effective deployment of nationalist rhetoric and engagement with radical activists would increase its popularity and cultural relevance. The strategy worked. The second phase of Stax was even more successful than the first, and many of the label's most prominent moments in the early 1970s— Isaac Hayes's Oscar-winning *Shaft* soundtrack in 1971, the 1972 Wattstax concert—appealed directly to Black Power's cultural and political assertions. In a very real sense, Stax owed its national success to its successful embrace of African American militancy.

Despite these triumphs, many have framed the story of Stax after 1968 around themes of decline and disintegration.[60] A key flashpoint in this narrative is Al Bell's hiring of Johnny Baylor and Dino Woodard, the founders of the Fair Play Committee, to management positions in 1968. The tenure of Baylor and Woodard at Stax remains just as controversial as their FPC careers; to this day, they remain the primary historical symbols of Stax's decline.[61] This narrative is oversimplified, but their work at the label undoubtedly provoked an extended and heated confrontation over its racial dynamics. Baylor and Woodard entered a black-controlled and black-focused record company that nonetheless remained an interracial workplace where whites remained important contributors on every level.

At least a few of these whites had problems with the newly confrontational tactics. Estelle Axton lamented that, in this period, "Al Bell had . . . gotten in so tight with the blacks, you could see division—both in the company and outside. I could feel it and see it, how he would have meetings with some of the blacks and no white was allowed."[62] Axton sold her shares in the company and left in 1970. Steve Cropper was even more forceful, blaming Baylor and Woodard for destroying the label's interracial camaraderie and introducing racial distrust to the Stax offices. "People were coming in and brainwashing our secretaries, the girlfriends of our musicians—even the maids were being brainwashed," he claimed, and he remained unsympathetic to the FPC's larger suggestion that soul artists had to be protected from white exploitation. "If any black man walking this planet has something against white people having a business, then he doesn't need to be on this planet. They can look at history. If it hadn't been for white record companies there would never have been such a thing as successful black artists."[63]

These vague swipes mask a more complicated story. Cropper had clashed with Al Bell since at least 1965 and later complained that Bell's ascent caused him to "lose his stick" when it came to decision making at Stax.[64] His similarly gendered remarks about "brainwashing" likely referenced a strike among African American secretaries at Stax, who were paid less than their white counterparts, that Baylor and Woodard helped organize.[65] Additionally, in light of Cropper's musical "history" lesson, it should be noted that the FPC duo loudly accused Cropper—as singers Sam Moore and Rufus Thomas would more recently—of taking too much credit and accruing too many royalties for his production and writing work at Stax.[66] Like the recollections of white musicians about the 1968 NATRA convention, Cropper presents his conflicts with Baylor and Woodard as the result of Black Power's intrusion into Stax in the person of two outside agitators.

Indeed, like Dan Penn's invocation of the NAACP, Cropper's language of "brainwashing" and general critique of the FPC echoes attacks levied against the civil rights movement by segregationists. But these tensions bespoke a longer tradition of black resentment at the label that went back as far as the first Mar-Keys recording session and paralleled a larger trend of nationalist activism in the soul business.

Many of Steve Cropper's criticisms are justified. Baylor and Woodard compromised the studio's finances, fractured its interpersonal relationships, and even physically attacked some of their coworkers. But, as with other aspects of the duo's career, whites like Axton and Cropper are quicker to say that the FPC's cofounders corrupted the good vibes—and perhaps the white-controlled power dynamic—that characterized Stax's early days. African Americans, in contrast, are critical of Baylor and Woodard but are less likely to say they destroyed an integrated Memphis sound. Marvell Thomas remembers being threatened with a gun by Johnny Baylor but also acknowledged that Baylor helped guard Stax artists against unscrupulous promoters.[67] Drummer Willie Hall credits Baylor with helping him to break into record production, while Deanie Parker notes that he "didn't go around all the time with his gun cocked. . . . Johnny allowed us to view him from time to time as an everyday guy who liked to have fun, who enjoyed laughing, who had a heart."[68] Further, both Thomas and Bell suggest that the duo's arrival was meant not to introduce strong-arm tactics into the label but to *protect* Stax from intimidation by local groups who sought to exploit its precarious position in the wake of the King assassination.[69] Stax's black musicians are just as aware of Baylor and Woodard's shortcomings as are white players like Steve Cropper, but they resist condemning the duo for shattering a racial utopia that—for many of them—never existed in the first place.[70]

Beyond this, both Baylor and Woodard were active participants in Stax's commercial resurgence. Al Bell has long defended their contribution to the label's success and allowed Baylor to run a subsidiary label, KoKo, where artists like Luther Ingram scored big hits. "Johnny was a hell of record producer," suggested horn player Mickey Gregory. "If he had spent as much time producing as he did trying to be a badass, he would have been recognized as a great producer."[71] Bell took the duo with him to NATRA conventions, and Baylor was even honored along with Bell at a 1970 dinner as an "Executive of the Year."[72] Ultimately, both men were important, if not always successful or well-intentioned, participants in Stax's moment of greatest political engagement and national popularity.

Al Bell accepts an award from NATRA in 1970. The support of industry organizations like NATRA became key to Stax's success in the Black Power years. Bell is seated in the center, holding the trophy. Dino Woodard is seated on the lower left. Stax Museum of American Soul Music.

The tale told by Cropper and others of Stax's racial exclusivity in the Bell years is most strikingly contradicted by the fact that, from 1969 until the label's closing in 1974, a large percentage of Stax's releases were recorded with the white studio musicians at Muscle Shoals Sound Studio, opened by the former FAME rhythm section in 1969. When he was not challenging the racial dynamics of Stax's Memphis headquarters, for example, Johnny Baylor visited Muscle Shoals Sound with his star client Luther Ingram. Although Ingram and others made big records there, the studio's most important Stax clients were the Staple Singers.[73] The major hits the family ensemble created at Muscle Shoals Sound crystallized Al Bell's vision of black cultural and political progress. The Staples' working relationship with the all-white Muscle Shoals Rhythm Section, meanwhile, demonstrated the degree to which musicians continued to work in interracial settings after the hostilities and transformations of the Black Power years. Into the mid-1970s, the Staple Singers and the Muscle Shoals Rhythm Section both reaffirmed and subverted Black Power's cultural expectations.

Al Bell saw the Staples as the cornerstone for his reimagining of Stax. "Ever since I've been in the record business," he told Rob Bowman, "one of my hidden desires was to record the Staple Singers. . . . The minute I got to Stax and got an opportunity to reach out for them I did."[74] Bell believed that the Staples, who became one of the most popular gospel groups of the 1960s with their civil rights–oriented "message music," could be huge secular stars if their soulful and socially conscious sound was combined with Stax's talented corps of producers, songwriters, and studio players. Bell's ambitious enthusiasm was shared by staff members like songwriter Homer Banks, who said the Staples shared his interest in songs that reflected "the cultural revolution."[75]

From their first Stax releases in 1968, the label marketed the Staple Singers as musical embodiments of the African American struggle for equality. "Their message is freedom and their media, song," extolled an early *Stax Fax* profile of the group, and an ad for their 1972 album identified the group's "message" as firmly connected to the black freedom movement: "You get it in the streets where people are looking for freedom. You hear it in tiny churches and one-room meeting halls where people are looking for truth. You find it at demonstrations where people are looking for peace and justice through equality. And you discover it in yourself if you have any kind of sense of all."[76] Though they had roots in the early integrationist phase of the civil rights movement, the Staples were equally willing to express a racially exclusive vision of soul politics. In *Stax Fax*, Pervis Staples bluntly claimed that "the white man can't relate to the black experience 'cause he hasn't had it, and now, we're trying to give it to him."[77] As with their parent label, the group's commitment to the struggle was more than rhetorical. They were involved in black activist campaigns throughout the period, including regular association with NATRA.

At first, Bell paired the Staple Singers with Booker T. and the MGs, then in their final days as the label's house band. The MGs were the backbone of Stax's early success and the popularization of the Memphis sound as both music and myth, but the group grew tired of the increased pressure brought on by Bell's ambitions. "The workload became enormous," Steve Cropper recalled of the period, lamenting that they could no longer devote enough time to crafting individual recordings. The MGs

The Staple Singers perform at the Wattstax concert, 1972.
The Staples became perhaps the best symbol of Stax's increased political
militancy, even as they recorded their biggest hits with an all-white ensemble
in Muscle Shoals. *Memphis Press-Scimitar* Collection, Preservation and
Special Collections, University of Memphis Libraries.

"would go in and spend our time, maybe sometimes we take three, four hours on one song. All of a sudden we're watching the clock."[78] Cropper, of course, was also resentful of the new racial power dynamics that he blamed on the entrance of Baylor and Woodard and perceived as an increasing hostility toward white involvement. He soon departed, opening a different studio in Memphis before ultimately moving to Nashville. Booker T. Jones also left the company, choosing greater autonomy and a more peaceful work environment as an independent producer in Los Angeles. Duck Dunn and Al Jackson Jr., stayed, working sessions at Stax until almost the very end. Faced with Cropper's and Jones's departure, and perplexed by the Staple Singers' failure to make a significant commercial impact with their first Stax albums, Bell sent the group to Muscle Shoals Sound.

The apparent incongruity of this choice—given Stax's politics and the connotations of soul music—should not be understated. The splintering of the MGs provided Bell with a perfect opportunity to surround the Staple Singers, who were deeply connected to African American cultural and political traditions, with black collaborators. In theory, this would lead to greater musical authenticity and economic control, thus simultaneously bolstering both the aesthetic and economic goals that Black Power activists hoped to achieve in soul music. Instead, he sent the Staples to work with an entirely white ensemble. Rather than ending in disaster or frustration, the Staples' sessions in Muscle Shoals became highpoints of southern soul as both art form and political symbol.

The Muscle Shoals Rhythm Section was a widely admired ensemble. "The Muscle Shoals guys were a rhythm section that a singer would just die for," recalled the Staples' lead singer Mavis Staples, who admitted that she originally thought the players were black because of their soulful reputation.[79] Steve Cropper said they possessed the same combination of musical talent and business savvy as the MGs. "They did it for the same purpose," both "out of the love" and "because they have commercial blood or something in them."[80] In fact, when it came to the Staple Singers, the Muscle Shoals Rhythm Section far surpassed the accomplishments of their celebrated Stax counterparts.[81] The Staples brought out the best in the Rhythm Section, too; all four members—particularly drummer Roger Hawkins—played with a creativity and fluidity that they rarely recaptured. The sessions produced the magic for which Al Bell hoped, and the Staple Singers entered their most successful period, defined by their hit singles "Respect Yourself," "I'll Take You There," and "If You're Ready (Come Go with Me)."

All three songs were direct commentaries on the state of the black experience: they combined the gospel funk of Black Power-era soul with explicit references to the historical and contemporary struggles faced by African Americans. They epitomized, in a sense, exactly what *Time* columnist Chris Porterfield meant when he said that soul represented the "primal currents of racial experience and emotion."[82] Still, the three songs emerged from thoroughly integrated musical spaces. In other words, the *contents* of each song affirmed soul's potential as an expression of black feeling while their *contexts* complicated that image. The creation of "I'll Take You There," which topped both pop and R&B charts in 1972, is a particularly fascinating illustration of this complexity.

"I'll Take You There" combined a gospel-influenced lyric written by Al Bell and Mavis Staples with a Jamaican-style rhythm track lifted from a recent ska hit. (This was also the period when the Rhythm Section worked with reggae star Jimmy Cliff, one of the many Jamaican musicians who developed their reggae sound after hearing R&B records on Nashville's WLAC.)[83] On top of the bubbling beat, Staples offered a series of gospel-style testimonies, promising to take the listeners to a place where racial discrimination and economic inequality are things of the past.[84] Driven by Hawkins's snapping snare and David Hood's thumping bass, the song never abandons its central groove, and the lack of formal song structure strengthens its gospel feel. It features no horns, one guitar, and only the barest keyboard work from Barry Beckett. In the middle of the song, each member of the band (except for drummer Hawkins) is singled out to take a solo. Beckett and Hood each showcase their supple playing. When it comes time for the guitar solo, Mavis calls out to "Daddy" to play one of his spare, powerful licks. But the guitarist playing the solo is not group patriarch Roebuck "Pops" Staples. It is young white guitarist Eddie Hinton, who plays a solo in Staples's trademark style.

The creation of "I'll Take You There," like the broader relationship between Stax and the Muscle Shoals Rhythm Section, demonstrates that even the soul label that most supported Black Power still recognized the talents of white musicians. Al Bell and Johnny Baylor proclaimed their music's blackness and called for greater African American control but nonetheless utilized the talents of white triangle players on Stax's soul releases. Ironically, given the importance of whites in helping develop southern soul, the use of integrated bands on soul records was actually closer to the music's "roots" than an all-black band would have been. But the integrated cast of musicians was incongruent with the racially essentialist rhetoric and racially driven political campaigns that Bell, Baylor, and others used during the late 1960s and early 1970s. Their characterization of soul was just that: a conscious construction that the music's producers, particularly those who were legitimately interested in furthering the cause of Black Power, could deploy for commercial benefit and political cover when necessary.

The deployment of these fiery racial politics is made even more significant by the fact that Stax routinely blasted white music-industry men in promotional materials sent to *those very white men.* Some may have stopped doing business with Stax because of this, but if so it never hindered Stax's climb. In fact, if anything, this approach likely contributed to the label's reputation as a cultural vanguard. The selling of blackness had always been a staple of the recording industry, and the manipulation of its musical contours structured the development of the country-soul triangle. But the late-1960s soul moment marked the first time that black militancy became a selling point in the U.S. music business. And nobody did it better than Stax Records—as the title of a 1972 Al Bell speech put it, "Black Is Beautiful . . . Business."[85]

Stax's musicians and executives were at the forefront of a major shift in U.S. cultural politics. They recognized the growing salience of Black Power language and iconography and used it to their commercial advantage. Additionally, Bell and other Stax leaders asserted the need for greater black representation in the Stax offices, a move that alienated some of the label's longest-serving white employees. These linked campaigns represented a broader trend in the music industry in which black-nationalist rhetoric and organizing reshaped the cultural understandings of soul music and the daily operations of the soul business. In turn, soul music—as both artistic expression and cultural commodity—became a central piece of the larger landscape of Black Power politics. This relationship brought Stax Records back from the brink and into a new position of prominence.

At the same time, in terms of both outward rhetoric and internal strategy, Stax defied the narrowest expectations of how black music was supposed to sound and how black-controlled companies were supposed to operate. Even as the company increased the sonic "blackness" of its records and the demographic blackness of its personnel, Stax continued to work with whites, utilize the integrationist rhetoric of the Memphis sound, and expand the stylistic palette of its releases. The story of Stax Records in the Black Power years reveals that musicians in the country-soul triangle were not primarily motivated by a quest for an essential black identity or the overwhelming influence of external racial divisions. They stood at the shifting center of a moment in which their music became a crucial marker of racial change, and they responded with an adaptive versatility that sprang from their musical work.

The openness of Stax's militancy was astounding. Still, it was surely easier for independent, black-controlled, soul-focused labels like Stax (or Motown, which also supported NATRA and other Black Power causes) to adopt such a platform than it was for major record companies that had far fewer African Americans either in the front office or on the artist roster. Unsurprisingly, Black Power activists directed particular ire at these majors and accused them of misrepresenting, mismanaging, or outright ignoring the potential of soul culture. Still, one label, Capitol Records, responded in a way that likely surprised the most aggressive critics. Capitol embraced Black Power, and—as evidence of its commitment to real soul music—went into business with white producer Rick Hall and his band at FAME Studios. Like the partnership between Stax and Muscle Shoals Sound, the deal between Capitol and FAME was one of the most important signals of the Shoals' rising national prominence as a home for soul and soul-influenced music. Muscle Shoals' mostly white cadre of music professionals responded to this prominence by reshaping the musical geographies of race in the United States. As they had always done, southern musicians both confirmed and confounded larger cultural expectations.

Four

TAKE THE WHITE MUSIC AND

MAKE IT SOUND BLACK

The Muscle Shoals Sound in the 1970s

The 1969 NATRA convention was far less chaotic than the previous year's meeting, where the organization demanded black control of soul music, but it was no less forceful. The convention's keynote speech was given by Stanley Gortikov, the white president of the corporation that oversaw Capitol Records. He did not mince words. "There is one thing wrong with the record industry," Gortikov said. "It is too damn white." Gortikov encouraged the group to keep up the fight and assured them that "if you can use the help of another honky record man please count me in."[1] Gortikov's remarks were part of Capitol's larger attempt to harness the energy of Black Power and answer the critiques of groups like NATRA. In 1969 Capitol launched a major effort to hire blacks in front-office positions and became the first major record company to establish a black-music division; it selected a former NATRA official as the division's leader. "Capitol is taking a corporate stand to increase employment of blacks in sales and promotion posts, while fostering the growth of black culture," *Billboard* reported on its front page, and both Gortikov and label vice president Bob Yorke spoke of their desire to establish what Yorke called a "purposeful and meaningful" relationship with the black community after years of distrust and exploitation.[2]

Central to this campaign was a new commitment to soul music. Capitol was slow to invest in R&B and soul and had only begun hiring African American salesmen in 1966, and Yorke claimed the company now possessed a "moral stake" in promoting black-oriented records. Capitol executives further believed that, in *Billboard*'s words, "the era of black nationalism and awareness has created a positive feeling among young blacks to be associated with music of their heritage."[3] They figured that a strong and steady line of soul products would mean more than giving newly hired black staff members something to sell or black listeners a chance to get excited about the label's catalog. It would prove the company's support of racial equality. As Capitol vice president Tom Morgan told *Billboard*, "The word is out . . . that Capitol is in the soul world with both feet and [has] a concern to hire more black people, to further NATRA, and to do something more than just scoop dollars out of the market."[4]

To boost their soul catalog, Capitol signed production and distribution contracts with independent soul companies throughout the United States. One of their first and most prominent deals was with FAME Studios in Muscle Shoals. Still smarting from the loss of his Atlantic contract in the aftermath of the disastrous Aretha Franklin session, FAME's owner, Rick Hall, eagerly joined with the company to establish FAME Records as a new Capitol subsidiary. The racial irony was overwhelming: one of Capitol's first acts in its push to promote the black presence in the record industry was to go into business with one of the most prominent white men in soul music.

The partnership between FAME and Capitol symbolized the complex position occupied by musicians in Muscle Shoals during the Black Power years. As in Memphis, the push for greater black control of soul music existed in tense partnership with the continuing presence of whites in Shoals studios. Labels like Atlantic, Capitol, and Stax sent African American artists to Muscle Shoals to make records that emphasized the rhythms, vocalizations, and lyrical imagery that signified musical blackness in the late 1960s and early 1970s. At the same time, the Shoals' studios remained staffed and controlled primarily by white musicians whose role in soul music had been directly challenged by Black Power's ascendance.

The musicians responded by remixing the Memphis sound for the Black Power age, creating a new conception of a "Muscle Shoals sound" in the 1970s. The Muscle Shoals sound fueled a boom period in Shoals recording and became a globally recognized slogan and symbol. Like its Memphis counterpart, the Muscle Shoals sound claimed its value through a simultaneous assertion of musical blackness and cross-racial blending of country, soul, and other styles. In another similarity, promoters of the Muscle Shoals sound suggested that it confirmed the importance of interracial cooperation at a time when blacks and whites in the United States were increasingly polarized. This narrative of friendship remains the primary trope through which the music of Muscle Shoals is presented in both popular and scholarly contexts.

But the popularity of the Muscle Shoals sound did not have racially equal benefits. As the 1970s progressed, many of the most important sessions held in Shoals studios involved white performers who wanted an authentically black sound. The Muscle Shoals sound gave whites from across the stylistic spectrum a chance to make soul-influenced records that could compete, creatively and commercially, with those by contemporary African American artists. In Rick Hall's words, Muscle Shoals musicians could "take the white music and make it sound black."[5]

Muscle Shoals was the only major site of 1960s soul that so fully transformed itself into a home for white artists, and its musicians played a crucial role in integrating soul's musical characteristics into other sectors of the pop mainstream. Building on their justified reputations as skillful players, Shoals musicians offered white performers from Liza Minnelli to the Rolling Stones a chance to immerse themselves in the culturally transformative sounds of southern soul. While this process has often been bathed in a reassuring rhetoric of cross-racial liberation, its primary beneficiaries were white. The use of soul sounds by white performers raised serious questions of racial appropriation, most strongly reflected in the 1971 controversy surrounding FAME's success with the pop group the Osmonds, and provoked a significant decrease in the number of black artists who made records in Muscle Shoals. Black soul stars remained an important part of the area's recording scene throughout the 1970s, but by decade's end the Muscle Shoals sound was an increasingly white thing.

Despite its black roots, the Muscle Shoals sound ultimately symbolized a rejection of Black Power's expansive racial militancy. The Shoals' studios earned their reputation as wellsprings of southern R&B and soul, but they now played host to the marginalization of black artists and the appropriation of soul music by whites. Even worse, Muscle Shoals' soul-trained musicians came to embody the very rip-off that soul culture—inaccessible to whites and empowering to blacks—was supposed to erase.

Capitol wanted to work with Rick Hall, but it recognized the importance of appointing a black man to head the new FAME Records venture. On Hall's suggestion, it recruited Sidney Miller, a former jewelry salesman whom Capitol hired in 1966 as part of its first wave of black promotion men. Miller was certainly up to the job. His friend and colleague Logan Westbrooks described him as "very knowledgeable [and] rather sophisticated"; as Capitol's southern promotions manager, Miller had built

Rick Hall at FAME Studios, 1969. After signing with Capitol Records, Hall became central to the label's promotional campaign and the emerging idea of the Muscle Shoals sound. *Memphis Press-Scimitar* Collection, Preservation and Special Collections, University of Memphis Libraries.

relationships with black radio and retail that made him perfect to head the FAME subsidiary.[6] After being hired, he declared that he would demonstrate to Capitol that it was "doing [itself] a disservice if it is not prepared to handle soul on a specialized basis."[7] Hall told a Shoals newspaper that Miller's hiring would be "of immeasurable benefit to both labels" because of his "close liaison with key Capitol personnel" and track record "in the areas of artist relations, sales, promotion and merchandising."[8] And, like Capitol leaders, he also probably hoped that Miller's presidency would assuage any fears that FAME Records was simply another exploitative or inauthentic white-controlled soul company.

Even though Miller was the official head of FAME Records, Hall was its public face. His name and image were prominently featured on Capitol promotional materials, which presented him as a singular white visionary who blended black and white sounds into a soulful and profitable mixture. The producer used his reputation as a musical integrator to attract black artists to FAME throughout the 1960s, but his name (and, crucially, his face) had never been featured so prominently in a national ad campaign. One advertisement, promoting Candi Staton's debut FAME single "I'd Rather Be an Old Man's Sweetheart (than a Young Man's Fool)," is particularly striking. In this full-page spread, an empty rural road is pictured with text on either side. One half features a brief biography of Hall: "And he comes from Alabama. There was a man with a bankloan [sic] who kept making the gut sounds. And Muscle Shoals became famous. The man's name is Rick Hall." On the other side is a similar profile of Staton: "And she comes from Alabama. And her name is Candi Staton. And the sound is a rich belt of blues."[9] Racial blending became central to Capitol ads that presented FAME Studios as a site of musical awakening that produced a unique mix of country and soul with Rick Hall as the mastermind. Staton had a decade of experience in gospel and R&B before she came to Muscle Shoals, but the ad campaign presented her as an ingénue who blossomed under Hall's mentoring. A Capitol Records press release announcing Staton's debut release repeatedly called her a "pretty young girl" whose previous musical work was less important to her success than the mysterious magic of FAME and Muscle Shoals. "Unless you see it," Staton remarked in the press release, "I can hardly explain it. But it's beautiful."[10]

A similar subtext marked the promotion of white singer Bobbie Gentry. Gentry, a singer-songwriter from Mississippi whose work blended country, pop, and R&B influences, had a massive hit in 1967 with her debut single "Ode to Billie Joe." Despite success on the country charts, she had yet to replicate her initial success on the pop listings. Both Gentry and Capitol

Candi Staton promotional photo, 1969. Staton was one of the
most prominent artists on FAME Records, the Capitol subsidiary
crucial to Rick Hall and the broader Muscle Shoals recording scene.
Memphis Press-Scimitar Collection, Preservation and Special
Collections, University of Memphis Libraries.

executives hoped that working with Rick Hall and the soul players at FAME
would provide the impetus. Gentry had always included a sizable dose of
R&B and soul in her recordings, but the album she recorded at FAME,
Fancy, foregrounded these elements in both the horn-driven arrangements
and the songs, which included several soul covers and Gentry's title composition. Released in 1970, the single of "Fancy" became her biggest pop hit
since "Ode to Billie Joe," and Capitol's promotional strategy situated Gentry directly in their burgeoning narrative of cross-racial and cross-stylistic
integration at FAME. "What happens when a country girl goes to Muscle
Shoals?," one Capitol ad asked, accompanied by a seductive photo of the
singer. "She gets Fancy. . . . And she gets her biggest hit yet."[11] Capitol ignored the fact that Gentry had long incorporated eclectic influences in her
music and instead credited Muscle Shoals (and, by implication, Hall) with
remaking this "country girl" into a modern, soulful pop star.[12]

Gentry's work at FAME Studios has justifiably been celebrated by critics and journalists, but not everyone had a positive impression of the singer's successful incorporation of the Muscle Shoals sound. One of the songs on *Fancy*, "He Made a Woman Outta Me," had recently hit the R&B charts in a gritty version by Nashville-based soul singer Bettye Lavette. Lavette hoped that the song would cross over to the pop charts, but Gentry's recording appeared to prevent that possibility. Lavette remembered that "someone said they'd heard the song on white radio sung by someone else. 'Who?' I asked. 'Bobbie Gentry.'" Lavette was not pleased: "When I heard her version of 'He Made a Woman Outta Me,' though, I knew I had outsung her. I knew I had a hit. . . . She got the hit. I'm still mad." Gentry's recording was not actually a major hit, but Lavette remained angry at both Gentry—"Years later, when I was asked to sing on a Bobbie Gentry tribute album I said, 'Hell, no.' Muthafucka."—and Hall. When she recorded a 2007 album at FAME, she titled the recording *The Scene of the Crime* in reference to her feelings about Hall's role in stopping her progress.[13]

Capitol's relationship with FAME may have stalled Lavette's career, but it came at a very convenient moment for Rick Hall. For one thing, the Black Power push to establish soul as the property of African Americans required Hall (and Capitol) to find a way to make his whiteness into a benefit rather than a liability. To do this, they borrowed from the playbook that produced the notion of the Memphis sound, but the narratives possessed one crucial difference. The Memphis sound was promoted as the product of a group of local black and white musicians, while the Muscle Shoals sound had a single white source. Capitol's partnership with FAME—a direct product of the Black Power movement—had the ironic effect of positioning a white man as the creator of a deep soul powerhouse.

Hall was unambiguous in linking his work to Memphis; in 1969 he even opened a branch of FAME Studios in the city. Reporter James Kingsley noted that Hall hoped to "take advantage of [the] 'Memphis sound'" by moving to its epicenter. The Memphis branch of FAME launched with a lavish party and a performance by Candi Staton of "I'd Rather Be an Old Man's Sweetheart (than a Young Man's Fool)," penned by local black writer George Jackson.[14] Hall hired an interracial staff of Memphis musicians and recorded artists ranging from white country singer Sami Jo to African American soul man Spencer Wiggins. FAME's office in Memphis was never as successful as its original location, nor did it ever compete with homegrown studios like American or Stax. Still, Rick Hall's invocation of the Memphis sound helped solidify his seeming ownership of the Muscle Shoals sound as creative approach and commercial entity.

Hall's newfound prominence was additionally helpful to him because he was now competing against his former studio band. The relationship between Hall and the FAME musicians, which deteriorated after the Aretha Franklin session in January 1967, collapsed completely during the Capitol negotiations. The musicians left in early 1969 and opened the evocatively named Muscle Shoals Sound Studios. It was only after this studio opened that Capitol advertisements began touting Hall as the style's originator. This suggests that Capitol's construction of the Muscle Shoals sound and centralizing of Hall within it was motivated as much by a Shoals-area turf war as it was by a larger desire to deflect the criticisms of black nationalists. Capitol's promotional heft provided a key means of support for Hall as he tried to maintain his studio's prominence after the departure of his musicians.

Ironically, Hall signed with Capitol in part to prevent his musicians from quitting FAME Studios. He was afraid that Jerry Wexler was going to hire the Shoals players to work exclusively for Atlantic Records, and—given that Wexler had flown them to New York in semisecret to record with Aretha Franklin—Hall's fear was perhaps warranted. Still, though Wexler's support was a primary source of income and respect for the players, guitarist Jimmy Johnson said they had no interest in an exclusive relationship. "We had a built-in clientele, four or five record labels coming to us [whereas Hall] was going to operation of a closed shop, and we didn't want to." While Johnson's use of "closed shop" differs from the standard connotation—unions' insistence on membership as a condition of employment in a workplace—his implication is not entirely dissimilar. The FAME musicians saw their ability to work a wide variety of sessions as a matter of professional protection and opportunity, and they viewed the Capitol deal as a dubious attempt by Hall to deny them the full fruits of their hard-earned reputation in the music industry. "We felt like [leaving FAME] was our only chance to do something for ourselves and not just be players," Johnson recalled. "We had aspirations of being publishers and producers too."[15]

Just as they did not want to work for one company, they also hoped to avoid being associated with one genre. The musicians wanted Muscle Shoals Sound to be a home for a variety of artists, including ones who did not perform soul music. Like other triangle musicians, Johnson proclaimed "adaptability" as the key to their success. "We pride ourselves on that. We can accommodate any artist and get the best sound out of him without forcing our sound on anybody."[16] Now calling themselves the Muscle Shoals Rhythm Section, the musicians marketed themselves to a wide range of clients.

Despite these ambitions, the Muscle Shoals Rhythm Section's early success depended on soul music and Jerry Wexler. The studio's first hit was "Take a Letter Maria," by Atlantic newcomer R. B. Greaves, and their other early clients included pop star Cher, who recorded a soul-inflected album that Wexler produced, and rockers the Rolling Stones, who came to Muscle Shoals on Wexler's advice. "The setup . . . had a legendary ring because some great soul records had been coming out of there for several years," remembered the Stones' Keith Richards. "So to us, it was on a par with going to [legendary Chicago blues label] Chess Records, even though it was out of the way and we had wanted to record in Memphis."[17] Wexler's support established Muscle Shoals Sound as a soulful alternative to studios in Memphis or Chicago (or to FAME, for that matter), and it is perhaps not coincidental that he did not widely publicize the fact that the Muscle Shoals Rhythm Section was white.

Their race was also underplayed by Stax Records chairman Al Bell, who regularly employed the Rhythm Section at the height of Stax's association with Black Power. The group played on some of Stax's biggest (and most political) hits, but the players were rarely pictured on album covers or advertisements, nor did they become stars like Booker T. and the MGs. Bell's intentions are unclear, but it is not hard to believe that he (like Wexler) wanted to avoid the obvious contradiction between his assertively black soul recordings and the image of the all-white players who helped create them. This was made easier, of course, by the fact that—unlike the MGs—the Muscle Shoals Rhythm Section was not famous and did not release recordings under its own name. It remained a faceless collective of soulful expression.

This lack of exposure, combined with the racialized expectations of the soul audience, meant that many people assumed that the Muscle Shoals Rhythm Section was black. Indeed, many of the stories most often used to buttress the notion that Muscle Shoals Sound and the Muscle Shoals sound were vehicles of racial progress are centered on these moments of unexpected realization. After hearing the Staple Singers' "I'll Take You There," for example, white pop-rocker Paul Simon told his record label that he wanted to work with the Jamaican musicians who played on the record. He even called Stax to ask Al Bell how to contact them, and was shocked to find that they were white Alabamians.[18] British rocker Rod Stewart was similarly perplexed when he came to Muscle Shoals Sound in 1976; he reportedly thought that bassist David Hood was merely setting up equipment for when the black players arrived.[19]

It was not just white rock stars who were fooled by the Rhythm Section's soul sound. Mavis Staples, for example, assumed the musicians were black when Bell sent her to record in Muscle Shoals. But the story of Senegalese deejay Idrissa Dia is even more striking. Dia wrote to guitarist Jimmy Johnson to congratulate the Rhythm Section for being more authentically connected to the black experience than their counterparts at Motown, which he considered too white. "He told us," Johnson remembered, "that he used to call our names on the radio there in Dakar in Senegal. . . . 'Our African brothers in America' kind of thing." Johnson also remembered Dia writing that "we'd done more for relations between Senegal and America than any of the ambassadors. The music tied the people together."[20]

Johnson's memories are confirmed by Dia's own recollections. When Dia realized for the first time that the Muscle Shoals sound was made by four white men from rural Alabama, he "could hardly believe it. The way they played sounded very black."[21] In a letter to Jerry Wexler, Dia admitted that the whiteness of the Muscle Shoals Rhythm Section challenged the ideas that he and other Afrocentrists developed about soul's racial character and racial politics in the United States. "Despite the headlines that [former Alabama governor] George Wallace was grabbing around the world," he wrote, "the brothers from Muscle Shoals showed that America was a far more complex society. Can you imagine, we were saying in sheer amazement, how . . . black these musicians born and bred in the same environment as Wallace sound?"[22]

These claims are made even more noteworthy given Dia's location. During this period, Senegal became a center for pan-Africanist thought and cultural activism under the leadership of President Léopold Sédar Senghor. Senghor launched a campaign to celebrate the artistic legacy of the African diaspora, hoping to make Senegal, in Dia's words, "the cultural and intellectual beacon of Africa."[23] Unlike some other Afrocentrists, Senghor welcomed American soul music as an equal part of that continuum. Dia's show on Senegalese state radio was part of this project and nothing held a higher place of prominence as an expression of the black diaspora than the music made by the white musicians at Muscle Shoals Sound.

Dia's story—like those of Simon, Staples, Stewart, or even Muscle Shoals Sound bassist David Hood, who assumed that Stax bassist Donald "Duck" Dunn was African American—represents far more than just a humorous error.[24] It illustrates the ways Muscle Shoals Sound's white rhythm section both confirmed and denied the musical expectations that became so crucial to Black Power conceptions of racial identity. Additionally, stories like Dia's—built around his surprising yet strangely reassuring discovery that the Muscle Shoals Rhythm Section was white—became crucial to the suggestion that the Muscle Shoals sound was a vehicle for white liberation. In this formulation, similar to contemporaneous uses of the Memphis sound, Muscle Shoals was where white people came to immerse themselves in black music to free themselves from the trappings of cultural racism.

Some of the first white musicians to do this became important members of the studio staffs. In fact, when he extolled the "very black" sound of the Muscle Shoals Rhythm Section, Dia was likely referring in part to the guitar playing of Eddie Hinton. A white Georgian who started playing sessions in Muscle Shoals in 1967, Hinton also worked at American Studios in Memphis. His piercing guitar could be heard on hits by the Staple Singers and others, and he cowrote hits for Shoals soul star Percy Sledge and pop artist Dusty Springfield. Hinton also possessed a growling tenor that bore the obvious influence of his vocal hero, fallen Stax star Otis Redding.[25] Hinton's vocal ability convinced Jerry Wexler that Hinton was a "wonderboy" who would soon be a "superstar" thanks to the unlikely combination of his credible soul sound and his whiteness.[26] In other words, he was what Sam Phillips might have called a "white man with the Negro feel," and the excitement about Hinton's commercial possibilities paralleled FAME's early optimism about Dan Penn. Like Penn, Hinton never realized his promise as a "blue-eyed soul" recording artist, but his skills and spirit made him one of the most beloved members of the Muscle Shoals Sound community.

Many of his contemporaries admired Hinton not only for his professional talents but also because they viewed him as one of the few whites who could unlock the deepest secrets of the African American musical approach. In fact, many of his friends and colleagues suggest that Hinton's desire to sound "black" exacerbated the personal demons that ultimately destroyed him. They note that Hinton abused his voice by screaming and shouting to acquire a rasp that sounded more like Redding or other soul singers, and some even believe this musical obsession played a role in Hinton's death from a heart attack at age fifty-one after years battling alcohol and drug addiction.[27] Pianist Jim Dickinson argued that Hinton's problems stemmed from his attempts to reach into "the racially black musical experience. There's . . . something out there that doesn't want you with it, and I guess Eddie just got too close to that because he certainly was the blackest of all the white boys."[28] Dickinson essentializes and pathologizes "the racially black musical experience," but he echoes others' conclusions about Hinton's avid and ill-fated attempts to mimic African American singers.

Hinton came to Muscle Shoals around the same time as George Soule. Like Hinton, Soule was a young white musician of multiple musical gifts, particularly valued for his ability to convincingly reproduce the sound of black soul singers. Born in Mississippi, Soule grew up on pop and R&B from the radio, especially WLAC, and joined several bands that performed at the region's clubs and colleges. After a brief sojourn to Nashville, where he sold a few country songs, Soule joined the staff of Malaco Records, a fledgling soul label in Jackson, Mississippi. Malaco provided Soule with helpful experience, but he soon realized that he would have to move elsewhere if he wanted to find full-time work. He arrived in Muscle Shoals in 1969. "There was a terrific amount of activity going on at all of the studios," Soule recalled. "Everybody came in, just everyone you could imagine."[29] Soule quickly found work at both FAME and Muscle Shoals Sound, working as a songwriter, producer, and "demo singer," recording rough versions of songs as a performance model for the artists who would later record them.

It was in this capacity that Soule scored a hit in 1972, when he recorded a funky political tune called "Get Involved." Over a brooding, horn-driven arrangement, Soule demands action from all the "brothers and sisters" whose political will has not yet translated into action. Despite the quality of the performance, Soule did not intend to release the track under his name. He recorded a demo version of the song at FAME as a favor for its black songwriter, George Jackson, who hoped to sell it to an African American artist. But Rick Hall decided that Soule's intense performance was convincing enough to release on its own. "Get Involved" reached the Top 20 on the R&B chart and became part of the soundtrack of black politics in that tumultuous election year. "It was a national anthem in Harlem," Soule remembered. He was thrilled with the success and proud that so many listeners assumed he was black, but he refused to do any live or television appearances to promote the recording. Soule made this surprising decision, in part, because of his race. Before "Get Involved" came out, Soule explained, "I [had] asked that we do a photograph picture sleeve . . . to be sent out to the radio stations. Because I just felt like the disc jockeys needed to know who was doing the record. And, of course, it wasn't done that way and, as a result, I just felt uncomfortable. . . . I felt like it was misleading to some extent."[30]

Soule's fear was not that African American audiences would automatically reject a white singer doing a soul record. Instead, he worried that not acknowledging his whiteness constituted a betrayal of the black audience (and maybe the white audience too) who heard the song as an authentic expression of African American political feeling. More than a fear of musical illegitimacy, then, Soule's unease reflected his awareness of soul as the cultural and political property of African Americans. Even though Soule got calls from as far away as Milwaukee and Seattle, he stayed home. He remembers only one performance behind "Get Involved," at a black club in Birmingham, Alabama, which he did as a favor to the deejay who put on the show. "I . . . was received very well," he has said. "I went out and did my thing, and the audience was very receptive." His fears may have been overblown.[31]

The few black employees at Muscle Shoals Sound in these years remain less well-known than their white colleagues. George Soule often wrote and produced with a man named Phillip Mitchell, a Kentucky native who worked in the music business for several years before coming to Muscle Shoals. He first arrived in 1966 and made a few records at FAME, but their lack of success led him to leave the area. He returned in 1969 to find that the former FAME musicians had formed their own studio and wanted to work with him. They were particularly interested in Mitchell's writing, discouraging the singer from making his own records. "I kind of got pushed away from the artist side of things," he recalled, and—while he recorded a few singles in Muscle Shoals—he became known primarily as a successful composer of soul songs.[32] Mitchell wrote and produced several major hits and became the lone African American member of the studio's management team in its greatest period of success.

In a 1970 issue of *Billboard*, Mitchell was pictured in an embrace with several white studio employees as part of an article celebrating Muscle Shoals Sound's recent expansion and declaring the studio to be "sort of a commune."[33] Mitchell's presence seemed to confirm the notion that the ascendance of the Muscle Shoals sound represented cultural progress. Still, Muscle Shoals Sound was a barely integrated operation that remained firmly in white control. And while Mitchell achieved success as a producer and songwriter in the 1970s, he has been largely forgotten in subsequent appreciation of the Muscle Shoals music scene. "He's one of the best writers I've ever known," remembered Shoals soul star Millie Jackson. "He sings pretty good too. He never got the recognition he deserved. I hope he got the money instead."[34]

Phillip Mitchell illustrates a troubling undertone of the Muscle Shoals sound as both a musical style and commercial project in the 1970s. Despite their origins recording African American soul artists, Shoals studios and their "sound" became famous primarily for the white men who worked there. This discourse underpinned a practical shift in the Shoals' recording economy in which a series of high-profile sessions refocused the studios' output toward white performers who wanted to incorporate the black influences of the Muscle Shoals sound in order to modernize their recordings and stay relevant. This process was both provoked and encapsulated by the Osmonds' smash hit "One Bad Apple," recorded at FAME in 1971.

Before they arrived at FAME, the Osmonds would not have been pegged as obvious candidates for the Muscle Shoals sound. The five brothers recorded for several record labels during their stint as featured performers on crooner Andy Williams's popular 1960s television show, but they never scored a major hit. They signed to MGM Records in 1970, and label president Mike Curb—a noted political conservative—planned to market them as a contrast to the sex-drugs-and-revolution acts of the late 1960s. With their Mormon faith, their clean-cut image, and their whiteness, the Osmonds were a perfect fit. But Curb also recognized that if the group was to be musically credible the brothers needed to shed that traditionalism and update their old-fashioned sound. He looked to soul music for a model, specifically noting the similarities between the Osmonds and another quintet of young siblings, Motown Records' Jackson 5, who burst onto the scene in 1970 with four consecutive number one hits on the pop and R&B charts. Sensing the potential, Curb called Rick Hall.

As usual, Hall's first step was to find the right song. Luckily, FAME staff writer George Jackson—the writer of George Soule's "Get Involved" and no relation to the Motown group—had previously pitched a song to Motown as a potential Jackson 5 single. George Jackson had a proven track record in Memphis and Muscle Shoals, and he came to FAME on the recommendation of the studio's cofounder, Billy Sherrill, who was by this point achieving massive success as a country producer and songwriter in Nashville. Sherrill recognized the value of good black songwriting talent and knew that Jackson would work well at FAME, even though—despite the studio's reputation—Hall had never before hired an African American writer. When the Osmonds needed material that mimicked the Jackson 5, Hall knew that George Jackson was up to the task.

Hall was equally confident in the musicians who would create the track. The ensemble known as the Fame Gang was his third studio band, replacing the Muscle Shoals Rhythm Section after its members left in 1969. The Fame Gang were just as talented as their predecessors, but—unlike the previous FAME musicians—the group contained an equal number of black and white members. Contrary to the persistent myth, it was only after the King assassination and the 1968 NATRA convention that truly interracial recording work began at FAME. It is also noteworthy that, though the Fame Gang recorded plenty of soul for Capitol Records and

other labels, the group had their greatest successes with white pop artists. In other words, it was with all-white bands that FAME did its most famous soul recordings and with an integrated band that FAME started working with white artists like the Osmonds.

The Osmonds' arrival in Muscle Shoals was inauspicious. After the glitz and glamor of national television, the spare surroundings shocked the five brothers. "While we were there, we lived in a trailer home," remembered Donny Osmond. "The fact that our 'home' was parked smack in the middle of a cow field, now that was different." He was equally unimpressed with FAME Studios, which "wasn't anything fancy either. With its walnut, recreation-room wood paneling, and location somewhere close to the middle of nowhere, it appeared surprisingly modest in view of the great music that came out of it."[35]

The fact that Hall put the Osmonds up in a trailer in the middle of a field seems strange given that several hotels regularly hosted the recording artists who came to the area. (A local Mormon resident also recalled that

The Fame Gang promotional photo, 1969. The third rhythm
section to record at FAME Studios, the Fame Gang was the studio's first
interracial ensemble. Standing, left to right: Aaron Varnell, Jesse Boyce,
Harrison Calloway, Freeman Brown, and Junior Lowe; seated: Harvey
Thompson, Clayton Ivey, and Ronnie Eades. Courtesy of Rodney Hall.
FAME Studio Records, Library and Archives, Rock and
Roll Hall of Fame and Museum.

the brothers' arrival in Muscle Shoals was big news in her temple, suggesting that local indifference was not the problem.)[36] Hall may have asked
the Osmonds to rough it as part of his attempt to strip away what Donny
Osmond called their "too stiff, too tentative," and—most crucially—"too
white" approach in the recording studio. During the session, Hall pushed
the brothers to more closely approximate the sound of the era's black soul
singers. "Standing on a soda crate so I could reach the mike," Donny recalled, "I listened as Rick exhorted me to 'give it more feeling' and 'sing
it from your gut.'"[37] This situation, in which the producer sought to craft
a more "natural" and soulful reaction from his singers by demanding

multiple takes, was repeated throughout southern recordings of the period, and Hall tried "One Bad Apple" in several different configurations. Hall finally hit on the right combination of Merrill Osmond singing lead on the verses and Donny doing a Michael Jackson–style falsetto on the chorus. After a great deal of work, everyone knew they had a hit. "One Bad Apple" spent multiple weeks at number one on the pop charts and also reached number six on the R&B lists. Thanks to the skills of the professionals at FAME Studios, the Osmonds effectively recreated the "Motown sound" in rural Alabama.

In this respect, "One Bad Apple" is a nearly perfect example of the larger racial and stylistic crisscrossing that the Muscle Shoals sound was meant to symbolize. A white producer known for deep soul produced a track written by his studio's first African American songwriter who came to FAME on the recommendation of one of the kings of country music, himself a former R&B musician. The players on the track were the first truly integrated studio band in Muscle Shoals, backing a clean-cut group of white singers from Utah on a record specifically designed to mimic one of the biggest Motown artists, released on a label run by one of the most conservative men in the music business. If one only considers the "Muscle Shoals sound" as a symbol of racial integration, "One Bad Apple" is the very height of its permutations—and it took place three years after the King assassination.

But the record provoked a very different reaction upon its release. In the spring of 1971, "One Bad Apple" was held up as the latest example of white people stealing black music. Particularly in the African American press, the Osmonds became a symbol of the longer debate over the racial character of popular music and the specific assertion of blackness within soul and the Black Power movement. For a few months in 1971, "One Bad Apple" was as controversial as any piece of U.S. popular culture.

Given the most essentialist of the era's rhetoric, one might expect that soul fans lampooned "One Bad Apple" as a silly attempt by white pop stars to recreate black music. But this was not the case. Instead, "One Bad Apple" was criticized for doing it too well. In fact, some listeners initially thought that the jubilant song was performed by the Jackson 5 and claimed that this was why it climbed so high on the R&B charts. Beyond this rumor, there were other race-based complaints about the record's success. Some said that black-oriented radio should not play "One Bad Apple," since— no matter how good it sounded—it was by a white artist. Some argued that, for the same reason, the Osmonds should not be listed on the R&B or soul charts. Others expressed outrage at the fact that "One Bad Apple" prevented the Jackson 5's fifth single from reaching number one and thus ended their streak of chart-toppers. Each of these claims shared a common root, summed up by Motown's vice president, Ewart Abner. Asked about the similarity between the groups, Abner promised that Motown would "go on doing our thing [while] they go on doing—our thing."[38]

As Abner's words suggest, the fundamental objection raised against the Osmonds was that they were participants in the white rip-off of black cultural resources, joining a dubious list of performers like Pat Boone and Elvis Presley, whose names could be invoked even to nonmusical audiences as examples of white thievery. Everyone from white rock critic Robert Christgau to African American comedian Richard Pryor leveled these charges, and actor Hari Rhodes linked the Osmonds' success to larger nationalist critiques of soul radio and the use of "soul" as a commodity.[39] "It's a shame!," he erupted. "Every time black people get something to go the whites come right along and imitate them and make a mint. And what gets me really mad is that the so-called 'soul' stations, beamed to black audiences and claiming they play only 'soul' stuff are playing the Osmonds' recording all day long—as if to say anybody sounding like black folk are assumed to sound is projecting 'soul.'"[40]

Rhodes's comment cut to the quick of soul music's racial conundrum. He defined "soul" as something that cannot be replicated by those outside the black community while also slamming the Osmonds (and, by implication, all of those involved in the making and marketing of "One Bad Apple") for successfully "imitating" the Jackson 5. Indeed, even many who had no issue with "One Bad Apple" argued that, no matter how much the Osmond brothers may have sounded like the Jackson 5, the two were fundamentally different because of soul's extramusical meaning. *Los Angeles Times* columnist Kathy Orloff wrote that "The J5, growing up in Gary, Ind. [and] facing the black experience, share very little with Utah-bred and Mormon-insulated Osmond exuberance. J5 style is tempered by the experience of knowing, while the Osmonds' appeal is innocence."[41] Michael Jackson himself told Orloff that there was "a difference in the sound. . . . It's really the feeling you get into what you're singing and in knowing what you're doing."[42]

No one attacked the Osmonds and the white appropriation of soul with more passion than Booker Griffin, a radio host and columnist for the *Sentinel*, Los Angeles's African American newspaper. In a column titled "Osmond Brothers Exemplifying Rape of Black Music," Griffin excoriated the group for attempting and failing to mimic the "native talent" of the Jackson 5. The success of the Osmonds, Griffin wrote, has "re-emphasized in my mind with raw brutality the full impact of being black in White America." For Griffin, "the Osmond Brothers have joined a historical parade of white rapists who have seen fit to seize upon the racist orientations of America and utilize them to take the native and creative musical outpourings of the black experience and rip them off in mercantile commercialism." Griffin dismissed as "ridiculous" the idea that whites could perform with soul and attacked African Americans who suggested it was possible; he specifically criticized Stax soul singer Carla Thomas, whom Griffin called a "handkerchief-head" and "Aunt Thomasina" for her defense of white soul artists. Griffin saved his harshest condemnation for the record industry. Despite its liberal image, Griffin assailed the music business as "one of the most racist and anti-black in its orientations and hiring practices."[43] Griffin's comments would have fit in perfectly at the era's NATRA conventions, and he was a regular attendee. On the occasion of the 1974 meeting, Griffin invoked the Osmonds as proof of the continuing need for NATRA's assertive campaigns.[44]

Despite the firestorm, the controversy over "One Bad Apple" did not have a negative effect on either the Osmonds or Rick Hall. In fact, the record's success significantly improved the fortunes of both. The Osmonds became a pop phenomenon and recorded several of their follow-up hits at the studio. Still, in his autobiography, Donny Osmond felt compelled to defend himself against charges of racial mimicry. He condemned the hypocrisy of critics who slammed his group as "whitewashed, counterfeit soul" while they praised other white artists who approximated a black sound. "The influence of Motown's chart-dominating style can be seen all over popular music of the time, and if we were 'guilty' of being white boys who sang 'black,' we were certainly not alone."[45] Osmond's need to address charges of racial appropriation nearly thirty years after the release of "One Bad Apple" demonstrates the song's continuing power as a symbol of the racial politics of soul music, as well as soul's continuing resonance as a marker of African American or even black-diasporic identity.

Rick Hall, meanwhile, used his success with "One Bad Apple" to cement his reputation as the Shoals' musical architect. A 1973 newspaper profile showed him surrounded by the Osmond brothers and cited the group's 12.5 million records sold as justification for its potent headline: "Rick Hall Started the Muscle Shoals Sound."[46] He used the success with the Osmonds to attract other pop stars to FAME. In a reversal from what he did after Arthur Alexander's "You Better Move On," Hall offered "One Bad Apple" as an appeal to other white artists—even the Osmonds' old boss Andy Williams made a record with Hall in the ensuing years. Hall unabashedly considered "One Bad Apple" one of his proudest moments and the culmination of his musical philosophy. "The Osmonds did the Jackson 5 better than the Jackson 5," he boasted in 1999. "That was my whole attitude—take the white music and make it sound black."[47]

The charge to "make it sound black" perfectly sums up the broader trajectory of Muscle Shoals recording during the early 1970s, and—despite the lack of attention to it in most appreciations of the Muscle Shoals sound— "One Bad Apple" is a definitive moment in the development of the Shoals' music industry and the construction of its legendary reputation. The record expanded Rick Hall's musical reach and gave his boosters (including, first and foremost, Hall himself) further evidence that he was responsible for the culture-crossing music that Capitol Records spotlighted in its advertisements. Further, Hall's belief that the Osmonds sounded better, and even "blacker," than the Jackson 5 signaled that Hall and other white musicians in Muscle Shoals would increasingly market themselves to white artists who wanted access to otherwise unavailable black sounds, specifically the powerful and nebulous quality of soul. This shift worked.

Throughout the 1970s, white artists made up a larger and larger percentage of Muscle Shoals session rosters. Most of these artists—rock, pop, and country singers alike—came to FAME and Muscle Shoals Sound to make soul-influenced music. Besides the Osmonds and Andy Williams, FAME clients included everyone from pop crooner Paul Anka to country singer Mac Davis to film/theater star Liza Minnelli. Muscle Shoals Sound, meanwhile, hosted sessions by jazz player Herbie Mann, psychedelic rockers Traffic, pop singer Lulu, as well as the aforementioned sessions by rock stars like Paul Simon, Rod Stewart, and the Rolling Stones. There were many others (some of whom I discuss in subsequent chapters), but the list of white performers who recorded in Muscle Shoals in the 1970s forms a constellation of sessions that put FAME and Muscle Shoals Sound in nearly every corner of the U.S. pop market. This, combined with the two studios' continued success with soul artists, gave legitimacy to a claim that local leaders emblazoned on a plaque at the entrance to the city. For a few years in the 1970s, Muscle Shoals could be considered the "Hit Recording Capital of the World."

But the Shoals' recording boom was accompanied by a decrease in African Americans recording in the area, a fact that did not go unnoticed among the musicians themselves. "I don't think that when those white guys opened their studios in the South their aim was ever to stick with black music," Clarence Carter, one of FAME's biggest black 1970s stars, remarked later.[48] Andrew Wright, musician and cowriter of Percy Sledge's massive hit "When A Man Loves A Woman," echoed these sentiments, claiming the Shoals' musical leadership "just got rid of all the black musicians and writers" during the area's rise to prominence.[49] Black horn player Harrison Calloway argued that "opportunities for black musicians were lessened" in Muscle Shoals as white stars increasingly took interest in the area. As Calloway noted, these white performers often came backed by more money and garnered more publicity than their African American counterparts. "I mean, what was [soul artist] Eddie Floyd against [rock star] Bob Seger?"[50]

There were other major reasons for the decline in black sessions in Shoals studios. FAME and Muscle Shoals Sound lost their Atlantic, Capitol, and Stax contracts in the first half of the decade, which was itself partly a result of a larger shift toward northern studios and northern-identified sounds in the soul business. It also must be remembered that African American soul stars like Millie Jackson and Bobby Womack recorded hits in Muscle Shoals into the 1980s. Additionally, while the studio personnel remained mostly white, black musicians and songwriters like George Jackson, Phillip Mitchell, and half of the Fame Gang remained crucial to the Shoals' success. (In all likelihood, the presence of some African American players made the experience seem even more authentic to the white visitors.) Still, the eager pursuit of white performers by both FAME and Muscle Shoals Sound played a key role in remaking the Muscle Shoals sound into an example of black music made by white people.

In recent years, many white musicians have blamed the decline in black sessions in Muscle Shoals on African Americans. Like their colleagues in Memphis, they have pointed to the King assassination, the 1968 NATRA convention, and the larger (and vaguer) arrival of Black Power politics as the key moments that triggered an abandonment of Muscle Shoals by black performers and musicians. This, in turn, ended the Shoals' interracial magic. Historians and journalists have generally followed their lead. But white musicians actually played a larger and more insidious role in the process.

When it came to Black Power, the musicians in Muscle Shoals had it both ways. They capitalized on soul's perceived blackness by attracting business from companies like Capitol and Stax that had an explicit interest in using soul records to promote Black Power. But they also played a crucial role in blunting the campaign by asserting that soul—the epitome of blackness—could nonetheless be accessed and even controlled by whites. In musical terms, the Muscle Shoals sound showed the fallacy of racial separation by demonstrating that white people (and in the South, no less) could be just as soulful as any black person. But it nonetheless affirmed the persistence of racial divisions and the privileged position of whites in the music business. From the Osmonds to the Staples, the musicians of Muscle Shoals demonstrated both the possibilities and ultimate limitations of soul music's power as a force for racial liberation. The Muscle Shoals sound, in turn, symbolizes the broader tension between southern soul's long history of black-white collaboration and the painful inequality of that partnership.

A final story illustrates this tension even further. One of the black artists who defined Muscle Shoals soul was Joe Tex. After launching his hit-making career at FAME in 1964, where he helped to establish the creative approach and interracial image of the Muscle Shoals sound, Tex spent the 1960s and early 1970s recording hits in all three cities of the country-soul triangle. With his white producer and manager Buddy Killen, Tex created a catalog of hits that mapped soul's stylistic fads and sonic innovations, from the country-inflected gospel of "Hold What You've Got" to the rocking dance anthem "Show Me" to the early funk of "You Said a Bad Word." These records exemplify the racial interactions that defined the production of southern soul. Some examples of this are comedic, like when Killen bused a group of elderly white tourists from the Country Music Hall of Fame in Nashville to be the audience on Tex's "Skinny Legs and All," a pseudo-"live" recording built around slangy celebrations of black women's physiques. All the sessions are warmly remembered by participants both black and white. Released in 1972, Tex's funky hit "I Gotcha" seemed to be the next chapter in this happy history of collaboration.

But following the success of "I Gotcha," Tex left the music business and devoted himself to the Nation of Islam, which he had joined in 1968. He changed his name to Joseph X and then Yusuf Hazziez, became a Muslim minister, and launched a speaking tour to raise money for Nation-sponsored children's hospitals.[51] As Brian Ward describes, his speeches conveyed "a message of black separatism born of profound disillusionment with white America," and Hazziez focused his harshest criticism on the recording industry.[52] He told one audience that he never wanted his music to consist of "clowning for whites," and another that "blacks are already the best singers and dancers. . . . we need to unite."[53] As Joe Tex, Hazziez had performed at NATRA conventions and other black political events for several years, and his association with the Nation of Islam allowed him to unabashedly express the nationalist rhetoric of soul's Black Power moment.[54]

His personal journey paralleled that of southern soul in the late 1960s and early 1970s. He never publicly criticized his white collaborators or disowned his Joe Tex recordings. Still, he nonetheless recognized that the soul era was a chance for African American musicians to "unite," gain political and economic strength, and transcend the "clowning" that he felt tainted the work of black singers in the white-controlled music industry. Through his complex negotiation of integrated recording work and black-nationalist politics, Joe Tex/Yusuf Hazziez embodied the larger tension faced by soul musicians in the country-soul triangle in this period.

Despite his enthusiasm for life as a Muslim minister, Yusuf Hazziez resurrected Joe Tex a few years later. He came out of retirement in 1977 at the encouragement of Buddy Killen, who felt that the new disco phenomenon would be a perfect way to reintroduce Joe Tex to the record-buying public. In the intervening years, Killen remained one of the most important figures in country music and watched as the genre underwent a series of transformations in the late 1960s and early 1970s. The sound of country music changed, thanks in large part to its incorporation of the soul influence, but it also became associated with the reactionary politics of the ascendant New Right. The question of race was central to this moment, and Nashville's country musicians shaped the genre's racial politics through their recording work. The consequences proved just as complex and significant as those produced by their soul colleagues.

Five

PRIDE AND PREJUDICE

Race and Country Music in the

Era of Backlash

Merle Haggard, one of country music's most popular and acclaimed singer-songwriters, bluntly expressed the genre's racial politics in the early 1970s in a song called "I'm a White Boy." Over Haggard's trademark shuffle, the song's protagonist laments that he's "just a white boy looking for a place to do my thing" and describes his alienation in a country that has cast him aside in favor of minorities who—thanks to government assistance and racial solidarity—have opportunities that he cannot access. He says that since his "Daddy's name wasn't Willie Woodrow, and I wasn't born and raised in no ghetto," he has no place in the contemporary United States. Still, he remains proud of his identity and unwilling to give up his independence. "Yeah, I don't want no handout livin' and don't want any part of what they're givin' / I'm proud and white and I've got a song to sing." In this period, that anthem of pride and defiance was most definitely a country song.[1]

By 1970 country music was firmly associated with the politics of white backlash that crystallized around opposition to the civil rights movement and catapulted Richard Nixon to the White House in 1968.[2] In this period, country artists—including Haggard, who scored major hits on Capitol Records with backlash anthems "Okie from Muskogee" and "The Fighting Side of Me"—became well-known symbols of the ascendant New Right and icons of a supposed "silent majority" whose needs and desires had been abandoned in the push for civil rights and social welfare. Like most of the era's prominent conservative politicians, Haggard did not make any explicitly bigoted statements in "I'm a White Boy," though he got close when adopting a caricatured voice on the phrase "I ain't black." Instead, he deployed a well-known series of code words and veiled imagery to assert that 1960s liberalism was not designed to protect hardworking white folks like himself. Haggard's recording of "I'm a White Boy" was not a hit, but the song made the airwaves in versions by two other singers—both on Dot Records, once the home of Arthur Alexander—in the first half of the 1970s. *Cashbox* reviewed one version by saying that singer Jim Mundy "has laid his claim to a minority group—this time he's a card-carrying 'white boy.'"[3]

This racial appeal was certainly not the only link between country music and conservative politics in the late 1960s and early 1970s, but it was unquestionably among the most important. In recordings and public statements, country performers deployed the same criticisms of civil rights that leaders like Nixon or George Wallace used to great electoral success. Country performers and executives endorsed conservative candidates and included political messages in their recordings to an unprecedented degree. Some industry leaders were certainly motivated by political ideology, but— as with the use of Black Power in soul music—their primary desire was economic. They hoped that the conservative connection would expand country's national audience and secure its future commercial fortunes and prominence on the cultural landscape. And they were right: country sales boomed in this period and made front-page news across the country.

Country's ascendance as the voice of white conservatism paralleled and opposed soul music's rise as the voice of Black Power in the 1960s. In "I'm a White Boy," for example, Haggard's protagonist notes that he likes to hear "guitar . . . and fiddle," because "that's the kind of soul it takes to fan my flame." As with soul, country did not simply reflect contemporary cultural schisms or historical notions of white tradition. Instead, country musicians played a crucial role in structuring the larger perceived difference between black and white in the post–civil rights United States.

But country musicians did not always regurgitate the language of reactionary racial politics. Just before he recorded "I'm a White Boy," for example, Merle Haggard released "Irma Jackson," a tender defense of an ill-fated interracial love affair.[4] The coexistence of these songs reflects a larger tension. At the same time as country's artists and executives embraced white backlash to sell records, they also continued to assert— as they had with the Nashville sound in the late 1950s and in reaction to the Memphis sound in the 1960s—that the Nashville-based industry and country music itself was tolerant or even progressive when it came to issues of race. They claimed, in short, that country music was color blind.[5]

Country's assertion of color blindness was usually muted, but the massive success of African American singer Charley Pride made it one of the genre's central narratives. As Pride ascended to stardom in the late 1960s, country's boosters in the industry and press heralded his success as proof of country listeners' racial tolerance and the Nashville industry's open-minded professionalism. Conversely, many black journalists expressed joy and surprise that Pride was able to break through country music's racial barrier and offered his success as a historical corrective to a longer history of white appropriation. But Pride also faced criticism from a third group of people, both black and white, who worried that his devotion to white music in the era of assertive soul constituted a betrayal of his heritage. Pride himself mostly eschewed any potentially divisive statements and instead presented himself as a figure of healing. Nearly everyone else, it seemed, viewed Pride in the context of fierce debates over U.S. race relations.

Additionally, Pride's seemingly incongruous position as an African American who chose country over soul illustrates the crucial role that soul's reputation as a symbol of blackness played in establishing country's whiteness in the popular imagination. In fact, as evidenced by Merle Haggard's suggestion that country was the only "soul" music that white people wanted to hear, it was ultimately the relationship between the two genres that made each into such an important part of the language of race in the United States. This relationship reached maturity in the late 1960s and early 1970s, when scholars, musicians, and fans all reiterated the idea that the two genres were racial opposites. Among certain communities—politically involved youth, soldiers in Vietnam—the opposition even became the basis for open conflict. One's musical preference, with country and soul as the supposed stylistic polarities, became a sign of one's deeper ideology and identity.

Country music's establishment as a contested symbol of white identity, combined with the country industry's continuing reliance on African American musical style and even some black personnel, created a series of fascinating juxtapositions between the music's outward rhetoric and its internal mechanisms. Haggard and Pride were perhaps the most prominent examples, but this apparent contradiction also structured the careers of Nashville entrepreneurs like Shelby Singleton, who released conservative country and assertive soul recordings simultaneously. One of the most controversial of Singleton's conservative country records, a reaction to the My Lai incident titled "The Battle Hymn of Lt. Calley," was written and recorded in Muscle Shoals, where musicians embraced the song at the very moment they trumpeted their city's status as a progressive center of soul. The success of "Lt. Calley" troubles the divisions between the cities of the country-soul triangle and offers a striking illustration of how triangle musicians manipulated the racial and political expectations surrounding country and its stylistic overlaps.

The tension over racial inclusion in country music also structured the careers of black musicians like Jerry "Swamp Dogg" Williams. Williams's creative and professional choices were shaped in part by his recognition that—despite his love for country music and the success of Charley Pride—he was not likely to become a star in Nashville. Williams became a successful soul artist and producer, specializing in material that echoed soul's larger focus on assertive and even confrontational blackness. But Williams also achieved a surprising moment of country acclaim in 1971 as the songwriter of "She's All I Got," a major hit for singer Johnny Paycheck. Like the broader story of country's racial politics in these years, Williams's experiences reveal the complex ways the musicians of the country-soul triangle created a musical genre that became central to the cultural understanding of whiteness even as it tried to uphold its color-blind reputation.

Country music's politics had always troubled the distinctions between conservatism and liberalism. Instead of expressing a coherent and identifiable political dogma, most country songs and performers offered variations on a set of traditionalist and populist beliefs that produced inconsistent and sometimes competing messages. Country's most common critiques involved class, regional identity, and patriotism, but country artists tended to eschew overt statements when it came to race. Instead, they instead offered a contradictory mixture of calls for brotherhood (often cloaked in Christian imagery) with traditionalist celebrations of the southern and American past. In sum, country artists laid claim to cultural and political values while mostly avoiding controversy and sloganeering.[6]

This changed in the late 1960s as country music embraced the newly rejuvenated conservative movement. As Diane Pecknold notes, "country music did not so much shift to the right as the right shifted to country," and New Right politicians recognized that country's traditionalist-populist orientation and (supposedly) white audience offered an obvious analogue to their attempts to galvanize a disaffected populace.[7] For their part, the industry's leaders used this symbolism in their promotional campaigns and understood the potential benefits of linking country to the rising tide of reactionary politics. This strategy worked, and country executives and producers won the favor of prominent conservatives like George Wallace and later—on the advice of strategist Kevin Phillips, who also developed the infamous "southern strategy"—Richard Nixon.

Politicians like Nixon and Wallace championed country as the voice of the hardworking and patriotic Americans under attack in both the streets and the legislatures. They played to country fans' long-held resentment of cultural elites by suggesting that the inability of snobs to understand the music's virtues exemplified their larger dismissal of traditional American values. Wallace toured with country bands, while Nixon visited the Grand Ole Opry and hosted artists like Merle Haggard at the White House. Both men benefited from their embrace of country. In 1969 journalist Paul Hemphill described the numerous Nashville artists who supported each man in his bid for the White House (Hemphill said that Wallace had far more support than Nixon) and described the supportive bumper stickers on the cars outside the Grand Ole Opry.[8] Famed cowboy star Tex Ritter even recorded a special birthday tribute, "Thank You, President Nixon," that offered both explicit and implicit assurances that country's audience stood with the president and not with the protesters, cheats, and elites.

Country artists also echoed the rhetoric of politicians like Nixon and Wallace. Dozens of records that spoke out against welfare, disorder, and the anti–Vietnam War movement appeared in these years, and many country artists included segments in their shows that served as simultaneous tributes to patriots and condemnations of radicals. Hemphill described one such segment during a performance by Opry star Bill Anderson: "He worked up a two-minute speech on the virtues of patriotism ('There are a lot of people around today with long hair knocking our country, and I'm glad to say there aren't any of those here tonight'). Then Jan [Howard, a featured performer in Anderson's show], who had lost a son in Vietnam . . . would sing 'God Bless America.' . . . Considering the politics of any country-music audience, it was a natural at every show."[9] Interestingly, Hemphill noted that "Anderson toned down his 'long-hair' monologue in Boston, home of such centers of student dissent as Harvard and Brandeis," assuring the crowd that he was "not talking about *everybody* who has long hair." Anderson's dialed-down dogma in front of a potentially hostile crowd suggests that his political convictions did not trump his desire to please or at least placate his audiences.[10]

Country artists performed a similar balancing act when it came to race. Craig Werner is right when he notes that the "real problem with country's racial politics during the sixties was that they pretended not to exist," but his take is slightly simplified.[11] Country performers and audiences did not pretend that race politics did not exist so much as they deflected charges of racism while also making thinly veiled appeals to white conservatives. As in previous years, few country songs made direct statements on race, and most country artists spoke of their love and admiration for black influences and collaborators. Since the 1950s heyday of the Nashville sound, the genre's studio musicians, songwriters, and producers had included black-identified music styles, including soul, as part of country's musical mix. Additionally, many African Americans continued to enjoy country and claimed the music as their own. But these black artists and listeners remained both implicitly and explicitly excluded from country's supposedly "all-American" community. Implicitly, country songs and performers presented blacks—if only through coded language—as the cause of the problems facing the average country listener, who was assumed to be white. Explicitly, there were no superstar black country performers in this period of such deep musical synthesis, with one very notable exception.

Country music never had much room for black artists, even though several of the genre's most prominent figures were African American. Harmonica player DeFord Bailey became the first star of the Grand Ole Opry and the first artist recorded in a Nashville studio before he grew disillusioned with his treatment by Opry leadership and the country industry.[12] More prominently, Ray Charles's country recordings in the Nashville sound era proved hugely successful and groundbreaking in their sophisticated approach to country arrangements and instrumentation, but Charles did not initially get any airplay on country radio stations.[13] So it is particularly noteworthy that the most successful African American country singer in history emerged in this period of deep racial polarization.

Charley Pride, a Mississippian, was discovered by country star Red Sovine, who supposedly convinced Nashville executives to listen to his protégé by saying, "You gotta hear my nigger."[14] Sovine's crude words symbolized the double bind facing Pride and any other African American who sought to become a country star. His race might alienate the majority-white country audience, or—perhaps even worse—it would make him a gimmick or novelty artist. The executive who signed Pride shared these reservations. In 1966 Pride inked a deal with Nashville-sound architect Chet Atkins, who earlier turned down Arthur Alexander because he sounded "too black" and now worried that Charley Pride's color would hinder his success.

Atkins's answer was to try to keep it a secret. On Pride's first recordings, Atkins billed the young singer as "Country Charley Pride," a sly attempt to reinforce his legitimacy in the minds of listeners, and—despite Atkins's long interest in incorporating the sounds of black-identified music into country recordings—he kept Pride's records free of any obvious R&B influence. (He was helped in this regard by Pride's classic honky-tonk sound.) Additionally, Atkins did not include Pride's picture on early releases or advertising materials. The ploy worked, and it was only after securing radio play and record sales that Atkins and Pride revealed that the young star was African American.

Pride was not immediately accepted by everyone; he recalled that some white audiences greeted him with skepticism and hostility that Pride learned to disarm through his talent and stage patter. (For example, he got laughs by referring to the depth and quality of his "permanent tan.")[15] Such objections were not enough to stall Pride's career. He climbed the charts with startling ease, with early hits like the joyous "Kiss an Angel Good Morning" and the aching "All I Have To Offer You Is Me" demonstrating the power and versatility of his resonant baritone. Pride quickly became one of country's biggest stars and one of the era's most prominent recording artists in any genre. Even those people who did not listen to country music knew Charley Pride's name and, more important, his face.

Pride became a key figure in the cultural understanding of racial politics in the United States during the late 1960s. His success as an African American country star offered a handy symbol for the many people who used popular music as a microcosm for broader tensions in American racial politics. For those who carried the torch for early-1960s integrationism, Pride personified the racial progress of country music and the country it came from. For those who preferred the racial solidarity of Black Power or the New Right, Pride was a questionable figure who abandoned the culture of his people in order to perform music by and for whites. Even as he tried to unite the races behind a musical vision of brotherhood, Charley Pride personified the growing division between country/whiteness and soul/blackness.

Pride's backers resisted marketing the singer as an African American artist, although the title of his 1968 album *Songs of Pride . . . Charley, That Is* could be interpreted as a cagey reference to James Brown's "Say It Loud (I'm Black and I'm Proud)," the empowering soul hit that was released the month before Pride's album came out. Generally, though, Pride's record company avoided the issue. Still, much of the substantive press coverage of Pride during his peak years foregrounded his racial identity. Part of this interest stemmed from the simple reality that so few black singers ever achieved any country success, much less topped the charts. But some coverage went further and presented Pride's breakthrough as an important moment in the push for racial equality, and—more specifically— as a needed reaction to a longer history of white musical appropriation. In March 1967 *Ebony* called him the "handsome singer [who] cashes in

Charley Pride onstage at Ronald Reagan's inaugural celebration in 1981. Pride was one of the only African Americans to achieve major success in country music, and his ascent in the late 1960s provoked larger discussions about the musical relationship between black and white. U.S. Department of Defense, found on WikiMedia Commons.

on his novelty as Negro in rich field of hillbilly music." Both Pride and Atkins likely flinched at the presentation of Pride as a "novelty," but the *Ebony* writer celebrated the singer as an avenging agent who reversed the theft most obviously symbolized by Elvis Presley and Sun Records and soon to be revived in the debate over the Osmonds and "One Bad Apple." "Most long-haired rock 'n' roll singers make no secret of having borrowed their beat-heavy music from the Negro," wrote the *Ebony* columnist, "but a ruggedly handsome six-footer named Charley Pride has turned the tables on them all by being a Negro who sings like a hillbilly—and loves it."[16] A few years later, *Jet*'s Ralph Metcalfe noted with wonder that Pride's fans were almost exclusively "people of rural, Southern extraction not usually thought to be kindly disposed toward Blacks."[17]

Within the music-industry press, Pride's potential as a figure of integration was an unqualified reason to celebrate. In the October 1973 issue of *International Musician*, the newsletter for the American Federation of Musicians (AFM), Nashville correspondent Bill Littleton won a rare cover story with his profile of the singer, in which he argued that Pride's success demonstrated the sophistication of Nashville's industry.[18] Here, Littleton aimed not just to debunk the perception that country music was white and racist but also to demonstrate that Pride's success was merely the latest manifestation of what he earlier termed Nashville's penchant for musical "cross-culturation," the synthesis that made the city a first-rate recording center for music of all genres.[19] Given how infrequently Littleton's pieces reached the front page of the newsletter, his profile of Pride underscored the degree to which both the national AFM and Nashville's industry leaders remained invested in pushing the narrative of musical integration, especially since this new black star of country music offered an unprecedented storyline.

Most coverage followed this celebratory tone, but some discussions of Pride's ability to transcend the black-white boundary took a more pessimistic approach. Writers worried that Pride's love of country music and refusal to speak out on racial issues might make him guilty of "deserting his racial heritage."[20] Some African Americans expressed this concern, but the most striking presentations of Pride as potential race traitor came from whites. In his influential book *The Americanization of Dixie*, for example, journalist John Egerton dismissed Pride's blackness with a particularly poetic flourish: "Pride's blackness is a pigment of his imagination—his style is pure country, not blues or soul—and he has made himself a wealthy man."[21] Setting aside Egerton's regrettable reductivism and terrible pun, he expressed a wider belief that Pride's love of country music made him a trespasser who breached the divide between country and soul, and thus between black and white America, with ambivalent results.

Pride himself mostly demurred when he was asked about his role as a pioneer. And he was asked about this a lot, so much in fact that his responses took on the well-rehearsed pithiness of a set of talking points. He said that his ability to cross musical boundaries was only a function of his personal tastes ("I just happened to hear music that appealed to my ears"), though he did not note that part of that "appeal" resulted from the predominance of country on the radio during his youth. He countered charges that his music was not "black" enough by claiming that all styles of music were inherently linked. Asked if he felt he abandoned his "musical heritage," Pride told *Jet* that "all American music is connected. It's just how society has gone and sliced it up."[22]

Just as he did not consider himself a musical boundary-buster, Pride addressed his role in combating racism only in the most noncontroversial terms. He initially embraced comparisons to Jackie Robinson, for example, but later insisted that he did not want to be thought of as country's version of the man who integrated baseball.[23] Additionally, though he sometimes talked about overcoming the skepticism of white audiences, he usually presented himself as healing black folks. He repeatedly told the story of a young African American listener who approached him and noted quizzically that "you look like us, but you sound like them," or of a tense moment at a USO show in Germany when black soldiers asked him to sing one "for the brothers." Pride responded that—unlike many soul singers—he sang for *all* the brothers, regardless of race.[24] He went so far as to dismiss the idea that being a black country singer meant anything to him at all: "I'm Black only so far as society wants to qualify, describe and categorize me. . . . From a kid on, I decided to be Charley Pride the person—not Charley Pride the colored or Charley Pride the Black."[25]

Charley Pride's success and devotion to the rhetoric of color blindness offered a microcosm of both the possibilities and limits of country's gestures toward racial progressivism in the 1960s and 1970s. On the one hand, his ability to achieve massive fame in country music challenged the real and perceived racial divisions in the recording industry. On the other hand, despite the excitement, Pride's potential as a figure of progress extended only so far, particularly since his music rejected the racial assertions that characterized the era's country or soul music. It would be wrong to suggest that Charley Pride needed to do something identifiably "black" in order to contribute to the cause of racial equality within the music industry. But it nonetheless remains significant that the only African American who achieved major country stardom in this period was someone who explicitly and implicitly distanced himself from racial confrontation and whose racially motivated criticisms were almost always directed toward other blacks.

Charley Pride further demonstrates the limits of country's color blindness because he remained the solitary black face in the top tier of a genre that—if not explicitly whites-only—embraced a political strategy that rendered it generally inaccessible to African Americans. Other African American singers had some success on the country charts in the aftermath of Pride's breakthrough, including Stax artist O. B. McClinton, and they became the subjects of similar profiles in the press. "Charley opened up the field for us and he is my idol," McClinton told a reporter in 1974. "I used to try and sing rhythm-and-blues but I never thought it was my bag. Then along came Charley and things have changed in the country field."[26] McClinton even recorded a remarkable tribute to Pride in 1976. "Black Speck," which McClinton also wrote, concerns a white country fan who is unpleasantly surprised to find Pride—the titular "black speck"—singing at a Nashville nightspot. "That nigger sounds like a redneck," the white man exclaims as he leaves the club. By the song's end, the fan has gained a grudging respect and even admiration for Pride.[27] The racial inverse of Latimore's aforementioned "There's a Red-Neck in the Soul Band," McClinton's single reveals the degree to which Pride's success seemed to herald a broader opportunity for black performers. Despite the optimism, though, neither McClinton nor any other African American country artist achieved anything close to Pride's level of popularity.

Additionally, despite the large number of triangle soul artists who recorded country and country-influenced material during this period, they found that Pride's success (like that of Ray Charles) had not forced open the door to country stardom. Singer Joe Simon summed up a common belief when he told *R&B World* magazine in 1968 that "I'll sing country, but in order to be successful, I guess I'd have to change my colour [*sic*]."[28] Simon was one of several southern soul stars who recorded entire albums of country songs, joining a list that also included Millie Jackson, Joe Tex, Bobby Womack, and others. These albums were designed not just to spotlight the singers' versatility but also to assert a specific affinity between country and soul (and country and African Americans) that the racially polarized music industry did not always acknowledge. They had evocative titles like *Simon Country* (Simon) and *Soul Country* (Tex), and the cover art often depicted the performers in identifiably "country" settings. And they were clearly meant to duplicate the crossover success of Ray Charles's 1962 *Modern Sounds in Country & Western Music*.[29]

None of these achieved anything like the success of Charles's breakthrough recordings. Several singers saw this as a result of the closely linked musical and racial distinctions between country and soul. Millie Jackson, whose entry in this trend was called *Just a Lil' Bit Country* and who also released a hit soul version of Merle Haggard's "If You're Not Back in Love by Monday," said that her country work "served me no purpose, because no one would let me cross over!"[30] In an image that recalls the early careers of Arthur Alexander and Joe Tex, Jackson remembered that "I was supposed to appear on the . . . Opry [but my] record company said, 'She's an R&B act. You can't promote her country.' So nothing happened."[31] To be fair, it is hard to imagine Jackson's funky arrangements and salacious vocals on the Opry stage. But other soul artists who offered a more identifiably country sound also observed a racialized boundary between the genres. In 1976 Bobby Womack released an album called *BW Goes C&W* that offered faithful arrangements of country standards. Originally, though, Womack wanted to title his release *Step Aside, Charley Pride, and Give Another Nigger a Try*.[32]

Charley Pride crystallizes the tenuous balance between exclusion and inclusion that many in the country industry walked during the late 1960s and early 1970s. Pride's ascendance also reveals that country's racial politics were based on the same mixture of commercial concern, artistic choice, and cultural imperative that affected the era's soul recordings. This mixture was not just faced by exceptional artists—it was ingrained in the corporate strategy of Nashville's top executives. There is no more instructive example of this than the story of Plantation Records and its founder Shelby Singleton.

Nobody symbolized the expansion of the southern recording industry better than Singleton. He began his career in his hometown of Shreveport, Louisiana, working on that city's influential *Louisiana Hayride* radio show—a country program that introduced Elvis Presley to a national audience—before joining the Nashville office of Mercury Records in 1960. At Mercury, Singleton worked in promotions and production before becoming vice president of artists and repertoire. From the beginning of his career, Singleton built his reputation on his versatility. His earliest successes included R&B singer Brook Benton, teen-pop duo Paul & Paula, and several novelty hits by former FAME Studios musician Ray Stevens.

Singleton had many interests in the 1960s, but his primary passion remained the promotion of the Nashville sound. He worked with the fledgling Country Music Association, cofounded Nashville's chapter of the National Academy of Recording Arts and Sciences, and arranged for country musicians to work pop and jazz sessions in New York. A *Billboard* profile in 1962 named him "Man of the Week" and noted that Singleton believed Nashville musicians to be better than their "Big Apple" counterparts.[33] In 1967 Singleton even partnered with the U.S. Department of Commerce to lead a campaign promoting Nashville's country music as a tourist attraction around the world.[34] Others may have done more to musically modernize the Nashville sound and improve Nashville's reputation as a center of the music business, but no one approached the task more enthusiastically then Shelby Singleton.

After leaving Mercury in 1966, Singleton went into business for himself. He hit pay dirt almost immediately with his production of Jeannie C. Riley's "Harper Valley PTA," a country crossover smash that symbolized Nashville's changing identity. The stomping release made an instant star of the go-go-booted Riley and turned the relatively long-haired Singleton into one of the wealthiest and most respected symbols of country music's new elite. The record itself also demonstrated the changing times: with its assertive female protagonist shaming the powerful men in her small town by frankly describing their sins and hypocrisy, the song had a liberal-mindedness that clashed with country's traditionalist image.[35] Singleton crafted the promotional strategy to exploit these political dynamics, and he was justifiably proud of his success. Still, he was quick to point out that he was not an overnight success. "I had thirty-nine Gold Records before I'd ever seen Jeannie C. Riley," he told Paul Hemphill. "Tuesday I'm producing a country-pop novelty, Wednesday an R&B novelty, Thursday a bubblegum, Friday it's a folk-rock. . . ."[36] Indeed, Singleton's first success as an independent producer—with his new company SSS International—was with a soul duo.

Singleton's recording empire grew rapidly following these early successes. Just as he had done at Mercury, Singleton marketed himself as a pioneer who would, in *Cashbox*'s words, make Nashville "a multi-market threat" in record production.[37] Singleton's numerous labels, including soul imprints SSS and Silver Fox, released a vast and eclectic library of recordings in the late 1960s and early 1970s. Despite the success of soul on SSS and Silver Fox, Singleton's most intriguing company was the country-focused Plantation Records. Singleton began the label as an outlet for Jeannie C. Riley and—though the label never came close to equaling her first hit— Plantation released some of the era's most politicized country recordings.

Despite the label's debut with the open-minded "Harper Valley PTA," the political orientation of most Plantation releases was distinctly conservative. The Plantation catalog was a laundry list of New Right bailiwicks, with attacks on everything from high taxes to the gay-liberation movement, but the two most illuminating examples of the label's politics each tapped into the language of white backlash. "The School Bus," released in 1972 by T. Tommy Cutrer, opens with joyful sounds of children playing before Cutrer relates the sad tale of a poor community where the races got along. Its humble schoolhouse now stands "decayed . . . an epitaph to [the] freedom" that disappeared when the town was ordered to integrate by busing its children to a school "across the river, where the races were combined." Though residents protested, the authorities stood firm, so— with their limited resources—the town purchased an old school bus to send their children to the integrated school. The children were bused "across the muddy river, 12 miles up the road," until a fateful day when a storm caused the rickety bus to crash into the river, killing all the black and white children on board. Cutrer draws out the concluding sentences for extra impact: "On the back of that old bus we had painted in despair: 'Compliments of your Department of Health, Education and Welfare.'" With that, a children's chorus sings "My Country, 'Tis of Thee," and the tragic tale ends.[38]

"The School Bus" is not a good record, and it was not commercially successful. But it remains remarkable for the ease with which it deploys the racial rhetoric of early-1970s conservatism. It avoids overt race-baiting and even supports integration in the abstract, but it condemns the specific practice of forced busing that became a national firestorm and had recently exploded with particular ferocity in Memphis.[39] Further, it suggests a bucolic community that was happy and racially harmonious before the intrusion of federal policies caused that harmony's literal destruction. (In this respect, it sounds a lot like how many writers present integrated southern studios before the arrival of Black Power.) It attacks the U.S. government for exploiting the disadvantaged and hardworking community, right up to that poignant final reference to the Department of Health, Education, and Welfare on the wounded bus as it is pulled from the river. All told, "The School Bus" is a deft piece of backlash propaganda, cleverly crafted—if poorly executed—to push buttons of white conservative resentment.

More significant, and more successful, was "The Battle Hymn of Lt. Calley," released by Plantation in 1971 to coincide with the verdict in the case of William Calley, the accused perpetrator of the My Lai massacre. This incident became an international flashpoint for debates over the morality and effectiveness of the Vietnam conflict as well as an illustration of its barely subsumed debates over race and manhood. The antiwar movement presented Calley as a tragic tool of a barbaric war effort, while war supporters offered him as a symbol of demonized American patriotism.[40] Sung to the tune of "The Battle Hymn of the Republic," the song took the latter position, defending him as a hero whose only real crime was believing in the cause of defeating the North Vietnamese. The lyrics swipe at antiwar protestors—"While we're fighting in the jungles they were marching in the streets / While we're dying in the rice fields they were helping our defeat"—and suggest that Calley's actions were an inevitable consequence of a hard-fought war and the valiant attempt of a regular (white) soldier to defend his country against a sinister (nonwhite) enemy.[41]

Given its conservative content and country sound, listeners could reasonably have expected that "The Battle Hymn of Lt. Calley" was a product of the Nashville system, but it actually came from Muscle Shoals. Local businessmen Jim Smith and Julian Wilson wrote the song in April 1970 and recorded it with Shoals-based country journeyman Terry Nelson. They made Nelson's record at FAME Studios, at the same time that FAME was cutting soul hits for Capitol Records and pop smashes like the Osmonds' "One Bad Apple." Indeed, at the very moment that Rick Hall and others nurtured the idea that Muscle Shoals was more soulful and more progressive than Nashville's country industry, Hall and other local musicians leaped at the chance to make a country record that tapped into the same resentments that drove Merle Haggard to the top of the charts. Simply put, they knew a hit when they heard one.

After completing the record, Nelson sold "The Battle Hymn of Lt. Calley" to Shelby Singleton, who waited to release it until Calley was convicted in April 1971. Singleton promoted the record as a dramatic and urgent counterpoint to the prevailing narratives surrounding Calley's guilt. His advertisements usually included vivid graphics and artist photos, but the full-page ads for Nelson's single presented a stark and simple message: "WAKE UP AMERICA" (also the title of the single's B-side, an apocalyptic broadside against the powers of creeping leftism), with the song's lyrics reprinted beneath.[42] The record proved instantly successful and controversial. "On the day following the verdict," *Cashbox* reported, Singleton's office "was flooded with phone calls from people who wanted to hear the single as a means of protesting the decision."[43] Country radio stations quickly added it to their playlists, propelling it into the Top 40 of the country charts. In just a few weeks, "The Battle Hymn of Lt. Calley" sold a million records, making it Singleton's most successful release since "Harper Valley PTA."[44]

Unsurprisingly, the recording also inspired immediate controversy. While some listeners championed the recording as a needed antidote to Calley's vilification, others deplored it as an opportunistic exploitation of a tragic crime and an obvious example of country's reactionary politics. Many jukebox programmers refused to play the record altogether, noting that it caused fistfights and arguments in their locations. "If we programmed this record in locations . . . near campus here our windows would probably be busted," noted an operator in Madison, Wisconsin, a college town then in the throes of antiwar demonstrations.[45] Singleton later alleged that there was a coordinated effort among radio stations to keep the record off the air, and—while he never proved those charges—the single did disappear from the charts and radio playlists less than two months after its initial appearance. (Another potential reason for this, mentioned by several program directors, was that the record's ripped-from-the-headlines subject ensured a short shelf life.) In its brief moment of notoriety, "The Battle Hymn of Lt. Calley" inspired reportage and commentary both within and outside the music industry, encapsulating and fueling larger political battles over the Vietnam War.

"The Battle Hymn of Lt. Calley" was one of the biggest hits to emerge from Muscle Shoals in 1971, a big year generally for the city's industry, and the area's first country hit. After "The Battle Hymn of Lt. Calley," Muscle Shoals studios started booking more country sessions, even as they marketed themselves as a soulful alternative to Nashville. That summer, local studio owners and musicians planned a multiday festival called the Muscle Shoals Music Celebration, which included performances by numerous national pop and soul stars along with some local studio mainstays. They also booked Terry Nelson, and one festival planner told a reporter that the organizers believed "the people of this area would give him a fine reception."[46] Indeed, Nelson was warmly received by the crowd and recognized at a banquet honoring important contributors to the Shoals' music business. Nelson stood with—among others—Rick Hall, Jerry Wexler, and Zelma Redding, who accepted a posthumous award on behalf of her late husband Otis. Otis Redding was the only African American honored that evening.

By 1971, thanks to the popularization of the Muscle Shoals sound, Muscle Shoals music professionals had succeeded in establishing the city as a forward-looking alternative to the musical and cultural intransigence of Nashville country. But "The Battle Hymn of Lt. Calley" proves that this was an illusion. In fact, even before the record's release, Jim Smith said that the "people in the Muscle Shoals music industry," including the studio staffs at FAME and Muscle Shoals Sound, "have all been most helpful, both before and after the record became a success and I am looking forward to working closely with them in the future."[47] In the very moment when Muscle Shoals music was becoming known for its trademark funky sound and race-bridging musical mixtures (including antiwar material from the Staple Singers and others), one of its most prominent success stories came from a record that appealed directly to white conservatives. "The Battle Hymn of Lt. Calley" thus reveals that Muscle Shoals musicians had no greater political integrity than their counterparts in Nashville. Whether or not they believed in the song's message, their decision to create and celebrate it was motivated by the same economic factors that had guided triangle recording studios since the beginning. Nelson and his collaborators had the money to pay for the studio, making them another in a long list of clients who would benefit from the expertise of Shoals professionals. Once it became a success, they championed "The Battle Hymn of Lt. Calley" because it could attract new and different business, particularly among country artists who may not have immediately associated Muscle Shoals with their genre. The same rules applied throughout the country-soul triangle.

Given how directly it contradicts the standard myth surrounding Muscle Shoals music, it is unsurprising that "The Battle Hymn of Lt. Calley" is missing from the published histories of Muscle Shoals music. Just as the Osmonds' "One Bad Apple" does not adhere to the narratives of racial and musical authenticity that have been nurtured by Shoals musicians from the early 1960s, so too does "Lt. Calley" complicate the implicitly liberal and explicitly anti-Nashville presentation of the Shoals recording industry that has become a promotional strategy for Shoals musicians and such a comfort and crutch for many writers.

For his part, Shelby Singleton was always consistent in his public statements: he wanted to sell records. He knew that a market existed for "Lt. Calley," and he was happy to exploit it. Singleton also knew there was a similar market for soul music, and he made no attempt to segregate the conservative country on Plantation from the soul music on SSS or Silver Fox. He even promoted the recordings side-by-side in the same advertisements and mentioned them together when speaking to the press. Additionally, Singleton used Plantation to release Linda Martell's "Color Him Father," one of the only country hits by an African American woman. The song, a cover of a soul hit, presents a sympathetic portrayal of a black family from the eyes of a child who, though her father died in "the war," is happy to embrace the new man who has entered her mother's life. "Color Him Father" was a direct rebuke to stereotypes about broken black families and a subtle critique of the Vietnam conflict. Like "Harper Valley PTA," it illustrated that Singleton was willing to release material that diverged from conservative rhetoric. Additionally, many of the music professionals who worked on records like "The School Bus" and "The Battle Hymn of Lt. Calley" were at the same time recording tracks with black and white artists who might have objected to those records' lyrical content.

The coexistence of country and soul in Muscle Shoals and Nashville served as a counterpoint to the fact that by 1970 the divide between country and soul provided a structuring image for the larger debate over race in the United States. Increasingly, the racially coded appeals of both genres drew not only from their individual meanings but from the increasing belief in their fundamental difference. More than just abstract rhetoric or a promotional strategy, this perceived opposition fueled activism and even violent clashes. Nowhere was this more obvious than among American military personnel.

Soldiers regularly defined their military experience and their expressions of racial solidarity in the Vietnam era through the music they liked. Within this, country and soul were the two polarities.[48] "It was unusual in the unit I was in for whites to be listening to soul music," said R. Guy Slater, "just as it was for blacks to be listening to country music."[49]

Harold Bryant told journalist Wallace Terry that he and other black soldiers chose to spend their free time at "soul bars" because "I would want to do my drinking somewhere where I'd hear music that I liked rather than hillbilly," he said, adding that white soldiers "who wasn't [*sic*] racially hung up would also be there."[50] For Bryant, the white soldiers who listened to soul music possessed a greater degree of racial open-mindedness.

Others were not so open-minded. James "Kimo" Williams, an Army engineer and musician, recalled that—while rock music could bring the races together—country and soul always resulted in racial separation.[51] Soldiers even erupted into violence over whether the songs played on jukeboxes and radio stations tended more toward country or soul artists, and the absence of black-identified records (or black artists on USO-sponsored concerts) inflamed the already smoldering conflicts over racism in the war effort.[52] As tensions grew, some officers hoped to use music to quell the animosity. In late 1969 Marine Commandant Leonard Chapman announced that the Corps—as part of its attempt to end discrimination and violence— had "directed base commanders to see that there is 'soul' music on the juke boxes in noncommissioned officers' clubs."[53]

These conflicts made "country" and "soul" into convenient symbols for journalists who attempted to explain the complex tensions in Vietnam to their civilian readers.[54] It also provoked writing from soldiers themselves. Airman First Class LeRoy Edwards wrote to *Ebony* in December 1968 to detail his futile attempts to convince his base's radio station—which featured two country shows every day—to include a program devoted to soul. "I feel a separate program would benefit all concerned because it would expose the black man's contribution to the field of music," Edwards told the station managers. They turned him down, which Edwards saw as a deeper insult. "They thought I was a crazy young radical with nothing else to do but complain about the system. But I refuse to allow my discontent to go unanswered," Edwards assured the *Ebony* readers. "If I have to serve in this man's war, I want an environment which recognizes my existence."[55]

Through both content and marketing, country records provoked and manipulated the divisions felt by Airman Edwards and other black listeners. Many black musicians felt that their musical "existence" was not fully "recognized" by the Nashville establishment. Indeed, even after the success of Charley Pride and despite the continuing influence of African American players on the country sound, there were real limitations on black musicians' access to the interior of the Nashville mainstream. Even the most talented and eclectic black musicians faced this dilemma. One of them was Jerry "Swamp Dogg" Williams.

Jerry "Swamp Dogg" Williams's *Cuffed, Collared & Tagged*, released in 1972 on Cream Records. Williams's choice of army camouflage and an American flag shirt reflected his combination of eclectic musical influences and blunt critiques of American politics. The previous year, Williams had scored an award-winning hit as a songwriter on the country charts. Album cover photograph by Norman Seeff. Designed by Dean Torrence, Kittyhawk Graphics.

Williams was born in Portsmouth, Virginia, and grew up listening to country music.[56] "There was one big country station in Portsmouth called WLOW," he remembered. "I used to listen . . . every night, and the people at my house listened to country." Williams's grandfather nurtured his love by shopping at a local record store that serviced the black community with a wide variety of country options. "If you heard some country music, you could go in there and buy it," and the store used country records to lure in potential customers. "They'd be blasting country out front," he remembered, "and it didn't seem to bother anybody." This early exposure gave Williams a love for country that predated his appreciation for music more habitually identified with African Americans. He remembers finding gospel and blues hard to understand and musically inaccessible, and only later did he include them in his personal mix.[57]

Williams also recognized that the love of country music among African Americans in Portsmouth did not mean that opportunities existed for black country singers. Despite success as a singer, producer, and songwriter in both pop and R&B in the 1960s, Williams—like Arthur Alexander—believed that the doors to success in Nashville were closed to all but the most exceptional African American performers. The success of Charley Pride only confirmed Williams's perception. "They always let *one* [succeed]. . . . They let a black guy in to sing some country, and the motherfucker went all the way to the top. And they're like, 'We're not letting any more of these cocksuckers in.'"[58]

But Williams was also critical of the contemporaneous racial politics in the soul industry. His brief and unhappy tenure as the first black staff producer at Atlantic Records, a hiring he felt was motivated only by Atlantic's desire to placate political organizations like NATRA, left him bitter at the lack of good faith he perceived there.[59] He did not get to work with the label's top artists and was given little opportunity to succeed. Weary of the tokenism in both the country and soul worlds, but still committed to an eclectic musical menu, Williams fully embraced the era's most confrontational politics.

In 1970 he started issuing recordings under the name Swamp Dogg. These albums contained pointed commentaries on everything from ecological deterioration to excessive consumerism, but his most passionate statements attacked the two primary components of New Right reaction and the favorite topics of conservative country performers: racial politics and the Vietnam War. "I turned out to be everything that [the record company] didn't want—Anti-War, Pro-Black, Peace Movement participant and very candid," he recalled.[60] His commitment even inspired him to join the "FTA" (or "Fuck the Army") tour in 1972, where he performed outside military bases and earned a place on the Nixon administration's "enemies list." He also issued a gospel-dirge version of folksinger John Prine's "Sam Stone," a mournful ballad describing a returning veteran's descent into drug addiction and ending with his overdose. "Sam Stone" became perhaps his most famous solo recording, heralded by striking advertisements that featured Williams—wearing an American flag shirt—inserted inside a large syringe.[61]

Even as he abandoned the idea of country stardom, Williams never gave up on the idea that country would be part of his musical mix. He repeatedly spoke of country's impact on his songwriting, pointing out that, for "a long time, the songs were the same, the country songs and the soul songs. . . . It was just instrumentation that changed it, and the vocal—a hard black vocal or a hard white country vocal, but I see a very large connection between them." Williams also noted the country influence on his production style. "My productions still have country flavor," he explained, "and that's why I use all of those horns." Williams admitted that his consistently horn-heavy productions were a conscious attempt to make country-influenced recordings sound more like soul. "It's almost like putting ketchup on something: it's not tasting like it's supposed to taste. When I go in there and cut R&B, it's not supposed to sound like country."[62]

Williams's reasoning reflected his understanding of the racial rules that governed the production and promotion of country and soul. This commercial awareness altered his creative process. "Everything I write and sing comes out country, and that's why I have to take so much time in arrangements and instrumentation, because if not I'd just be cutting a bunch of country records with black people. And we *know* that black people are not makin' it in country."[63] Williams's recollections offer a striking inversion of the tenacious belief that soul music was built from inherently black musical characteristics, including the use of horn sections. Williams admits that he used horns not because he wanted to tap into a timeless tradition of black expression but because he wanted to make sure that his recordings did not sound *too white*.

His negotiation of country and soul makes it especially appropriate that Williams did most of his Swamp Dogg records—along with countless sessions for other artists—in Muscle Shoals. "I loved Muscle Shoals, that was paradise for me," Williams recalled, and his recording colleagues there remember his talents and personality fondly.[64] "I had great times with him," remembered David Johnson, a white man who engineered forty albums with Williams producing. "We had a great working relationship because he loved my ears. He always knew that I was going to give him what he wanted, and he always knew I understood what he wanted."[65] George Soule, who played drums on many of Williams's productions, said he "loved" Williams in part for his tireless work ethic: "We would stay in the studio eighteen hours," Soule recalled."[66] This mutual respect is evident on all of the recordings that Williams helmed during this period, even those—like "Call Me Nigger" or "God Bless America (For What?)"—that directly attacked the treatment of African Americans by whites in the United States.

Given all this, it is highly ironic that Williams's greatest moment of mainstream success came on the country charts through a smash version of Williams's "She's All I Got" by Johnny Paycheck in 1971.[67] But even this moment reveals the central tension at work in country music's racial politics. "She's All I Got" was a Top 10 R&B hit in 1971 for Nashville soul singer and WLAC deejay Freddie North. North's success piqued the interest of white producer and FAME Studios cofounder Billy Sherrill. Sherrill was one of Nashville's top producers by 1971, and he cemented his reputation as one of the biggest hit-makers in country music by bringing in influences, songs, and studio musicians from the pop and R&B that he made in Muscle Shoals. Sherrill liked the pulsing desperation of "She's All I Got," and he knew Freddie North as a successful demo singer who had recorded numerous songs for him in previous years. Convinced of the song's potential, Sherrill recorded versions by a number of country stars and found the magic mix when Johnny Paycheck applied his twangy vocals to an arrangement essentially identical to North's original. Paycheck's version soared to number 2 on *Billboard*'s country chart, crossed over to the pop Top 40, and earned a Country Music Association award nomination. In the same year that Swamp Dogg released an album featuring the soul song "Call Me Nigger," Jerry Williams was honored as country songwriter of the year by Broadcast Music International (BMI). Williams did not attend the Nashville awards dinner that preceded the ceremony, however. BMI's white secretary claimed that somebody had simply forgotten to send him an invitation, but Williams saw racism in the supposed coincidence. "I'm not pissed at anybody," he later claimed. "As a matter of fact, I thought it was funny. Most of the things that happened to me as a black man, I think was [*sic*] funny."[68]

Regardless of BMI's intentions, "She's All I Got" shows that—despite the country industry's desire to promote its racial progressivism—capable and enthusiastic black musicians like Jerry Williams remained marginalized. In the late 1960s country became thoroughly identified with white conservatism and marketed in opposition to the soul music and militant politics associated with black people. Even as they continued to overlap on the level of production, country and soul became increasingly understood as two extremes around which the continuing racial division in the United States could be articulated and confirmed. The country-soul division insured the terms of those debates, whether they took place between quizzical writers in *Ebony* magazine or angry soldiers in a PX in Vietnam. The people who created country music, like those who produced soul, exploited and constructed this relationship in ways that belie any simplified attempt to reduce country's racial politics to a story of either integration or backlash. In Nashville, Muscle Shoals, and even Memphis, the musicians of the country-soul triangle gave life to the key expression of whiteness and racial tension in this tumultuous era.

Even at his most scathing and profane, and despite his keen awareness of white supremacy, Jerry Williams understood that his hybrid music offered a way out of these divisions by presenting a vision of a southern future where the best traditions of the past coexisted with the social and political transformations of the 1960s. He explored this throughout his work, but no part of his recorded legacy demonstrates it more effectively than his versions of songs by a white man named Joe South. "His material painted an immediate picture," Williams recalled of South. "He could make you see things so vividly. His shit was simple, but it got to the point and got there quick."[69]

The two musicians followed a very similar path. Like Williams, South began with radio shows and small independent releases in the early 1960s, but he found his greatest success as a songwriter and session player in the middle of the decade. A mainstay of all three points of the country-soul triangle, South produced and wrote hits for pop and soul stars, and his bluesy guitar style—modeled after the playing of Roebuck "Pops" Staples—graced hits by artists from Bob Dylan to Aretha Franklin. Like many of his triangle colleagues, South was described in the day's press as a pioneer whose versatile talent would expand the South's musical fortunes and make Nashville safe for noncountry artists.[70]

South released his debut album, *Introspect*, on Capitol Records in early 1967.[71] Like the Swamp Dogg albums, *Introspect* and South's subsequent releases combined a cross-racial blending of musical influences with probing critiques of the political and social dynamics facing the South and the United States in that turbulent time. *Introspect* contained contemplative songs that attacked racism, class prejudice, and other hot-button topics in vibrant compositions that drew equally from country, gospel, rock, and soul. The mixture worked: South scored a major hit in 1968 with the troubled "Games People Play," which won the Grammy for best song and was recorded by a wide variety of other artists. Other South songs were routinely covered as well, making him a consistent presence on pop, R&B, and country charts in the early 1970s.

Jerry Williams recorded two songs from *Introspect*, as well as one from South's second album, on his Swamp Dogg releases. Each remained faithful to South's musical template but contained an increased dose of racialized critique. He infused the rollicking "Redneck," which lambasts a privileged young white man who loves to beat up hippies and laugh at the people in the ghetto while using his connections to "outsmart the draft board," with a righteous anger that surpasses South's more dryly humorous take. He added a winking racial recognition to South's critique of class snobbery, "These Are Not My People." And he expanded "Don't It Make You Want to Go Home" into an eight-minute epic that calls back even further than the original version. Joe South laments the loss of the bucolic Georgia landscape of his childhood, but—as Bill Friskics-Warren observes—Williams's version recalls "the continent his ancestors never chose to leave in the first place."[72]

Jerry Williams correctly recognized that Joe South was both a musical colleague and political kindred spirit, but South achieved much greater success than his African American counterpart. There were many reasons for this, of course, but race was unquestionably one of them. Williams's ambitious sound and confrontational politics left him marginalized in the pop marketplace while his skin color prohibited him from entry into certain sectors of the music business. Meanwhile, South's similarly eclectic and political material earned him the title of "visionary" from writers and record promoters. "HE SEES YOU," Capitol Records declared in one striking ad campaign,

Joe South at the Memphis Music Awards, 1971. South's eclectic songwriting style and willingness to address social issues made him a favorite among both audiences and critics. Photograph by James Reid. *Memphis Press-Scimitar* Collection, Preservation and Special Collections, University of Memphis Libraries.

adding that—while South's "vision isn't always what you'd like"—he nonetheless "speaks to something inside that you always knew was there. Joe South makes people uneasy. He sees you. And himself. Sometimes too clearly."[73]

The disparity became particularly evident as the 1970s progressed and Joe South became a symbol of a new breed of white southerner who abandoned the musical and political restrictions of Nashville's country establishment and the South's racist past. In the mid-1970s, the development of three new styles—"swamp music," "Outlaw country," and "southern rock"—became crucial symbols of the social and economic potential of a changing and modernizing South. However, as evidenced by the divergent paths of Joe South and Jerry Williams, the rise of these white musicians had the effect of culturally and commercially marginalizing their African American colleagues. The studios of the country-soul triangle became ground zero for a broader transformation in southern identity in the aftermath of civil rights, Black Power, and white backlash.

Six

THE SOUTH'S GONNA DO IT AGAIN

The Racial Politics of the

New Southern Music of the 1970s

In 1970, at the height of his fame as a singer-songwriter, Joe South appeared on the cover of *Cashbox* magazine. Inside, in language that may well have been copied from a label press release, an unnamed writer suggested that the commercial ascendance of the Capitol Records recording artist represented nothing less than "the South rising again."[1] Five years later, the language reappeared, in a similar context, in a song by another iconoclastic performer. In 1975, Charlie Daniels had a Top 30 hit with "The South's Gonna Do It Again," his raucous tribute to a new generation of southern musicians. Shouting out everyone from country singer Willie Nelson to rockers Lynyrd Skynyrd to white blues guitarist Elvin Bishop, Daniels's roll-call climaxes in an evocative assertion to his audience: "Be proud you're a rebel . . . 'Cause the South's gonna do it again."[2] Then, in 1982, Hank Williams Jr., whose rowdy sound bridged country and rock, released "The South's Gonna Rattle Again." This song also used the success of the region's musicians, including Charlie Daniels, to celebrate the South and hail its imminent resurgence.

The provocative use of this language—a battle cry of Confederate nostalgia revived in the backlash to the civil rights movement—served a similar purpose in all three cases. The *Cashbox* columnist, Charlie Daniels, and Hank Williams Jr. all asserted that a new and stylistically eclectic southern music demonstrated the South's continued strength in the face of historical marginalization and recent tensions. This musical claim linked to a larger project. In the aftermath of civil rights turmoil, southern leaders worked to rehabilitate their region's national image by declaring the emergence of a New South that transcended the backwardness of the past and entered a new phase of political relevance and economic power. This new breed of musicians would lead an accompanying renaissance in southern culture.[3]

Although it promoted a wide variety of artists, the rhetoric coalesced around three new genres: swamp music, Outlaw country, and southern rock. Writers, marketers, and the musicians themselves described performers in these styles as authentic products of southern musical tradition, representatives of the blend of black and white cultures created through integration, and symbols of the region's renewed vigor. In short, they were the soundtrack of the New South.

The new genres offered a specific counterpoint to mainstream country, which by the mid-1970s had thoroughly established its association with the perceived musical conservatism of the Nashville sound and the overt political conservatism of the New Right. "Country music is shit," Joe South told *Rolling Stone* in 1969. "It just isn't honest anymore." South's primary complaint was the narrowing of the genre to a specifically defined set of old-fashioned characteristics that he felt did not correspond to the versatility of the musicians. "The young guys, they sit around a studio in Nashville playin' jazz licks. They're playin' country only when they have to, to make a livin'."[4] Of course, given the jazz and R&B influence on two generations of the Nashville sound, South was observing a creative dynamic that had long existed in the city. But his comments reflected a larger belief that Nashville's lack of musical adventurousness corresponded to an absence of cultural inclusion.

Conversely, the incorporation of black influences by white insurgents like Joe South or Willie Nelson became coded as a broader rebuke of the South's racist past. Indeed, one of the key things that distinguished these new southern musicians in the minds of writers and fans was their embrace of African American music. They spoke of their black influences, performed covers of blues and soul songs, worked the musical textures of black-identified genres into their sounds, and recorded with soul musicians in Memphis and Muscle Shoals.

The notion that the new southern music represented a more racially progressive alternative to mainstream country has remained a common trope in both scholarly and popular discussions of the South in the 1970s. Journalists Frye Gaillard and Jan Reid, chronicling the rise of Outlaw country, presented it as a breakthrough moment of southern progress.[5] More recently, numerous scholars and journalists have depicted the genres as more racially inclusive than their mainstream counterparts, with music critic Mark Kemp even suggesting that southern rock initiated a "healing process" for young whites like himself who chafed at the South's legacy of racism and culturally constrictive mainstream country.[6] Like the Memphis sound of the early 1960s or the Muscle Shoals sound of the early 1970s, these genres have become a favorite narrative of racial change and redemption in the United States.[7]

But such progressive rhetoric has obscured the fact that swamp music, Outlaw country, and southern rock were just as segregated as the most conservative corners of mainstream country. Nashville artists had long incorporated the sounds of black pop and worked with some black musicians, and the success of Ray Charles and Charley Pride in the 1960s and early 1970s demonstrated that country audiences were at least somewhat willing to accept black faces on country stages. By contrast, essentially every performer associated with the new music was white. More insidious, the genres themselves were routinely promoted as being rooted in the experiences of white southerners who rejected white supremacy in favor of racial inclusion. This left little room for African Americans, except as inspirations and occasionally as behind-the-scenes collaborators. All three styles remained popular primarily among white audiences, and some southern rockers and country Outlaws appealed to these audiences by using Confederate iconography and visions of a romantic southern past that juxtaposed awkwardly with their more progressive lyrics and statements. No mainstream Nashville country artist of the period used Confederate imagery as enthusiastically.[8]

Finally, and perhaps most profoundly, the national marketing of swamp music, Outlaw country, and southern rock made the black-influenced music of southern whites—rather than music recorded by black southerners—into the primary musical symbol of the South's cultural progress. Southern soul, considered the vanguard even in the early 1970s, remained popular and relevant, but these new white-oriented genres quickly supplanted soul as the musical accompaniment to regional transformation. Instead of Aretha Franklin, the Staple Singers, or other black artists who harnessed the energy of civil rights while drawing from the South's rich musical heritage, the image of southern musical innovation became a white artist who rejected the sins of the past while holding on to the valuable elements of regional identity. Black musicians who attempted a similar alchemy, from Arthur Alexander to Swamp Dogg, were not included in this movement, despite sharing the same cultural and physical spaces as many of the white artists.

Certainly, the presence of white southerners who offered a counternarrative to the era's divisive politics had real value for individuals of any race.

Artists like Delaney & Bonnie or the Allman Brothers offered a powerful challenge to the era's dominant cultural and political narratives. Nonetheless, this discourse also had racially specific benefits by returning white musicians to the forefront of the southern recording industry. The rise of southern soul challenged the historically privileged position occupied by white performers and musicians in the country-soul triangle. In the Black Power years, thanks to the activism of black musicians at Stax and elsewhere and the emergence of "soul" as a cultural symbol, the music was increasingly understood as the artistic and economic property of African Americans. This left southern whites—some of whom had, of course, helped developed southern soul as musicians and songwriters—with the challenge of authenticating themselves in a suddenly unfriendly cultural marketplace. One reaction was the popularization of the Muscle Shoals sound among white artists. The new genres gave these musicians a similar and sometimes connected opportunity to once again capitalize on their diverse tastes and experiences.

The success of these artists fueled the insidious idea that whites were more musically adventurous than blacks. This notion has long infected musical discourse in the United States, but even in the richly integrated soundscape of the late 1960s many critics increasingly associated white southerners with style-blending and innovation and presented their African American counterparts as adherents to narrowly defined racial traditions. *Rolling Stone* critic Jon Landau encapsulated this view in 1968, writing about Stax stars Sam & Dave: "In music like soul, the artist doesn't seek to grow by expanding, but by penetrating. Sam and Dave's idea of musical growth is not the assimilation of eclectic influences, but the refinement of the essence of the basic ideas and forms which dominate their own style of music."[9] This was demonstrably untrue, but the association of soul with black essence—which, to be fair, was also a major component of Black Power rhetoric—became foundational in the contemporaneous assertion of the superior creativity and thus cultural relevance of the new white southerners. In his influential book *The Sound of the City* (1970), critic Charlie Gillett suggested that, while southern soul "lacked . . . a figure who could be seen to be developing his art stylistically," both Joe South and Tony Joe White had "manage[d] to put soul to good effect" on their solo recordings.[10]

Some journalists and advertisers took the narrative even further and presented these men (and they were almost all men) as nothing less than civil rights heroes. This heroic narrative had many uses. It offered a vision of reconciliation to a nation torn over racial issues. It demonstrated the continuing value of integration in both music and society, and (especially for northerners) told a story of southern redemption that provided a tidy happy ending to the nation's favored civil rights morality play. It affirmed the interracial narrative of the "sounds" in both Memphis and Muscle Shoals, while bridging the gap between the racially exclusive milieu of Black Power soul and the racially reactionary tone of New Right country. And it presaged the 1976 presidential campaign of Jimmy Carter, who articulated some of the same cultural dynamics and even enlisted the Allman Brothers, Willie Nelson, and other musicians in his events.[11]

The new southern artists both illustrated and structured the racial tightrope walked by white politicians like Carter who sought to transcend the South's reputation for racial bigotry. They celebrated southern tradition and identity in ways that could appear racially regressive—the most obvious example of this is the widespread use of Confederate iconography in both Outlaw country and southern rock. But they could also be powerfully subversive, as in the cultural critiques of swamp artist Tony Joe White or the jazz-influenced jamming of the interracial Allman Brothers. Despite these ambivalences, and though they differed in important respects, all of the new genres affirmed the notion that the hippest and most progressive southern music of the 1970s had a white face.

From its inception, swamp music was explicitly marked as the property of whites. In 1972 Atlantic Records executive Jerry Wexler—the hugely influential soul producer who signed many swamp acts—wrote in *Billboard* that it was "a fusion of country and funk" made by "people who have been subjected to the same influences as blacks."[12] He repeated this assessment in his autobiography, saying the style was "the Southern sound, R&B played by Southern whites."[13] Wexler certainly loved the sound, which possessed the cross-racial stylistic blend that originally brought him to the country-soul triangle in the early 1960s. It also fulfilled his long interest in stories of white redemption through black music. But it is additionally important to remember that Wexler, who was condemned by NATRA activists and alienated from southern soul in the Black Power years, was perhaps also motivated by the desire to reestablish his dominance in a southern musical style that could satisfy his eclectic musical tastes and allow him to maintain economic control.

Wexler and others promoted swamp music as representing a region that remained tied to cultural roots but rejected bigotry. Ads and artwork for artists like Tony Joe White, Delaney & Bonnie, and Don Nix (who began his career at Stax with the Mar-Keys) placed them in rural settings with acoustic guitars and other symbols of musical rusticity. But the musicians also sported the clothes and hairstyles of the hippie movement and stood side-by-side with African Americans presented as friends, collaborators, lovers, and sometimes as exoticized (and eroticized) fetish objects. Musically, swamp artists performed a similar mixture. They melded older southern-identified styles like blues, country, and gospel with the current sounds of rock and soul, making for a distinctive mixture of twang, funk, and volume that could appeal to both sides of the era's infamous "generation gap." The mixing extended to live performance. Delaney & Bonnie toured with black background singers and explicitly utilized the performance traditions of African American gospel, and Don Nix joined an interracial collection of artists called the Alabama State Troupers that toured the United States in 1971.

This revue-style performance was heralded in *Billboard* as reflecting "the diversity of modern Southern musicians."[14] Besides Nix, it featured African American Memphis blues veteran Furry Lewis and white Muscle Shoals singers Marlin and Jeannie Greene, backed by an assemblage of Shoals studio personnel personally selected by Nix. But the Troupers' "diversity"—at least in terms of race—was controversial. For one thing, their integration was merely accidental, since Furry Lewis was a last-minute replacement for white guitarist Lonnie Mack. Also, Nix later recalled that the young white audiences were not always interested in Lewis's traditional acoustic blues. "It was kind of the reaction that the Mar-Keys had on black audiences," he said, referring to Stax's white R&B band. "They had to be [won] over, but he always won them over."[15]

Furry Lewis's role in the Alabama State Troupers tour—last-minute replacement, sole African American performer, and keeper of the musical roots—underscores the fact that the blacks who took part in swamp music shows were almost always relegated to a secondary or token role. Lewis was the Troupers' musical authenticator, but most blacks who appeared onstage were female background singers who sometimes performed a familiarly uncomfortable role as sexual provocateurs for white audience members. Jan Reid described one performance of swamp star Leon Russell as featuring "a black girl [singer] thrusting and jiving" behind Russell "as Anglo males rushed forward like lemmings bound for the sea."[16]

Swamp music did not just leave blacks in the background: it put them firmly in the past. Like Furry Lewis playing acoustic blues for rock audiences, African Americans appear in swamp songs and iconography as representatives of a bygone era that inspired a new generation of white musicians. One of the most obvious examples of this is "Willie and Laura

Furry Lewis and Don Nix in the early 1970s. Lewis and Nix recorded together and performed as part of the Alabama State Troupers. Images of their collaborations became part of a larger attempt to link the rise of the new southern genres to broader cultural changes. Stax Museum of American Soul Music.

Mae Jones," a Tony Joe White song that became one of the most notable songs about race to appear in the swamp catalog. (It was also recorded by Dusty Springfield during her *Dusty in Memphis* sessions.) "Willie and Laura Mae Jones" tells a seemingly progressive story about the friendship between two families—one black, one white—who worked next to each other as sharecroppers. "When you work the land," the protagonist suggests, "you don't have time to worry about another man's color."[17] White's narrator looks back with nostalgic regret on his days working and living next to the Joneses on the plantation. His primary image of the Jones family's goodness is that his family used to play music with them in the evenings. At one point, Willie Jones even complements the white father for his ability to play the blues, a musical metaphor for the inspiration and validation that the African American family provided to White's young protagonist.[18] In the end, the white family of "Willie and Laura Mae Jones" moves away to find a better life and leaves the Jones family behind. White's narrator laments the loss of this bucolic scene and contrasts it with the racial hostilities faced by those outside of the sharecropping cabins. "That was another place," he bemoans, "and another time." "Willie and Laura Mae Jones" joins a line of U.S. racial fantasias that stretches from *Uncle Tom's Cabin* to *The Help*, and—like much of swamp music—it leaves African Americans in the disadvantaged but somehow friendlier past.

Swamp was historically important, but it was easily the least commercially successful of the new genres. Far more popular was Outlaw country.[19] Primarily associated with Waylon Jennings and Willie Nelson, Outlaw country sought to shake up the country establishment and offer an antidote to both the musical and political conservatism of the Nashville sound. These artists wore long hair, talked openly about smoking marijuana, and refused to yield artistic control to Nashville's powerful production and songwriting corps. The Outlaws' rejection of Nashville provoked the rise of an alternative country scene in Austin, Texas, which exploded as a site for performers—some homegrown, some Nashville refugees—who challenged the restrictions of the country mainstream.[20] This binary was far too stark to accommodate the complexities of the music being made in the two cities, but it was crucial to the success of an Outlaw sound that offered musical eclecticism and cultural acceptance as a chance for young whites to distance themselves from both George Jones and George Wallace.

One of the key ways Outlaw artists articulated this distance was by embracing black-identified music, specifically the R&B and soul that came from the country-soul triangle. Jennings and Nelson each relied on musicians, producers, and songwriters who gained their fame in Memphis and Muscle Shoals. Nelson worked with Atlantic's Jerry Wexler and Stax's Booker T. Jones, made an album at Muscle Shoals Sound, and recorded several songs by triangle songwriters.[21] Jennings, meanwhile, enjoyed a long and successful association with American Studios producer Chips Moman and several members of the American band, who by then had all left Memphis and—like the original Muscle Shoals rhythm section—quickly established themselves as sought-after studio players in Nashville.[22] In perhaps the most striking example of the overlap between Outlaw country and triangle soul, Jennings and Nelson's famed recording "Luckenbach, TX," a 1977 ode to outsider living in the Hill Country west of Austin that became perhaps the anthem of the Outlaw movement, was cowritten by Moman (who also produced it) and American pianist Bobby Emmons. Thus, the Outlaw country movement was literally defined by some of the players who earlier established the soulful Memphis sound as a musical and cultural icon.

An additional, if less prominent, soul touchstone for the Outlaws was Arthur Alexander. After being dropped from Dot Records in 1965, Alexander remained in Nashville, performing at local black venues and briefly recording for Monument Records, whose eclectic and interracial artist roster ranged from soul singer Joe Simon to a young Dolly Parton.[23] (Willie Nelson also worked there for several years.) Alexander's tenure at Monument failed to produce any hits, but it did lead him to employment at a songwriting house called Combine Music in 1970. Alexander was invited to Combine by his old FAME colleague Donnie Fritts, and Alexander joined an eclectic group of writers that in addition to Fritts included swamp-music pioneer Tony Joe White and an iconoclastic country hit-maker named Kris Kristofferson. Kristofferson, while on the outskirts of the Outlaw movement, played a similar role in expanding the songwriting and performing language of country in the 1970s. Outspokenly liberal and influenced by the counterculture, he attained significant success as both a singer and songwriter on the country charts.[24] Like the rest of his colleagues at Combine, Kristofferson loved Arthur Alexander.

The Combine staff had "great respect for Arthur as a person and as a musician," Kristofferson remembered, and they felt that his connection to soul would provide the country genre with a needed boost of artistic integrity and cultural inclusion. "When he was making his early music," Kristofferson described, "that was back in the days when race lines were still drawn down South. He was kind of a crossover. Like Ray Charles, he brought the heart and soul to country music."[25] Just like at FAME Studios at the beginning of his career, Alexander's blackness represented both musical authenticity and commercial opportunity for Kristofferson and his other Combine coworkers.

Despite this encouraging creative environment, Alexander failed to achieve any success at Combine even as his colleagues—Kristofferson, Parton, White, and others—became major stars in the 1970s. As Kristofferson's fame grew, he hired Donnie Fritts as his regular keyboard player, along with a Memphis-based group called the Dixie Flyers who worked a series of soul sessions for Jerry Wexler. Kristofferson worked with Fritts for two decades, giving the singer a literal connection to the southern soul that he considered so important to his iconoclastic country records. "Like Donnie," Kristofferson said, "[Arthur Alexander] was from Muscle Shoals, the real thing."[26]

As the Outlaws grew in national prominence, critics and journalists routinely echoed Kristofferson's words. They celebrated the Outlaws' connection to the black-identified music of the country-soul triangle as a demonstration of their greater authenticity and opposition to the restrictive country mainstream. *Los Angeles Times* writer Robert Hilburn, for example, said that Willie Nelson's recording an album at Muscle Shoals Sound symbolized a creative transgression against the "conservative, tradition-bent country music establishment."[27] But writers extended this argument beyond the music. In 1978 the *New York Times*'s Al Reinert suggested that until Nelson came along "country music was the smoothly polished product of the Nashville sound studios. . . . It involved precious little empathy and even less subtlety and was typified most blatantly by [Merle Haggard's] 'Okie From Muskogee,' . . . a song as strident and self-righteous as a Spiro Agnew speech."[28]

Reinert went on to credit Nelson with the success of Charley Pride, whose pioneering breakthrough began in 1967. That same year, Reinert wrote, "Lester Maddox was inaugurated Governor of Georgia, freedom buses were afire across the South, and the United States Congress was timorously preparing to dodge the President's civil rights program. Willie Nelson nonetheless concluded that his basically redneck audience was prepared to accept the first black singer in the history of country music."[29] Beyond the historical inaccuracy and snobby tone, Reinert ignored Pride's talent and courage and instead credited his success to Nelson's willingness to serve as Pride's white authenticator. Jan Reid concurred, calling Nelson "the real Nashville rebel" who "ushered Charley Pride through that . . . territory at a time when black churches were being bombed and blacks were confronting police dogs in Selma."[30]

Nelson deserves credit for championing Pride; he took the young singer on tour with him and opened their first show by kissing Pride on the mouth. But both Reid and Reinert replace Pride's success as an African American in a potentially hostile environment with the visionary progressivism of his white patron. Pride was a convenient target, since his mainstream country sound struck many observers—both black and white—as oppositional to the civil rights cause or even a racial sellout. The removal of Pride from both the civil rights story and the South's larger historical shifts made it easier for journalists like Reid to conclude that it was Nelson and his "successful defection from the 'Nashville sound'" that "startled Music City like the Civil Rights Act."[31]

The lionization of Willie Nelson and subsuming of Charley Pride is a perfect encapsulation of the white-centered rhetoric that structured the promotion of Outlaw country. Reid and Reinert are particularly emphatic in their hero-worship, but their general conclusions are very much in keeping with a larger discourse in which Nelson and his Outlaw compatriots are credited with saving a moribund genre and bringing the white South more firmly in step with a changing society. But, although Outlaw expanded the landscape of country music, it failed to extend this spirit of inclusion to actual participation by African Americans. The soul-trained musicians who benefited from their association with Jennings, Nelson, and the rest were almost exclusively white, and—despite the love and respect for musicians like Arthur Alexander—there were no African Americans in the Outlaw ranks. Additionally, as Travis Stimeling has recently shown in his study of the Austin scene, the Outlaws' eclecticism had the side effect of deracializing the many musical styles (like soul and Tejano) that they incorporated, making the white artists into the musical innovators and silencing the nonwhite musical communities that contributed to Outlaw's development.[32] Outlaw country remained music by and for white people, but with a comforting veneer of interracial brotherhood lain on top of it.

A similar tension occurred in southern rock. This raucous combination of country, soul, blues, and rock became associated primarily with the Allman Brothers and Lynyrd Skynyrd, each of whom had roots in the studios of Muscle Shoals. Duane Allman had been a session guitarist at FAME, and Skynyrd made its first recordings at Muscle Shoals Sound. They reaffirmed their Shoals origins in the musical blends that became their trademark. Additionally, like most of their southern rock followers, both the Allmans (who featured an African American member, making them one of the only integrated ensembles in the genre) and Skynyrd tried to present the 1970s South as a more progressive—or at least tolerant—place in terms of culture, custom, and comportment.[33] But the celebration of southern identity by white performers, some of whom used Confederate imagery and performed songs like "The South's Gonna Do It Again," existed on the very knife-edge of racial exclusivity.

Skynyrd's "Sweet Home Alabama," perhaps the southern rock anthem, illustrates this vividly.[34] The song features a trio of black female background singers, whose presence provides the song—like so many others in the period—with a soulful and interracial flavor. But at least one of the singers, Merry Clayton, found it difficult to reconcile her personal beliefs with the song's defiant message and celebratory tone. In the 2013 documentary *Twenty Feet from Stardom*, Clayton revealed that she almost refused to participate in the session until her husband convinced her that her presence offered an important counterweight to the song's more unseemly racial connotations. "He understood why it was important to have black voices on it," Clayton told a reporter. "There was nothing sweet about Alabama. You can hear our anger."[35]

Indeed, as Clayton suggests, the complexity extends into the song itself. In one verse, lead singer and songwriter Ronnie Van Zant sings of George Wallace, "In Birmingham, they love the governor," after which Clayton and the other background singers (along with Van Zant) sing three syllables that band members and others later claimed were actually "Boo, boo, boo," a subtle stab at Wallace and his administration.[36] This interpretation is certainly plausible, but the near-subliminal criticism of Wallace did not stop the song from being championed as a celebratory anthem of defiant white southernness. It is still performed by the contemporary version of Skynyrd in front of a giant Confederate flag.[37]

Regardless of how one interprets "Sweet Home Alabama," Lynyrd Skynyrd was one of southern rock's best groups and Van Zant one of its most thoughtful songwriters. He even wrote "The Ballad of Curtis Loew," a song that attacked racial discrimination, although this song too was a redemption narrative about an old black musician who inspires a young white man to reject prejudice and pursue his musical dreams. Still, most southern rock artists lacked Skynyrd's artistry and deployed problematic imagery with the same lack of creativity with which they churned out their increasingly hackneyed guitar riffs.

Although the genre remained popular through the early 1980s, southern rock's most lasting influence was on country music, both in terms of its rock-inflected sound (which became popular among stars like the band Alabama, which started its career in Muscle Shoals) and in helping popularize some of the genre's most conservative performers. These artists included both Hank Williams Jr., who recorded in Muscle Shoals and cowrote a song with Arthur Alexander, and Charlie Daniels, who later admitted that musical influence is not the same thing as interracial solidarity. "The one thing the South has always done," he attested, "is respect black music. Whether you respected black *people* or not, you respected the music."[38]

More than either Outlaw country or swamp music, southern rock fueled an expansion in the southern recording industry that became a crucial part of the South's larger economic rebirth in this period. After the success of Memphis, Muscle Shoals, and particularly Nashville in earlier decades, the 1970s saw the development of several profitable satellites heralded by journalists and politicians as crucial to the region's larger revitalization. John Egerton, for example, saw the expansion of white-identified music—which he called "southern to the core"—to be a crucial engine in the "southernization" of the United States. Beyond Egerton's romanticism, the growth of the southern recording industry exhibited several of the dynamics that structured the larger process.[39]

Perhaps the most obvious connection was the industry's sheer profitability. In these years, musicians, studio owners, and record executives were regularly pictured alongside other entrepreneurs as the faces of the New South's economic rebirth. But there was a further link between the music boom and the broader prosperity. The economic revitalization of southern states largely resulted from the relocation of industries that had been based in the cities of the northern "Rust Belt" but moved to southern states in search of lower taxes, laxer regulations, and fewer union members.[40] While nearly every musician in the country-soul triangle belonged to the AFM and followed its tight requirements concerning payments and schedules, upstart recording scenes often did not have such a rigid relationship to the union.[41] It was thus more profitable to record in a place that had not achieved the success of Memphis, Muscle Shoals, and particularly Nashville.

Joe South provides a fitting illustration of this. Despite his many experiences in triangle studios, South decided to base his solo career in his hometown of Atlanta. South appreciated the musicians who had tried (with little success) to establish the city as a prosperous recording center since the late 1950s, and he also described an atmosphere of "looseness" at Atlanta's studios that made it preferable to the hustle and bustle in more successful cities. This "looseness" had a more practical application that surely played as important a role in Joe South's choice of Atlanta as the friendlier environment. "The union is looser than [Nashville]," he attested in 1969. "Here [in Nashville], man it costs too much to make a record. It Atlanta, you can play all day and all night if you like."[42] The lack of AFM oversight allowed both for greater creative freedom—since the union's three-hours-per-session rule sometimes made it difficult for a recording to be satisfactorily completed—and a lower cost, which surely included reduced pay for musicians. This enticing arrangement mirrored the South's broader attractiveness for businesses looking to cut their rising personnel expenses. And, unlike in most other industries, the cost-cutting measures could be successfully cloaked in the benevolent language of southern "looseness" and cultural authenticity.

The expansion of the southern recording industry performed a similar role in relation to the political shifts that transformed southern states. In the 1970s the South embraced a rightward political drift symbolized by George Wallace and Richard Nixon and scored by the period's mainstream country music. Even as they promoted the region as the cradle of the new conservatism, though, political leaders—buoyed by the new economic prosperity—also presented the region as the forward-thinking engine of American success. This required some careful and sometimes contradictory rhetoric, particularly as it related to race. Promoters of the New South worked to assure the nation that the South's ugly legacy of bigotry was past even as African Americans found themselves without a significant voice in the leadership of southern states.

The new music scenes played a striking and surprising role in the silencing of African Americans. In Texas, for example, both Austin and Houston earned national attention as musical accompaniments for the New South, whose celebrated artists were almost entirely white. Beyond Austin's key role in the Outlaw movement, Houston—which boasted a wide and multiracial music scene—became particularly famous for the explosion of blues-rock trio ZZ Top.[43] In 1976, the year that Jimmy Carter won the White House, *New York Times* reporter Wayne King invoked Carter's election when describing ZZ Top as "the tip of the iceberg or the butter on the mound of grits in terms of the emergence to prominence of the southern music industry." With only the briefest references to either their African American influences or the continuing presence of black and brown musicians in the Houston scene, King argued that ZZ Top represented a "homecoming" in both the creative and commercial orientation of southern artists. This shift, he suggested, joined Carter's election and other factors in signaling a regional reinvigoration. "The South was somewhere a musician was from, not somewhere he was at," a member of ZZ Top told King.[44] That certainly had changed—at least for the white folks.

The best example of this tension is Macon, Georgia, which became the most celebrated of the new recording economies thanks to the success of Capricorn Records. In the late 1970s, Capricorn was southern rock's most influential label, the home of the Allman Brothers, Charlie Daniels, and other successful artists. The label was founded by Alan and Phil Walden, who previously ran a successful booking agency for black artists and managed several of them, including Arthur Alexander and Otis Redding, and the Waldens initially planned to make Capricorn a soul outlet. (Jerry "Swamp Dogg" Williams was one of the label's first artists.) But like Sam Phillips, Rick Hall, and others before them, they found it more profitable to record white artists who displayed a black musical influence. The Waldens' success with these artists made Capricorn a hugely successful and influential label by the mid-1970s, and the brothers were heralded as pioneers of southern rock and key players in the birth of the New South.[45] The company embraced this association and made little effort to disguise its overwhelming whiteness. In 1977, for example, Capricorn released a compilation album called *The South's Greatest Hits*, which featured an all-white collection of southern rock artists and was promoted with an evocative and provocative slogan: "You ain't just whistlin' Dixie with the South's greatest hits."[46]

Despite the national notoriety, not everyone was convinced that Capricorn's success represented a move forward. Southern soul star Clarence Carter, for one, specifically mentioned the Waldens when he recalled, "I don't think that when those white guys opened their studios in the South their aim was ever to stick with black music."[47] Carter's complaints were part of a larger feeling among southern black musicians that the new genres not only threatened their creative relevance but also endangered their economic livelihood. In the 1970s, as Carter suggests, southern studios increasingly filled their calendars with white artists, particularly white artists influenced by black artists like Carter. I examined how this transformation occurred in Muscle Shoals in chapter 4. The new genres of swamp music, Outlaw country, and southern rock joined the Muscle Shoals sound as key mechanisms through which previous strongholds of African American recording became increasingly white.

Like their counterparts in Nashville country, the musicians behind the new, white-identified southern genres were pivotal to the cultural understandings of whiteness and southernness in the post–civil rights United States. Their careers also illustrated the practical applications of those understandings. Despite the racially progressive impulses that motivated many of them and their boosters, they reinforced a white-dominated political and economic hierarchy in the South. In the process, they pushed soul music—perhaps the most obvious cultural manifestation of the new black politics—into the creative and commercial background. In a sad irony, they did so precisely by incorporating the sounds of soul into their iconoclastic musical mixtures.

At the end of the 1970s, even though they maintained significant connections in the ears and fingers of many listeners and musicians, country and soul became oppositional in nearly every other meaningful respect. Country music remained firmly associated with whiteness, even as Nashville musicians continued to integrate the newest sounds of African American music into their hit-making blends. Meanwhile, southern soul contracted into a regional scene, with an audience composed almost entirely of black southerners and a group of performers and promoters who marketed soul as the expression of tradition. The white musicians who developed soul music in Memphis and Muscle Shoals almost all ended up working in the country industry in Nashville, while their black counterparts largely did not follow them. As the musicians of the country-soul triangle approached the Reagan era, they continued to structure the racial geography of U.S. cultural politics.

Seven

DISCO AND DOWN HOME BLUES

Country and Soul at the End of the 1970s

In 1978 producer Buddy Killen wanted to introduce the latest development in soul to the country audience. "I thought it would be a good idea to make a disco record with [country singer] Bill Anderson, whom I was producing at the time. No one in the country field had done a disco record. Since I was always looking for something unusual to try, I felt that the climate was right."[1] Killen's gamble paid off and Anderson's "I Can't Wait Any Longer" went to number one on the country charts and crossed over to the pop Top 40. In a *Cashbox* profile following the record's success, Anderson—a popular performer in Nashville for over a decade—took full credit for the record, noting that his love of "the disco beat" convinced him that he could be "a country version of [soul star] Barry White." According to Anderson, Killen played only a secondary role at the session by helping to convince the Nashville studio players to play the disco groove. "All the session pickers looked at him like he was crazy," Anderson told *Cashbox*, "but once they got into it and understood what we wanted, it worked out great."[2]

Neither Killen nor Anderson acknowledged that "I Can't Wait Any Longer" had direct roots in the work of a prominent black soul artist, Killen's longtime client Joe Tex. In 1976 Killen asked Tex, who had changed his name to Yusuf Hazziez and was living in semiretirement on his Texas ranch, to help him capitalize on what Killen correctly identified as "the disco craze." By this point disco had transcended its origins in the multiracial gay dance clubs of U.S. cities and fully entered the cultural mainstream. Killen knew that the multitalented Tex, who had recorded hits in a variety of soul subgenres ever since his breakout sessions at FAME Studios in 1964, would be the perfect collaborator. Together, the duo wrote "Ain't Gonna Bump No More (with No Big Fat Woman)," which paired disco's throbbing rhythms with the singer's trademark gritty humor. Recorded in Nashville with some of Killen's favorite session players and released as a Joe Tex comeback in 1977, "Ain't Gonna Bump No More" returned the artist to the R&B Top 10 and gave him one of his biggest pop crossover hits.[3]

When Killen worked with Bill Anderson the next year, he used "Ain't Gonna Bump No More" as its foundation. He instructed the musicians who worked the Anderson session to "use the same groove" as Tex's song and even played them the record so they could model the soul smash as closely as possible (the principal bass lines on the two recordings are almost identical).[4] Although Killen admitted this in his autobiography, it was not discussed in contemporaneous press about "I Can't Wait Any Longer." Instead, writers credited Anderson and Killen as the creative visionaries who successfully married country and disco. More significant, they are the only credited writers, meaning that Yusuf Hazziez received no royalties for cowriting Anderson's smash.

This story encapsulates the tangled paths taken by country and soul at the end of the 1970s. In these years, country musicians from mainstream stars to Outlaws continued the decades-long process of incorporating black-identified sounds into their genre's musical core. By the early 1980s, nearly every important country artist used soul as a stylistic touchstone. Additionally, many of southern soul's most important white creators—from FAME's Billy Sherrill to American's Chips Moman to Muscle Shoals Sound's Barry Beckett—worked as powerful country producers and executives. For the most part, their African American counterparts did not share in their success.

The infusion of soul was the prime component in the country industry's assertion that its music was ready for the 1980s. Executives marketed contemporary country as an expression of the changing status of its urbanized and upwardly mobile fan base that could also appeal to a wider national audience. Thanks to these promotions, country achieved a level of crossover success that the music's creators had hoped for since the era of the Nashville sound. Country records sold in unprecedented numbers, country radio stations opened around the country, and writers in both the popular press and the emerging scholarship on the genre described the new music as the symbol of an economically energized, socially transformed, and politically relevant white South. Both musically and symbolically, the black-identified music of the 1960s and 1970s stood at the heart of this transformation. Bill Anderson's "I Can't Wait Any Longer," like other soul-and-disco-influenced country records, became a symbol of country's wide appeal and forward-thinking attitude.

But the erasure of Joe Tex's involvement in the creation of "I Can't Wait Any Longer" symbolized a connected trend. Southern soul's black talent pool—even a major star like Joe Tex—did not share in country's success at the dawn of the Reagan era. Simultaneously, southern soul was marginalized on the national pop landscape by the end of the 1970s. The rise of disco hastened the genre's commercial decline, and it also lost much of its cultural cachet. In the early 1970s journalists and activists described southern soul as the vanguard of U.S. popular culture, but it entered the 1980s being identified primarily as a nostalgic regional music that harkened back to the southern black past rather than pointing the way to the future.

This had a profound effect on the country-soul triangle. Soul artists still drew large crowds in the South and had hits on regional radio, but they no longer commanded the same national attention that Aretha Franklin or the Staple Singers had enjoyed just a few years earlier. Major record companies abandoned the South's black artists and studios, even stalwarts like Atlantic that had fueled the growth of southern soul. Stax and American closed. FAME and Muscle Shoals Sound completed the shift they began during the Black Power years, promoting their soulful Muscle Shoals sound among white artists. And country and southern rock performers became seen as the primary agents of southern musical innovation.

But, contrary to some subsequent portrayals, southern soul did not simply disappear with the rise of disco.[5] For one thing, many of its artists recorded disco tracks, and their work had an important influence on the genre's musical and lyrical parameters. Additionally, numerous smaller labels filled the vacuum left by departing national companies. Though these labels had neither the finances nor the prominence of Atlantic and Capitol, they recognized the continuing existence of listeners and musicians in the black South who could sustain their business. The most important of these by far was the Mississippi-based Malaco Records. Malaco marketed its releases as the expression of a southern black tradition as fundamentally different from the rhythms, futurism, and northernness of disco. The pinnacle of the strategy came with Z. Z. Hill's 1982 song "Down Home Blues," which became an anthem for Malaco's southern-oriented style and a direct counterpoint to disco as both musical style and cultural symbol.

Disco was a controversial cultural touchstone almost as soon as it appeared on the national scene in the mid-1970s.[6] The genre's fans celebrated its deep grooves while its detractors condemned it as a "mush of vacuous Muzak" that represented a clear downturn from the serious-ness and supposed authenticity of 1960s rock and soul.[7] This musical debate encapsulated a larger battle. The music's opponents—including former Stax collaborator Rev. Jesse Jackson—claimed that disco both represented and contributed to a degeneration of cultural values. (These criticisms were often tinged and sometimes totally suffused with racism, misogyny, and homophobia.) Conversely, disco's supporters heralded it as the soundtrack of racial and sexual liberation. For both sides, disco was anything but meaningless "Muzak." It was a metaphor for the moral and political condition of the United States.[8]

Despite their differences, many on both sides of the debate believed that disco was fundamentally different from both country and soul on musical, geographical, and cultural grounds. Those who criticized disco claimed that it was less musically authentic and socially valuable than the two genres, while disco's supporters clumped country and soul together under the umbrella of the old-fashioned and politically retrograde. Though both sides recognized important stylistic and political differences between the two, they still asserted that country and soul possessed a similar charac-ter rooted in large part in their shared southern origins. This dichotomy, though false, structured both contemporaneous reaction and subsequent analysis.

In this sense, then, disco performed the seemingly impossible task of reuniting two styles of music that had diverged so widely in the popular consciousness. But disco's success also resulted in a further separation be-tween country and soul. Country's successful incorporation of disco sounds and iconography contrasted with soul's inability to maintain its commer-cial footing or cultural relevance in the wake of disco's ascendance. This divided path became a crucial component of a broader shift in the nation's cultural and political geography.

Increasingly in this period, "the South" came to mean "the white South." This conflation had long been present in the national consciousness, but the erasure of black southerners became particularly acute during this pe-riod. It was in the era of disco and "Down Home Blues" that, as Thadious Davis observes, "whites in the South became simply 'southerners' without a racial designation" while "blacks in the South became simply 'blacks' without a regional designation."[9] Southern music—both disco-fied coun-try and nostalgic soul—became the sonic apparatus for a larger narrative in which the expressions of the black South became both less southern and less relevant to the contemporary African American experience in the 1980s.

The stark musical imagery masked a more complex reality for African American southerners. For one thing, the 1980s marked the beginning of the "reverse Great Migration" that saw African Americans returning to southern states in large numbers after decades of northern movement.[10] Additionally, while white conservatives increasingly became the face of the South as governors, U.S. senators, and members of Congress, a dramatic increase in black voting led to the election of African Americans across the South in unprecedented numbers that exceeded northern representation.[11] Country and soul drove a narrative of black southern irrelevance that contradicted much of the quantitative evidence and structured the national dialogue of race and region in the divisive Reagan years. "[The] obscuring of a black presence," notes Davis, "simultaneously asserted changed conditions in the region and denied one significant aspect of those changes: the post–civil rights political and social progress of black southerners."[12] The musicians of the country-soul triangle stood at the center of this process, literally and figuratively "playing the changes" of U.S. cultural politics.

A nyone wanting to understand the complicated nature of life in the post–civil rights South simply needed to turn on country radio. Just by playing the current hits, country stations presented listeners with a mix of the competing stylistic and ideological strains that defined the music, and southern life, in that decade. The backlash anthems of Merle Haggard might follow the singles of black hit-maker Charley Pride. A deejay could transition from the buttoned-up balladry of Tammy Wynette to the roughhouse rock of an Outlaw like Waylon Jennings. But one common factor united this diverse and sometimes polarized musical landscape: every country star used sounds and musicians that came from soul music.

This ubiquity contradicted one of the primary narratives driving the music industry. Fans of Outlaw country and southern rock, not to mention many soul partisans, repeatedly presented Nashville's mainstream music as bereft of black influence. Still, a quick glance at the charts demonstrates how deeply the interchanges of the country-soul triangle infused the era's country hits in the mid-1970s. Soul-influenced singers like Conway Twitty and Ronnie Milsap (each of whom had hits written by Dan Penn) mingled with performers like Jerry Lee Lewis who employed soul veterans in their bands. Jerry Reed, who started his career as a session guitarist in Muscle Shoals, shared space with Lynn Anderson, whose first hit was a Joe South cover. Most significant were the large number of artists whose hits were produced by FAME Studios cofounder Billy Sherrill, who was by that point one of the most important people in country music.

Sherrill owed his rapid rise to his role as a key architect of the "countrypolitan" sound in the late 1960s. As the name indicated, countrypolitan updated the jazz-and-R&B-influenced Nashville sound, using pop and soul sounds to appeal to listeners outside of country's core audience. A radio station manager described countrypolitan in 1972 as "[the] sound and rhythm of today with the basic country still there . . . but with an uptown sound," while journalist Mary Campbell noted in 1967 that countrypolitan records (what she called "sophisti-country") were explicitly "aimed for city-suburban consumption."[13] Countrypolitan was the next step in the Nashville industry's ongoing attempt to use black-identified musical forms to stake country's claim to broader relevance.

Billy Sherrill was one of countrypolitan's most proficient practitioners, mastering the synthesis that blended the sonic signifiers of country's roots with the musical textures of other pop genres. He demonstrated a particular talent for incorporating soul music. Of course, Sherrill started in R&B, playing saxophone as a teenager and cofounding FAME Studios. He later described his departure from Muscle Shoals in 1962 as a larger break from black-identified music, recalling that he "was a rock 'n' roller in a band playing sax until I heard George Jones. I said 'This guy's cool.' Then I got switched around and came up to Nashville and got caught up in the big country deal and had a lot of fun doing it."[14] But Sherrill's involvement in the development of countrypolitan was predicated on his interest in using R&B and soul to achieve country success. He always kept one ear tuned to black-oriented radio so that he might pick up the latest hit songs, which led—for example—to his previously discussed production of Johnny Paycheck's "She's All I Got." Beyond using individual songs, Sherrill also brought soul's broader stylistic characteristics (including copious use of horns and electric piano) into the modern country sound, which made him a key part of Nashville's music economy in the 1970s.

Sherrill's alchemy met resistance in some country circles. "I did a duet one time on George Jones and Brenda Lee, on [a Ray Charles song]," Sherrill told one reporter, "and in the middle of Ray's record there's a sax break. So I put overdubbed sax on there, too, and got a call from a country station here in town that said 'If you take that sax off and put a steel there, we'll play it.' . . . They ended up playing it anyway."[15] (This provides an interesting parallel to Jerry "Swamp Dogg" Williams's story about adding horns to his country-inflected records to identify them as soul.) The station's fears demonstrate how deeply the supposed divide between country and soul permeated the music business, but Sherrill had immediate and consistent success in bridging this gap. In 1977 he even cowrote a number one hit for Joe Stampley called "Soul Song," in which the protagonist tells his partner how he feels by calling her "my soul song. And that's why I sing all the time."

Stampley's hit certainly offers a powerful image, but there is no better example of Sherrill's use of soul than his work with a silver-haired and velvet-voiced singer-pianist named Charlie Rich. Though the lush, soul-soaked recordings made by the duo were thoroughly products of the countrypolitan moment, Rich was neither a newcomer nor a studio construction. He was a veteran of the country-soul triangle whose diverse set of musical influences and experiences prepared him creatively and professionally for his breakthrough success.

Rich was born in Arkansas in 1932. Unlike most of his musical contemporaries, who Pete Daniel describes as "the last generation of sharecroppers," Rich was economically privileged, the son of a landowner whose farm employed over two hundred tenant-farming families.[16] Like most of his contemporaries, Rich learned a variety of music from an early age, picking up blues and gospel from the farm's black workers and country and pop from the radio. Rich learned piano from one of his family's employees, and his affection for white jazz bandleader and pianist Stan Kenton gave Rich a unique sound that distinguished his later recordings. When he was a teenager, he began using his versatility when playing gigs throughout the mid-South. "I guess probably you get as much experience doing that and playing for and with different people than any other way," Rich noted, recalling the crucial lesson he learned in these early performances. "Your music didn't have to be perfect, but you" learned to play "some blues," "some country," "dance music," or "whatever the situation called for."[17]

Rich continued playing clubs when he moved to Memphis in the late 1950s and fell into the circle of musicians at Sun Records. Rich backed many of Sun's rockabilly artists as a session pianist and also recorded his own material, an expert synthesis of pop, country, jazz, and R&B that nonetheless did not catch commercial fire. According to Rich, Sam Phillips felt that Rich's records were doomed by his tailored professionalism, which did not correspond to Sun's wild rockabilly image. Throughout the 1960s, Rich worked throughout Memphis and Nashville, playing sessions, selling songs to other artists (including a hit by soul star Bobby "Blue" Bland) and recording for several adventurous record companies that hoped Rich's genre-blending talent would reap commercial dividends. He even recorded for Memphis's Hi Records in the aftermath of its breakthrough as an early home for the Memphis sound. Rich later said that one such recording "sounded more like Ray Charles than me."[18] For the most part, commercial success eluded this idiosyncratic talent.

Rich finally broke through when he started working with Billy Sherrill in 1967. Rich's unique mix of interests and skills made him perhaps Sherrill's greatest project, and the pair's work reflected a heavy soul influence from the beginning. 1969's "Life's Little Ups and Downs," paired Rich's pleading vocal with an organ-based arrangement that could have come from Stax, and he recorded a weepy Dan Penn ballad ("A Women Left Lonely") in 1971. These were only minor hits, but Rich's reputation as the "white Ray Charles" soon found massive success with his 1973 album for Epic Records, *Behind Closed Doors*, which went platinum and spawned several crossover hit singles, including the title track and "The Most Beautiful Girl."[19] Rich toured the country with a live show that resembled a soul revue, complete with a trio of black women as backup singers. When he won several Country Music Association awards in 1974, fellow singer Roy Clark celebrated Rich as "the man who brought jazz and blues to country music."[20]

Rich symbolized country's use of soul sounds as part of the genre's broader push for national acceptance. Unlike the conservative stars of the late 1960s or the Outlaws who were shaking up Nashville, Rich was marketed by Epic as the suave and sophisticated voice of a newly uptown country audience. His gauzy vocals, wrapped around Billy Sherrill's slinky arrangements, sounded less like the rough-and-tumble voice of the white working class and more like the luxurious soundtrack to social climbing and economic aspiration. "Just during the past few years," Rich told reporter Nat Hentoff in 1974, "even the audiences in some of those Southern honky-tonks were becoming more open-minded" to his synthetic musical style, and Rich perceived this as representative of a broader change.[21] Rich's efforts were symbolically repaid in 1979 when Motown soul star Stevie Wonder performed Rich's "Behind Closed Doors" at the Grand Ole Opry.[22]

Nearly every major countrypolitan star of the 1970s followed the Charlie Rich model, using a soul-influenced sound to demonstrate crossover potential. Some artists simply dabbled by recording a cover or experimenting with instrumentation. But artists like Rich, Barbara Mandrell (a Billy Sherrill client), or Ronnie Milsap (who started his career in Memphis) made soul an integral part of their sound and marketing. Mandrell even got played on black-oriented radio with her cover of Luther Ingram's Stax hit "If Loving You Is Wrong (I Don't Want to Be Right)."[23] This soul-focused strategy was central to a broader country boom that the music press presented as the result of country artists' willingness to embrace other musical styles and pursue commercial crossover.[24]

Charlie Rich, Epic Records president Ron Alexenburg, and Billy Sherrill pictured with gold records for Rich's 1973 album *Behind Closed Doors*. Rich recorded in Memphis before partnering with Sherrill, a cofounder of FAME Studios, to record some of the most significant, soul-influenced country recordings of the 1970s. *Memphis Press-Scimitar* Collection, Preservation and Special Collections, University of Memphis Libraries.

The countrypolitan moment also concerned some in the critical and scholarly community who worried that country was further abandoning the roots it had started to leave behind with the Nashville sound in the 1950s. In his book *Country Music, U.S.A.* (1972), the first major history of country music, Bill C. Malone wondered if the crossover urge "saved the music and made it possible to thrive" or "headed it down the road to accommodation, homogenization and possible extinction."[25] Malone was unsure of the answer, but in *The Americanization of Dixie* journalist John Egerton linked the "homogenization" and "modernization" of country to his larger fear that the South was losing its distinctiveness. "Country music, and the people in it, and the people around it, have survived some hard times," he wrote. "Now the test is to see whether they can survive the good times."[26] Writers like Egerton and Malone set up Outlaw country and southern rock in opposition to this supposed "homogenization" and argued that the insurgent sounds—with their connections to black music and black people—were the true sites of integrity and authenticity.

Still, despite the rhetoric, no Outlaw country or southern rock performer was more engaged with African American music than artists or producers in the Nashville mainstream. In fact, the sounds emulated by such performers as Rich and Mandrell were more current than those preferred by their insurgent counterparts. The Outlaws and southern rockers tended to favor the rawness of 1960s southern soul or an even earlier blues-based model, and writers presented this as evidence of their authenticity in contrast to Nashville's "homogenized" pap. But the mainstream Nashville stars skillfully adopted the current trends among black listeners. By the mid-1970s, soul (like country) turned toward smoother and more lushly orchestrated recordings. Just as Nashville-sound creators like Chet Atkins had been the first to recognize the creative and commercial potential of southern R&B in the early 1960s, so too did a new generation of country executives—now including soul veterans like Billy Sherrill—hope to incorporate (or perhaps appropriate) soul's most modern variations.

As with country, the stylistic changes in mid-1970s soul reflected attempts by the music's creators to react to the audience's changing socioeconomic demographics. Soul studios from Motown to Muscle Shoals increasingly integrated string sections and lush arrangements into their sound, and newly popular labels like the Philadelphia-based Philly International Records sought not to reflect the traditions of black musical life but to explore the contemporary desires of an upwardly mobile black community.[27] African American stars of the 1950s and early 1960s, including Carla Thomas at Stax Records, had once used strings and choirs to make R&B more palatable to the ears of an unfamiliar white audience, but 1970s soul artists now offered their swirling soundscapes as affirmation of the increasing urbanity and modernity of the black audience.

The most notable recordings signaling this shift were crafted in the studios of the country-soul triangle. This strategy brought great success to soul artists like Memphis's Al Green and Ann Peebles, who recorded for Hi Records under the direction of its longtime producer (and former Memphis bandleader) Willie Mitchell, or Muscle Shoals–based artists like Millie Jackson and Bobby Womack. Southern soul musicians were both willing and able to expand beyond the understood parameters of the Memphis sound or the Muscle Shoals sound in order to cater to a changing market.

The rise of disco provoked a similar reaction. Although they did not have the same success as their country colleagues, triangle musicians demonstrated a similar commitment to updating their trademark music by incorporating the day's most popular sounds. They recorded disco songs with most of the soul artists they worked with in the late 1970s. Studio bands and songwriters in Memphis, Nashville, and Muscle Shoals all explored the possibilities of the newly popular style. Homegrown stars like Green, Jackson, and Womack integrated the style's swirling rhythms and string-heavy arrangements into their hit recordings. Isaac Hayes's late-1960s explorations with extended, string-heavy tracks made for an easy transition to the new style, while Joe Tex proved the continuing power of his chameleonic talent with "Ain't Gonna Bump No More." More tellingly, perhaps, outside artists came to the triangle expressly to record disco tracks. Even James Brown, the legendary "Godfather of Soul," recorded his 1979 album *The Original Disco Man* at Muscle Shoals Sound. Backed by the Muscle Shoals Rhythm Section, Brown's album was—in *Billboard's* words—clearly "designed for the pop market."[28] Southern soul artists and studio personnel also used disco's flashy iconography and sexual frankness to update their images. Artists like Hayes and Jackson accompanied their funky rhythms with explicit lyrical content, and their album art and press photos featured them in flashy clothes and urban settings that seemed far removed from the rural-South fantasias of early-1970s southern soul advertising.

These changes were not just the reactions of musicians who feared for their economic livelihood. They were, in fact, the continuation of musical and lyrical tropes that southern studios helped to pioneer. As Alice Echols notes, Millie Jackson's lyrical focus on sexuality and Isaac Hayes's musical experimentation predated disco's rise in the marketplace, and their records—like those of Al Green, the Staple Singers, Bobby Womack, and other triangle artists—were important parts of the early club mix that defined disco's lyrical and musical characteristics.[29] The musicians of the country-soul triangle embraced the new commercial and creative possibilities, but disco still accompanied and provoked a clear decline in the fortunes of southern soul artists.

Just as in country, this transitional moment prompted a larger debate over the future of the music and its audience. Many soul journalists and scholars viewed the collision between disco and southern soul as representative of something more than just changing musical tastes. Instead, they presented southern soul's commercial decline a sign that a larger set of societal and racial values had collapsed in the late 1970s. Some even suggested that it helped end the civil rights movement. As with the commercial ascendance of the Memphis sound and soul's prominence in the Black Power years, the black-oriented records of the country-soul triangle again became well-known symbols of a larger cultural transformation.

Most scholars presented the rise of disco as the final nail in southern soul's coffin for two connected reasons. One was commercial and nearly inarguable. Given that disco was primarily associated with northern studios and dance clubs, its success meant that southern studios (and the supposedly distinctive southern sound) were less in-demand among artists and record companies. This is generally true. The other reason was much more debatable and reflected the cultural discourse that had surrounded southern soul since the emergence of the Memphis sound. In this interpretation, disco's rhythms and orchestration were somehow fundamentally incompatible with the gospel roots and communal spirit that southern soul represented. Barney Hoskyns, for example, wondered if soul "was too ingenuous and heartfelt to survive" the rise of disco. "Can pop music," he asked, "ever regain such innocent intensity?"[30]

Hoskyns was particularly flowery in his appraisal, but the larger link of disco to cultural degeneration and the end of the civil rights movement became common in the first generation of soul scholarship. Gerri Hirshey suggested that disco "drowned out" the voices of soul with its tyrannical rhythms, while Nelson George blamed disco for what he famously termed "the death of rhythm and blues." George believed that disco, with its synthesizers and its promotion of hedonism, symbolized the "symptoms of the illness" plaguing African Americans' "political and economic conditions" in the 1980s.[31] For George, Hirshey, Hoskyns, and others, disco reflected a larger abandonment of soul's musical integrity and commitment to social progress. This narrative of downfall has been complicated in recent years, but the suggestion that disco was musically and culturally oppositional to southern soul remains tenacious.[32] The work of the musicians reveals that this was not the case.

There is no doubt, though, that disco's popularity quickened the decline of southern soul as a national commercial force. It had a stunningly opposite effect on country. Indeed, disco finalized the process begun in the 1950s with the Nashville sound and perfected by the Billy Sherrill–led countrypolitan movement. Country artists used disco to stay musically current, demonstrate their contemporary relevance, and ultimately achieve crossover success. Although country's embrace of dance rhythms only lasted a few years, it reflected the previous three decades of the music's history, represented the genre's response to a changing demographic, and had a profound effect on its future.

In 1978 Buddy Killen took a chance by releasing a country single with a disco beat, and the massive success of Bill Anderson's "I Can't Wait Any Longer" convinced Killen and others in Nashville that disco-influenced country material had real potential. In the next several years, numerous country artists—from young upstarts like the Bellamy Brothers ("Let Your Love Flow") and Sylvia ("Drifter") to established stars like Ronnie Milsap ("Get It Up") and even George Jones ("I Ain't Got No Business Doin' Business Today")—cut disco songs, some of which became big hits.[33] (At one point, two versions of the Nashville soul/disco song "Everlasting Love"— by Narvel Felts and Louise Mandrell, respectively—reached the country charts simultaneously.) Country artists used disco sounds to assert the genre's continuing relevance to the upwardly mobile and increasingly urban orientation of its core audience. By the late 1970s country listeners were primarily middle-class urbanites and suburbanites, living either in suburbs, northern endpoints of migration, or bustling southern metropolises like Dallas–Fort Worth or Atlanta. Country's fan base had never been entirely or even predominantly working-class and rural, and the tension between traditionalism and modernism defined much of the genre's creative development and promotional strategy. But country's disco boom was a particularly potent crystallization of this long-standing dynamic.

No country artist embraced disco more effectively and controversially than singer-songwriter Dolly Parton, who transformed herself from the homespun "Tennessee Mountain Girl" of the early 1970s to a flashy crossover superstar at the end of the decade.[34] Starting in 1976, Parton began incorporating a heavy soul influence into her records, which helped her score a series of pop crossover hits and ensure her position as a musical representative of the changing region. In 1977 *New York Times* reporter Blair Sabol mentioned Parton next to the Allman Brothers as the musical symbols of the New South.[35] Parton changed her image, abandoning the floral-print dresses and subdued hairdos of her early years for flashy gowns and gravity-defying wigs. (She even donned a blond Afro when she performed a Merle Haggard song with black disco stars the Hues Corporation on her television show.)[36] And she released several dance-inflected tracks and remixes of singles "Baby, I'm Burnin'" and "I Wanna Fall in Love," leaving one flummoxed record storeowner to claim that it "would be ridiculous to put Dolly's pink vinyl disco single in the country section, so we stock it in our disco section."[37] Her transition into the disco market was complete by 1978, when legendary New York club Studio 54 honored Parton with a rural-themed party to honor her recent success.[38] Parton's success with disco made her perhaps the most frequently mentioned example of country's late-1970s crossover.

Parton's biggest hit, "9 to 5," symbolized her personal transformation and that of her genre. The 1980 release was the title song from a film in which Parton costarred about three women's revenge on their misogynist boss. "9 to 5" topped the country, pop, and adult contemporary charts simultaneously, confirming Parton's role as the symbol of the new Nashville. The track throbbed with disco beats and stabbing saxophones, while its lyrics described the drudgery and indignities of contemporary labor, from traffic jams to the lack of opportunity for promotion. The song's lyrics do not mention sexism directly, but Parton includes enough references ("You would think that I would deserve a fair promotion," "You're just a step on the boss man's ladder") to mark her song as directed specifically—though not exclusively—toward the large number of women fighting for respect in the 1980s workplace.[39] Still, there is nothing inherently contemporary about the lyrics' overarching sentiment; economic frustrations (and contested gender roles) had always been at the core of country's thematic palette. The song "9 to 5" is made modern solely by its incorporation of disco. Lyrically, it could have been written in the 1930s, but musically it was made for the modern dance floor.

Country's embrace of dance culture also fueled the "urban cowboy" phenomenon that, even more than Parton's success, became a symbol for its changing audience and stylistic orientation. The phenomenon began with the 1980 film *Urban Cowboy*, starring John Travolta—fresh off his success in the disco-themed *Saturday Night Fever*—as a young oil worker and country fan who frequents Gilley's Nightclub in Houston. There, Travolta and other country fans dance to the latest sounds in the glow of Gilley's colored lights. As Tyina Steptoe notes, the title, themes, and popularity of *Urban Cowboy* reflected larger tensions among an urbanizing country audience in Houston and elsewhere.[40] The film's soundtrack included dance-inflected tracks and a cover of a popular soul song, and it became one of country's biggest crossover successes. It also inspired a rash of copycat releases—also appropriately called urban cowboy—that recreated the dance-centered sound and citified orientation of the film and its soundtrack.[41] The success of urban cowboy pushed country to its most profitable period of crossover success.

Despite its obvious black influence, urban cowboy was not immune to the argument that country and soul represented diametrically opposed political and racial philosophies. In 1981 journalist Mark Hunter implied that the success of the *Urban Cowboy* soundtrack "signaled an end to disco music's black power, and is spreading a white pop sound from New York . . . to San Francisco."[42] This link was drawn further by disco pioneer (and former Black Panther) Nile Rodgers, who saw the release of disco records by artists like Parton as a "disgusting" example of white appropriation.[43] More recently, disco historian Peter Shapiro provocatively suggested that country, the "racial inverse" of black-identified styles, had "hogtied" disco's commercial ascent and that the era's popular country "ditties" (including those by Parton and other soul-and-disco-influenced acts) represented a white reaction to disco's transformative capabilities.[44] Hunter, Rodgers, Shapiro, and others presented country fans—whom they defined as white southerners—as somehow incapable of appreciating disco, and they saw urban cowboy's popularity as simply the latest chapter in the backlash to the civil rights movement and the historical marginalization of African American culture.[45]

Country's disco moment also attracted attention from critics who worried that the massive success of these crossover syntheses represented a further betrayal of the music's roots, following the earlier tensions over the Nashville sound and countrypolitan. "We couldn't help but feel that some of Nashville's soul was being lost in deference to gaining crossover appeal," *Cashbox* editorialized in 1978, and the crossover success of Dolly Parton and the urban cowboy acts renewed the debate over whether country music's pursuit of pop success—specifically its incorporation of disco and other contemporary sounds—was causing it to lose its uniqueness.[46] In the disco era, country and soul occupied a similar discursive position even as they diverged in terms of commercial success.

Many soul musicians in the country-soul triangle envied the success of urban cowboy and admired the effectiveness with which Nashville's musicians included the hottest soul and disco sounds in their releases. "That's when it became the number-one [music] format in the country," said George Soule, a producer and songwriter who had been a Muscle Shoals mainstay since the late 1960s. But Soule and others also cited this phenomenon as the moment "when it really went downhill Muscle Shoals–wise," the turning point in the larger commercial decline of southern soul.[47] Still, the music did not become a thing of the past. In fact, one of Soule's earliest employers, Malaco Records, played the most crucial role in sustaining and reframing southern soul in the wake of the impact of disco and disco-influenced country.

More than any other entity, Malaco understood and exploited southern soul's rapidly changing economics and cultural symbolism.[48] Though it aimed for national success and occasionally achieved it, the label's marketing department explicitly targeted its promotional efforts at southern listeners. Moreover, rather than attempting to compete with disco, Malaco's executives presented their soul releases as rootsy reminders of the black musical past. As southern soul's market and cachet eroded, Malaco jumped into the breach.

The company opened in 1962 as a booking agency, Malaco Attractions, started by two enterprising white southerners, Tommy Couch and Wolf Stephenson. Couch and Stephenson—both of whom grew up on the same eclectic musical diet as their southern contemporaries—hoped to exploit the profitable frat circuit, the network of southern white colleges that hosted countless R&B and soul performers in this period and through which Couch and Stephenson were exposed to numerous African American artists.[49] Malaco Attractions quickly became one of the most successful sources of live black-identified music in the South.

Though the duo was initially happy promoting live shows, the success of another southern musical entrepreneur led them to expand their ambitions. "I wanted to have a recording studio," Couch told Rob Bowman, "because Rick Hall had a studio in Muscle Shoals."[50] In 1966 Couch and Stephenson launched recording sessions in their hometown of Jackson, Mississippi, and performers and studio players, including a young George Soule, soon filled the studio's schedule. The musicians who came to Malaco admired Couch's and Stephenson's ambition and hoped to make their own mark in the South's expanding recording industry. "That's where we just started hanging out," Soule recalled. "And we started going over as often as possible, and eventually got an apartment over in Jackson and stayed at the studio most of the time."[51] Through the end of the 1960s and into the 1970s, Malaco was another important location on the landscape of southern recording houses. It nurtured local talent, attracted national artists, and made several important production and distribution deals with other triangle studios. Al Bell, for example, signed a deal with Couch and Stephenson that led to Malaco-produced recordings being released on Stax. One of these—Jean Knight's "Mr. Big Stuff"—hit the pop and R&B Top 5.

For the first decade of its existence, Malaco released recordings that ran the gamut of R&B and soul music. The label promoted itself as part of the same fertile bed of expression that produced Stax, FAME, and other southern soul companies. But in the mid-1970s the label shifted its marketing strategy. Sensing the changing times and the shifting cultural position of southern soul, Malaco put all of its promotional energy in the regional radio stations and independent record retailers that serviced the black South. Malaco's leaders recognized that this audience was smaller, but they also believed it to be more loyal and more receptive to Malaco's brand of old-fashioned southern soul. Although the label scored a huge disco hit in 1977 with Anita Ward's "Ring My Bell," its releases of the period were predominantly the sort of gritty, small-band performances that could have come from Memphis or Muscle Shoals in the mid-1960s. Both in terms of musical style and business strategy, Malaco returned to the regionally based model that formed the basis of the country-soul triangle in the 1940s and 1950s. The label's leadership remained explicitly and happily southern in its approach.

Malaco promoted itself as the final holdout of a bygone era; by the end of the 1970s its slogan was "The Last Soul Company." Veterans of the country-soul triangle, particularly the black musicians and songwriters who had not joined their white colleagues in Nashville's country studios, found steady work at Malaco. The label built its artist roster and studio personnel on the wealth of regional talent that had not found a place in the disco craze. Singer Denise LaSalle remembered that, until her Malaco success, "I stayed on the sidelines because there was *nobody* interested in me. . . . The only thing that could get played was disco music."[52] The label further affirmed its role as the keeper of southern soul tradition in 1979 when it relaunched Muscle Shoals Sound Records as a primarily gospel label; Malaco later purchased the studio and its assets.[53] This move contained added symbolic resonance. Muscle Shoals Sound (and the Muscle Shoals sound) attracted a large number of white artists by the mid-1970s but was now repurposed to cater to Malaco's almost entirely black clientele.

Malaco's efforts sustained the market for southern soul and played a crucial role in asserting the genre as an antidote to the cultural changes represented by disco. This dynamic is embodied most strongly in the label's most enduring song, and perhaps the last nationally significant soul recording to emerge from the South, Z. Z. Hill's "Down Home Blues." Born in Texas, Hill had worked in gospel and blues groups since the 1950s and recorded a few R&B hits in the 1960s and 1970s. (Hill recorded one album in Muscle Shoals with producer Jerry "Swamp Dogg" Williams.) In the last part of the decade, Hill signed with Malaco and found a perfect home for his warm blend of blues and soul. "Down Home Blues" became his trademark.[54]

The song's writer, George Jackson, was another black triangle veteran who found a home for his soulful craft at Malaco. At the beginning the 1970s, Jackson was one of the hottest songwriters in popular music, penning numerous hits as a staff songwriter at FAME Studios in Muscle Shoals. Most famously, Jackson wrote the Osmonds' "One Bad Apple," and his success with that song and others—including Candi Staton's debut FAME Records hit "I'd Rather Be an Old Man's Sweetheart" and the politicized George Soule hit "Get Involved"—made him an important player in the triangle's early-1970s prominence. As the decade progressed, though, Jackson found less room for his compositions on the national charts. But his fortunes improved in the early 1980s, when two of his songs—"Old Time Rock & Roll," recorded by Detroit-based rocker Bob Seger, and "Down Home Blues"—became anthems. Neither were released as singles, and they were marketed to different audiences, with "Old Time Rock & Roll" aimed at the mostly white rock crowd and "Down Home Blues" almost exclusively at black consumers. But the songs shared a nostalgic rejection of disco and pined for the halcyon days of the country-soul triangle.

"Old Time Rock & Roll," recorded by Seger at Muscle Shoals Sound in 1978, chugs along with a mid-tempo 1960s groove that suits the passionate request of the lyric written by George Jackson and collaborator Thomas Jones: "Today's music ain't got the same soul / I like that old time rock and roll." The second verse gets even more specific, rejecting "disco" in favor of "some blues and funky old soul."[55] By framing his ode to the past through this evocative comparison, Jackson tapped into the then common belief that disco represented cultural degeneration, particularly in relation to the older soul music that came from places like Muscle Shoals. Of course, Seger's performance of the song also symbolized the increased use of the Muscle Shoals sound by white artists and the accompanying decline in Shoals sessions with black performers. But this neither hindered the song's message nor hampered its reception. "Old Time Rock & Roll" remains a staple of Seger's live shows and "classic rock" radio to this day.

"Down Home Blues" employed a similar rhetorical device but was perhaps even more effective in articulating the growing distance between contemporary pop and southern soul. Over a loping blues beat, Hill tells the story of a woman who prefers the sounds of the past: "She said, 'Take off those fast records and let me hear some down home blues.'"[56] Like the protagonist of "Old Time Rock & Roll," the main character here prefers the sound of the older records and views them as possessing greater cultural value. Between this song and "Old Time Rock & Roll," George Jackson became perhaps the most popular purveyor of antidisco nostalgia in U.S. pop music.

"Down Home Blues" remains Malaco's most enduring release. Rob Bowman argues that "it is truly impossible to exaggerate" the recording's importance for the label and for southern soul more generally.[57] Hill's album of the same name spent two years on the R&B charts, several artists recorded "Down Home Blues" after Hill's recording, and journalist Bill Dahl notes that the song has "graduated into the ranks of legitimate blues standards."[58] Additionally, numerous writers championed "Down Home Blues" as a theme song for the disco backlash and a return to the musical traditions of African Americans, particularly in the South. Bill Minutaglio heralded it as "an anthem [that brought] blues back to black audiences," while Alan B. Govenar called it "a turning point" after disco faded in popularity.[59] David Whiteis rhapsodized that the song "[arose as] an avenging spirit of blues righteousness from amid the mechanized pounding of disco and early rap."[60] Most tellingly, perhaps, Nelson George suggested that Malaco's success with the record and proud status as "a black traditionalist label" showed the persistence of African American culture in the face of "the death of rhythm and blues."[61]

The success of "Down Home Blues" also symbolized how synonymous the cultural expressions of black southerners had become with the past by the 1980s. This process had been ongoing since at least the beginning of the 1900s, when mass migration to northern cities shifted the geography of African American culture and made the South into the mythical repository of black tradition. Music provided a primary articulation of this discourse. Southern-identified styles like blues and gospel were described, for both better and worse, as expressions of a bygone age, while northern-based sounds like ragtime and jazz became the sound of new opportunities. This dichotomy was disrupted in the 1960s and 1970s, when the seemingly rootsy soul of black southerners became crucial to the era's cultural and political transformations.[62] But the era of disco and "Down Home Blues" provided this long-standing discourse with a contemporary remix.

The era also coincided with a major and surprising shift in African American demographics. In the 1980s the "Great Migration" began to reverse, and black folks started moving back to the South. They were lured by new economic opportunities, heartened by the elimination of legal segregation, and propelled by the frustrations of living in northern cities that did not represent the "land of hope" for which many black migrants planned.[63] Many southern-bound African Americans credited their decision to move back in part to their desire to reconnect with southern family members and community structures that they left behind when they traveled north.[64] "I've never lost my love for the richness and culture of the South," Stella Shepherd wrote in 1998. "Millions of Blacks in their search for who they are find that their heritage is firmly planted in the rich soil of the South."[65] In this context, "Down Home Blues" was a reassuring reminder of how the black past (both real and mythological) could represent a workable black future. According to Clyde Adrian Woods, the song "expressed for many African Americans the intellectual need to escape a seemingly meaningless existence by returning to a place and a state of mind where they could 'take off their shoes.'"[66]

The nostalgia in "Down Home Blues" also paralleled a larger erasure of black southerners from U.S. political narratives. In the 1950s and 1960s, southern states were the perceived ground zero of the nation's racial conflicts, but changes in the national civil rights landscape in the late 1960s and 1970s shifted the hotbeds of black activism to the North and urban West. Simultaneously, a reinvigorated Republican Party returned the South to one-party, white electoral dominance. Black voting rates skyrocketed in the wake of 1965's Voting Rights Act, and black voters elected African Americans to powerful local, state, and even federal offices in the South. But several factors—the continued white dominance of southern politics, the election of Ronald Reagan (who campaigned on a racially divisive, anti–civil rights movement program) and nagging cultural ideas about the relative racism of the South versus the North—limited southern blacks' political relevance on a national scale. Politically, too, African Americans in the South became symbols of the past.

The success of "Down Home Blues" was an anomaly, a rare nationwide success for Malaco's regional commercial strategy. More broadly, too, even as African American southerners lived a complex economic and political reality in the 1980s, they were starkly eliminated from the national pop-music landscape. In the Reagan years, southern-identified black music retained its regional popularity but found little space on national charts or radio playlists. Southern soul, blues, and the hybrid "soul-blues" style became a common descriptor for Malaco and Malaco-style recordings made by former national soul stars like Clarence Carter and Johnnie Taylor as well as newer hit-makers like Z. Z. Hill, Denise LaSalle, and Latimore, whose releases included "There's a Red-Neck in the Soul Band." Soul veterans worked behind the scenes, as well, with former Stax stalwarts Homer Banks, William Bell, and Lester Snell all opening independent labels in the 1980s and 1990s; even Al Bell got into the business with his BellMark label. These records—many of which were made in Memphis—remain almost unknown outside of African American communities below the Mason-Dixon Line.[67]

In a sense, southern soul had doubly lost its place. In black-identified pop, disco and then hip-hop became the artistic, commercial, and political vanguard. At the same time, white country and southern rock artists cornered the national market on explicitly southern-identified recordings. In keeping with the broader erasure of black southerners from national discourse, these white performers helped make the musical South into a primarily white space in the minds of many listeners throughout the United States. These narratives ultimately contributed to a larger cultural perception that the music of the black South was a relic to be cherished rather than a dynamic pop form that could transform the nation's culture as it had done in the past. African American southerners were essentially written out of the national pop-music story until the late 1990s, when southern hip-hop artists—many of whom took their musical cues directly from soul—brashly and brilliantly reclaimed the cultural prominence of the black South. As they did so, they often described themselves not just as black and not just as southern, but also as country.

Arthur Alexander would have been perfect for Malaco Records. He helped establish the template for southern soul in the early 1960s, and he worked with many of the important studio musicians and producers in the country-soul triangle during his long and turbulent career. Though he had not duplicated the success of the hits he recorded at FAME Studios back in 1962, he worked as both songwriter and recording artist in Memphis and Nashville in the fifteen years that followed. He even scored another hit, "Every Day I Have to Cry," which he wrote back in 1963 and finally recorded in Muscle Shoals in 1975. It is not hard to imagine that he would have found the same success at Malaco that many of his contemporaries did. But Alexander did not take the opportunity. In 1978, tired of the constant grind, disappointed with his lack of consistent success, and fed up with what he saw as the injustices of the recording industry, Alexander moved to Cleveland. He left the music business and became a bus driver.[68]

Two years later, Alexander's former collaborator Billy Sherrill recorded an album by George Jones and Johnny Paycheck, two of his most successful clients and each a beneficiary of the creative and commercial overlaps of the country-soul triangle. George Jones worked with the Staple Singers and cut a disco record, while Johnny Paycheck had a number one hit with Jerry "Swamp Dogg" Williams's soul song "She's All I Got." Working together for the first time, Jones and Paycheck expected Sherrill to provide great material for their collaboration.

One of the songs Sherrill chose was Arthur Alexander's "You Better Move On," a song he helped develop back in Muscle Shoals in 1961. Since the time of Alexander's initial recording, "You Better Move On" had been covered by a wide variety of artists, but it had been a few years since a country artist recorded the song. Sherrill knew that the time was right to revisit his old collaborator's debut masterpiece. Rather than add any countrypolitan or urban-cowboy flourishes, Sherrill and the Nashville musicians faithfully recreated the graceful sweep and melancholy textures of Alexander's original, and both Jones and Paycheck delivered vocals that made clear how much Alexander had been influenced by country singers. The duo's version of "You Better Move On" was a stunning testament to the blurring of musical divisions that formed and defined the country-soul triangle.

The record was also a clear demonstration of how deeply country music had integrated the sounds of soul by 1980. Whether it was Dolly Parton going disco, Willie Nelson recording with Muscle Shoals studio players, or George Jones and Johnny Paycheck covering Arthur Alexander, country artists of all sorts fully incorporated soul's stylistic markers into their sound. By this point, they had direct help from the many white musicians who came to Nashville from Memphis and Muscle Shoals and applied their hard-earned musical versatility to the records of primarily white artists who catered to primarily white audiences.

Indeed, just as in the triangle's previous history, the musical blending could not disguise a racial disparity. The commercial opportunities awaiting whites who started out playing soul in the studios of the country-soul triangle were simply not available to their African American counterparts. As southern soul's commercial prominence faded on a national level, most of its black talent was working for Malaco, scuffling along without a recording contract, or—like Arthur Alexander—abandoning the music business for more stable work elsewhere.

George Jones and Johnny Paycheck's cover of "You Better Move On" went to number eighteen on the country charts in 1980. Perhaps Arthur Alexander heard it while driving his bus in Cleveland. After all, he loved country music.

CODA

On Accidental Racists

Interracial Friendship, Historical Memory,

and the Country-Soul Triangle

On April 8, 2013, the Internet exploded with discussion of "Accidental Racist," a collaboration between white country singer Brad Paisley and black hip-hop artist LL Cool J. The song features a white southerner and a black northerner discussing the historical legacies and contemporary realities of U.S. racism and ultimately achieving a friendly, though tentative, understanding. "Accidental Racist" was widely criticized and lampooned as a failure that misrepresents U.S. history and suggests that white supremacy can be eliminated simply if everyone let bygones be bygones and got to know each other as individuals. The song deserves much of the criticism—it seems well-intentioned, but "Accidental Racist" presents a view of race in the United States that is oversimplified and sometimes grossly inaccurate.

Still, the laughter and derision that marked the reception of "Accidental Racist" obscured the fact that the song's message of brotherhood and transcendence is not really all that different from the central narrative that drives the contemporary understanding of southern musical history. In recent decades, the South's musicians have been widely promoted as symbols of interracial cooperation and southern music as a space where the races have come together as equals and even friends. This notion has become central to nearly every aspect of the memory and marketing of southern musical genres. Writers, filmmakers, and playwrights use it as the foundation of their works.[1] Museum curators and tourism officials make it central in their appeals to tourists and enthusiasts.[2] Producers and record executives use the theme of racial crossover in a growing series of reissues that map out the shared spaces between styles, as well as to structure the promotion of new artists and recording projects.[3] Educators and politicians use the music of the South to celebrate a more expansive vision of racial togetherness and progress.[4] And many of the musicians themselves have made it central to the way they present and remember their careers.

When knitted together, these stories of cooperation offer an alternative narrative of southern history, a tradition of racial interaction that complicates or even contradicts the conventional understanding of the South's conflicted past. Interracial musical collaborations from Jimmie Rodgers and Louis Armstrong in the 1920s to Nelly and Tim McGraw in the 2000s are offered as counterpoints to racial polarization. The interracial intermingling of 1850s string bands or 1950s rock 'n' roll becomes evidence for the limits of segregation and white supremacy. And contemporary artists from black country star Darius Rucker to white rapper Yelawolf to interracial soul band the Alabama Shakes are all promoted as the latest participants in this continuum of cross-racial blending.

This historical reappraisal coincided with a series of attempts to demonstrate the specific connection between country and soul. Just as the genres became symbols for racial divisions, images of their reunification become a potent metaphor in the 1990s and 2000s. Politicians from George H. W. Bush to Barack Obama signaled their desire to build coalitions and transcend the "blue state"/"red state" divide by mixing country and soul in their campaigns.[5] In the recording industry, numerous projects have explored the crossovers between the two. Perhaps the most prominent example was the hugely successful 1994 album *Rhythm, Country and Blues*, a star-studded collection of duets that was designed to show how a shared musical heritage can heal old wounds and transcend societal difference. Numerous similar projects followed in its wake. One of the most successful occurred in 2012, when Alabama-born soul singer Lionel Richie topped the country charts with an album that recreated his old hits in countrified duets with contemporary Nashville stars.[6] From the L.A. riots to the rise of the Tea Party, these partnerships affirmed the notion that country and soul, and black and white musicians in the South, possessed a meaningful historical affinity.

Unsurprisingly, the musicians of the country-soul triangle became central to this assertion. Soul became a symbol for 1960s integration, where—in studios like Stax or FAME—black and white musicians played together in the heat of racial turmoil and supposedly either did not see race or did not care about it. "In the '60s and '70s, Memphis knew its share of division and discord and injustice," Barack Obama recounted at a 2013 event honoring Memphis soul. "But in that turbulent time, the sound of Hi . . . and Sun and Stax Records tried to bridge those divides—to create a little harmony with harmony."[7] The Outlaw country, southern rock, and swamp rock of the 1970s were made into symbols of an alternative, racially liberated southern whiteness that emerged in the aftermath of the civil rights movement, while mainstream country was celebrated for the success of Ray Charles and Charley Pride or the visits of soul stars like James Brown or Stevie Wonder to the Grand Ole Opry. In the current understandings of the southern music of the 1960s and 1970s, Peter Guralnick's "Southern dream of freedom" has become the dominant analytic.

But, as this book's examination has demonstrated, the "Southern dream of freedom" obscures a more complex history. It is true and significant that even in the worst days of racial turmoil, musicians in the South worked together to produce something that defied both the ideology and practice of white supremacy. But those who promote this narrative (and there are lots of us, from Barack Obama to me at some points in my career) have taken it further and exhibit a disquieting tendency to imply that the music existed outside of history.[8] Statements like "racism did not exist in this studio" or "on the bandstand, everyone was the same" or "we saw no difference between black and white" are commonplace in this discourse. Southern musical spaces—both literal and figurative—have become a kind of ahistorical interracial dreamland.

This is a fallacy. Nothing mattered more to these musicians than race. Nothing structured their work more than the racial divisions and disparities that structured life and music making in the South and the rest of the United States. And African Americans did not share equally in the benefits of the music that is now routinely heralded as a demonstration of racial progress. To remove race and racial history from their experiences is to ignore this painful reality and deny the musicians' rightful place in the messy history of race and culture in the United States.

To remove race in this way also ignores the fact that the narrative of interracial friendship was, in large part, created by the musicians themselves. In the 1960s and 1970s they filled press releases and advertisements with this rhetoric, tailored their music to appeal to the new dynamics, and sometimes—as in the case of Jerry Wexler's work at Atlantic—made the pursuit of interracialism into an overarching theory of their activities. In part, this was designed to spotlight the musicians' accomplishments and skills. It was also meant, though, to exploit a broader shift in U.S. politics in the mid-twentieth century, in which overtly racist or racially divisive imagery was replaced by images of tolerance and the language of color blindness. By situating their music within this ascendant rhetoric of reconciliation and togetherness, the triangle's musicians ensured their continued commercial success and cemented their cultural significance.

But the rhetoric of togetherness masked a more insidious trend in U.S. politics in the post–civil rights years. In recent decades, interracial friendship has not only become a favorite defense against charges of racism— "But some of my best friends are black"—but also the foundation to the argument that individual relationships can either supersede or outright disprove deeper structural inequalities. This idea, which Benjamin DeMott calls "friendship ideology," fueled the backlash campaigns of the 1970s and beyond by suggesting that black people have gone too far in their push for greater equality and opportunity.[9] "Friendship ideology" has also become crucial to the popular memory of U.S. race relations. Moments of interracial alliance are idealized while movements grounded in racial solidarity or separatism are either minimized or demonized.

The same thing has happened to the story of the country-soul triangle. The privileging of interracial friendship in southern music has disproportionately credited whites as racial heroes, even in cases (like those of Steve Cropper, Rick Hall, or Sam Phillips) when black musicians have voiced significant complaints about their conduct. Black musicians, meanwhile, have been criticized for their racial assertions and marginalized as the influences who helped the white innovators achieve their breakthroughs. In a sad echo of Confederate and segregationist apologists, the dominant narrative suggests that everything was fine until outsiders showed up, black people got too uppity, and the alliances with whites were shattered. The primary beneficiaries and heroes of the supposed color blindness are white people. And that is neither exceptional in U.S. history nor a cause for celebration.

I do not reject the idea that we should celebrate the interracial collaborations of the country-soul triangle. After all, these collaborations did exist—even if they have been mischaracterized—and they often took place in open defiance of legal and cultural codes. We rightly honor these musicians for their unique role in demonstrating the fundamental absurdity and evil of white supremacy and in helping to bring about the revolutionary transformations of the civil rights era. Near the end of his life, Rufus Thomas—who recorded at both Sun and Stax and registered his own complaints about their racial politics—said that, in the country-soul triangle, "we found out that whites and blacks as entertainers and as musicians could work together . . . You have people who say 'It can't happen[,]' . . . one of the biggest lies ever told."[10]

We must all remember and cherish Thomas's words. We must also better contextualize them, understanding that the popular narrative of interracial friendship is a product of the history it purports to explain. We must remember that, first and foremost, musicians "work together," and that a full appreciation of their accomplishments requires us to frame the story around their working experiences. They insist that we interrogate the conventional wisdom about what makes music racially progressive and what makes it reactionary. They teach us that music's potential as a liberating force exists in constant dialogue with its more divisive consequences. And, ultimately, they prove that there is no limit to what we can learn from popular music and the people who make it.

In the end, the musicians of the country-soul triangle force us to reconsider the ways that race has been expressed and lived in the United States. They used their deep and diverse skills to create music that both reflected and shaped the nation's rapidly changing cultural and political terrain. As they did so, they negotiated a specific and complex set of racial expectations, limitations, and opportunities. They had a job to do and they did it well. And they changed the world.

Acknowledgments

I suppose that this book might exist without Ariel Eisenberg, but—like everything else in my life—it would feel a lot less important to me. Ari is my reason for waking up in the morning and my solid foundation in the many times I waver. She saw me through most of this process, and I know that I would never have finished this thing without her reassurance and support. Her brilliance as a historian and writer helped me formulate ideas, clarify language, and untangle this work's many snarled components. But her impact goes so much deeper. She's the best friend I ever had, who brings out the best in me while somehow finding a way to tolerate my many flaws. The everyday joys of laughing, singing, traveling, and simply being with her have given my life purpose. I'm the luckiest person in the world, and I love her with everything I have.

There are many others who contributed greatly to this work's completion. I am incredibly lucky to work with such a talented group at the University of North Carolina Press. Mark Simpson-Vos is an inestimable editor and advocate. Alex Martin greatly improved the book's clarity and cohesion. Cait Bell-Butterfield, Mary Caviness, Lucas Church, and Heidi Perov have been extremely helpful. David Perry's early and sustained interest in this project helped bring it to fruition. Thanks also to the two anonymous readers whose profound and pointed comments significantly improved the final product. I received crucial financial support from the Mellon Foundation, the Smithsonian Institution, Case Western Reserve University, the Rock and Roll Hall of Fame and Museum Library and Archives, the E. David Cronon Memorial Fund of the University of Wisconsin–Madison History Department, and the UW-Madison Vilas Travel Grants Program. Thanks to Rodney Hall, Norman Seeff, and Dean Torrence, who graciously allowed me to use images from their collections. Additionally, I offer my deepest gratitude to my interview subjects, who were extremely generous with their memories and insights. Finally, I am especially indebted to Richard Younger, both for his excellent biography of Arthur Alexander and for his generosity in letting me use a number of the interviews he conducted for that book. This book is much better because of his work.

While training at the University of Wisconsin–Madison, I was privileged to work with many passionate and brilliant individuals. Will Jones was a tireless source of help and encouragement. Craig Werner shaped my life as an intellectual, citizen, and human being in more ways that I can possibly detail here. Tim Tyson helped me discover who I was and wanted to be. Nan Enstad, Steve Kantrowitz, Ron Radano, and Bill Van Deburg remain trusted mentors and good friends. I am also grateful to Leslie Abadie, the late Jeanne Boydston, Cindy I-Fen Cheng, the late Jeanne Comstock, Tracy Curtis, James Danky, Richard Davis, Christina Greene, Michele Hilmes, Dolores Liamba, the late Nellie McKay, Tony Michels, Thomas Mitchell, Brenda Gayle Plummer, Jim Schlender, Robin Schmidt, Freida High Tesfagiorgis, and Carrie Tobin. And, of course, my students were a constant source of inspiration.

After leaving Madison, I was fortunate enough to work for two years at Rhodes College, where the faculty, staff, and students made every day a pleasure. During my time in Memphis, I was able to expand and enrich many of the ideas contained in this work. I am so grateful to Milton Moreland for his guidance, support, and friendship. Tim Huebner is a great scholar, fearless leader, and passionate advocate; I owe him a great deal. John Bass makes astounding things happen, and I'm excited to collaborate more with him in the future. Russ Wigginton was a true ally and will be one for a long time. I'm glad that I got to spend so much time with Rin Abernathy, Angela Frederick, Nannette Gills, Jeff Jackson, Leigh Johnson, Tait Keller, Jim Lanier, Charles McKinney, Evie Perry, and Robert Saxe, each a great companion and a role model. My deepest appreciation also goes out to Carole Blankenship, Suzanne Bonefas, Tom Bremer, Liz Daggett, Hamlett Dobbins, Skyler Gambert, Dee Garceau, Lori Garner, Huntley Hudgins, Jonathan Judaken, Brooks Lamb, Mike LaRosa, Seok-Won Lee, Gail Murray, Kenan Padgett, Joel Parsons, Natalie Person, Buffie Rice, John Rone, Anthony Siracusa, Phoebe Strom, Etty Terem, Elizabeth Thomas, Molly Whitehorn, and Lynn Zastoupil.

I am extremely excited to now be a part of such a fantastic group of colleagues and students at Oklahoma State University. They have welcomed me with open arms, and their support of this project has helped me through the final push in both tangible and intangible ways. I have immensely enjoyed our conversations and collaborations, and I look forward to many more in the years to come. Thanks especially to Laura Arata, Laura Belmonte, Thomas Carlson, Brian Frehner, Diana Fry, Emily Graham, James Huston, John Kinder, Michael Logan, George Moses, Susan Oliver, Lesley Rimmel, Richard Rohrs, Elizabeth Williams, and Evan Woodson.

One of the best things about being a music historian is that any visit to the record store can qualify as a research trip. While I'm not delusional enough to believe I made all of my purchases only for my professional benefit, I'm nonetheless grateful for the many great retailers that have brought me such musical pleasure and wisdom. Number one with a bullet is Inner Sleeve Records, owned and operated by my friend Mike Capista. I owe much of my formative musical experience to my long hours spent at Inner Sleeve, and I have endless adoration for Mike's great ear and warm heart. I'm also really glad to have spent time and money at three great independent stores in Madison—here's to Steve Manley at B-Side Records, Ron Roloff at Strictly Discs, and Dave Zero at Mad City Music Exchange. Thanks also to the staffs of Electric Fetus in Minneapolis, Ernest Tubb Record Shop in Nashville, Pegasus Records in Muscle Shoals, and Shangri-La Records in Memphis.

This project repeatedly took me to more traditional "archives," and the remarkable archivists, librarians, and others who worked at these sites made my research such a pleasure. Thanks to Wayne Dowdy at the Memphis & Shelby County Room of the Memphis Public Library, Ed Frank and Chris Ratliff at the Special Collections Department at the University of Memphis, Andy Leach and Jennie Thomas at the Rock and Roll Hall of Fame and Museum Library and Archives, Brenda Nelson-Strauss at Indiana University's Archives of African American Music and Culture, Matthew Turi at the Southern Folklife Center at the University of North Carolina–Chapel Hill, and Levon Williams at the Stax Museum of American Soul Music. I want to especially recognize the many Smithsonian curators and staff members I met as a research fellow at the National Museum of American History in 2010–11. David Haberstich, Kay Peterson, Wendy Shay, and the entire staff at the NMAH's Archives Center helped me immensely. Susan Ostroff helped me access important materials. I know that Paul Gardullo, John Hasse, Kip Lornell, Jeff Place, Mark Puryear, Dwandalyn Reece, and Kevin Strait will all be collaborators for years to come. Most of all, Pete Daniel's mentoring and friendship gave me all the validation I needed to keep on pushing. I look back on lunches, parties, and Pete's legendary Tuesday night happy hours with tremendous fondness. LuAnn Jones, Bill Mansfield, and Grace Palladino helped make these times even more special, as did the outstanding group of fellows that I worked with. Thanks to Ryan Lee Cartwright, Perla Guerrero, Israel Pastrana, Maia Surdam, and Michelle Zacks (along with her husband, Eric Applegarth), brilliant folks who brought joy to the day-to-day research grind and made my time in D.C. so pleasurable.

I've also gained a lot from various academic meetings, and none has been more important to me than the Experience Music Project Pop Music Conference. The EMP has exposed me to new ideas, helped me improve my own thoughts, and brought me into a vibrant and open-hearted community of listeners and thinkers. I'm so grateful to have gotten to know Michael Bertrand, Daphne Brooks, Jon Caramanica, Jeff Chang, J. D. Considine, Kandia Crazy Horse, Chuck Eddy, Holly George-Warren, Camara Holloway, Mike McGonigal, Charles McGovern, Karl Hagstrom Miller, Diane Pecknold, Ann Powers, Ned Raggett, Jody Rosen, John Sharp, R. J. Smith, Ned Sublette, David Suisman, Gayle Wald, Oliver Wang, Eric Weisbard, and Andy Zax. Special thanks to David Cantwell, a wonderful guy and brilliant scholar who has inspired me with his friendship and insight.

Both this book and my life would be far less rich if not for the many friends that I've worked, played, and plotted with over the years. Bill and Bobbie Malone have been a constant source of great support and good fun. Simon Balto is a gentleman and a scholar. Joanna and Wyl Schuth prepare a welcome table at which I'm so happy to sit. I've shared a lot with Brian Bischel over the years, and I can't imagine how I would've made it through either the good times or bad times without him. Alexander Shashko is a first-rate colleague, confidante, and conspirator. The multitalented Jeff Kollath cuts a great promo and always keeps it on The One. Eddie Hankins is one of my most trusted authorities on Memphis music as well as one of my favorite hangout partners. Finally, I've been blessed to walk many paths (and share many drafts) with Dave Gilbert, who is a peerless intellectual and musical collaborator, as well as a close friend.

Many others deserve to be mentioned. I'm sure that I'm forgetting some names, but I want to acknowledge John Adams, Brad Allen, Danny Alexander, Scott Barretta, John Beifuss, Britt Bjornson, Matt Blanton, Kenneth Burns, Andrew Case, Ellen Daugherty, Catasha Davis, Piko Ewoodzie, Karlyn Forner, Daniel Frederick, Trudy Fredericks, Will Freiman, Bill Friskics-Warren, Joe Fronczak, Mark Goldberg, Michelle Gordon, Robert Gordon, Aram Goudsouzian, Brenna Greer, Laura and Patrick Helper-Ferris, Bob Hemauer, Jenn Holland, Justin Horn, Roland Jackson, Doria Johnson, Patrick Jones, Lauren Kennedy, Daney Kepple, Doug Kiel, Jennifer Kaye Kollath, Yumi Kusonoki, Michael Kwas, Dave LaCroix, Adam Malka, Wayne Marshall, Story Matkin-Rawn, Danielle McGuire, Natalie McKinney, Nic Mink, Leah Mirakhor, Perri Morgan, Crystal

Moten, Ryan Murphy, Raka Nandi, Steve Nathans-Kelly, Mark Anthony Neal, Leslee Nelson, Daniel O'Grady, Ted Ownby, Haley Pollack, Ryan Quintana, Megan Raby, Melissa Reiser, Ashley Roach-Freiman, Zandria Robinson, Meredith Beck Sayre, Fritz Schenker, Eric Schumacher-Rasmussen, Jud Sojourn, William Sturkey, Libby Tronnes, Hope and Sam Tyson, Zoe Van Orsdol, Dan and Kate Venne, Eric Wenninger, Kaylee and Riah Werner, Naomi Williams, and Anna Zeide.

Several communities deserve special recognition. The students and staff of Freedom Ride 2001 fundamentally changed how I view the past and present. Blixie, the mighty country band that I played in from 2003 to 2008, is the subject of some of my fondest memories. Dave Gilbert, Kori Graves, Holly McGee, and Tyina Steptoe taught me a great deal, and I hope we get to tear the roof off the sucker at least once more in the future. Finally, I hail the Friday Night Music Club, a social and spiritual cornerstone for me from the moment we started it a decade ago. Shout-outs to club cofounders Brian Bischel, Jerome Dotson, Dave Gilbert, Alexander Shashko, Tyina Steptoe, and Craig Werner, plus mainstays Brian Bieniek, Anthony Black, Doug Bradley, Judy Brady, Scott Carter, Tracy Curtis, Theresa Healy, Jeff Kollath, Leah Mirakhor, Yvette Pino, Wendy Schneider, Joanna Schuth, Wyl Schuth, Heather Stur, and Jay Van Orsdol. I also have to recognize some of Music Club's satellite members. Lauren Onkey and Bob Nowatzki are great friends and brilliant thinkers who showed me such hospitality when I did research in Cleveland. Stewart Francke is a true soul man and a brilliant writer. Dave Marsh has been very generous and helpful over the years. And John Floyd has significantly influenced my understanding of southern music and been a consistent source of great tunes and conversations.

I am so fortunate that many of my oldest friends also remain my closest. Charlie Alden has made me laugh, sing, and think longer than anyone else. Matt and Mike Cepress are my blood brothers. I do not deserve the caring and company that I have been shown by Greg and Lee Ann Venne, and I daily try to live up to their example. I met John Capista when we were just a few years old, and I've come to rely tremendously on his wit, wisdom, and kindness. Erica and Kevin McCool are the best running buddies anyone can ask for. And, when I grow up, I want to be like Chris Jarvis.

I am also fortunate to have a truly remarkable extended family. My aunts and uncles—Raymond Foster, Mary Hoppe, Mike Hoppe, Barbara Hughes, Eileen Hughes, Jean Hughes, Karen Hughes, Maureen Hughes, the late Michael Hughes, Bob Mason, and Ita Hardesty Mason—have given me immense amounts of love and guidance. I cherish being a part of a large group of relatives that also includes cousins Emily Foster, Rebecca Foster, Myron Hooks, Ben Hoppe, Bridget Hoppe, Amy Hughes, Erin Hughes, Kevin Hughes, Michael Hughes, Tim Hughes, and Megan Nyberg; great-aunts Helen Goetsch, Marjorie Mason, and Genevieve Plant; and a sizable set of second-cousins and beyond. Although Bobby Anderson, Peter Bukowski, Dick Crump, Kathy Sheahan, John and Darlene Roseth, and Greta Zeller are not blood relations, their long friendships with my parents and me make them all crucial parts of my family. I have also been so lucky to be welcomed into the wondrous Eisenberg/Silver clan by Ari's parents, Woody Eisenberg and Ellen Silver, her brother Jesse Eisenberg and his partner Aynnie Sionas, and other family members. I regret that my grandparents—Althea Hughes, Miles Hughes, Dorothy Jean Mason, and Lawrence Mason—did not live to see this moment.

My story begins with my parents, and I hope this work reflects well upon their efforts on my behalf. Beyond giving me a peerless level of love and encouragement, for which I love them both deeply and can never thank them enough, they raised me to understand that words and ideas were necessary parts of a well-rounded life. Both of my parents surrounded me with art, books, and music; they included me in deep and complex conversations; and they imparted to me that my intellect could not develop separately from my conscience. My father, Ron Hughes, remains a central influence on me, and—while I'm sure he's sometimes frustrated that I haven't figured it all out yet—I'm so grateful for his love and help, along with that of his wife, Pat Tyberg. My mother, Lee Ann Hughes, died while I was in high school. I miss so many things about her, and I'm so sorry that she isn't here to see this book, for I know it would make her proud. This is for her.

Notes

ABBREVIATIONS

JBR&BC	Jonas Bernholm Rhythm & Blues Collection, Archives Center, National Museum of American History, Smithsonian Institution, Washington, D.C.
JWC	Jerry Wexler Collection, Southern Folklife Collection, University of North Carolina, Chapel Hill, N.C.
JWP	Jerry Wexler Papers, Rock and Roll Hall of Fame and Museum Library and Archives, Cleveland, Ohio
MPS Collection	*Memphis Press-Scimitar* Collection, Preservation and Special Collections, University of Memphis Libraries, Memphis, Tenn.
PKMC	Portia K. Maultsby Collection, Interviews, SC 18, Archives of African American Music and Culture, Indiana University, Bloomington
RSVHPC	Rock 'n' Soul Video History Project Collection, Interviews, National Museum of American History, Archives Center, Smithsonian Institution, Washington, D.C.
SOP	Spooner Oldham Papers, Rock and Roll Hall of Fame and Museum Library and Archives, Cleveland, Ohio

INTRODUCTION

1. Lyrics from "There's a Red-Neck in the Soul Band," written by Steve Alaimo and Willie Clarke. According to David Whiteis, the song is a tribute to Latimore's longtime guitarist, Joey Murcia. See Whiteis, *Southern Soul-Blues*, 43.

2. It also predates the more famous "Play That Funky Music," a number one hit in 1976 for white Cleveland-based band Wild Cherry. That song concerns a very similar incident of racial surprise, where the protagonist is shocked and happy to find a "white boy" playing "funky music" for a black audience.

3. James Dickerson argues for a similar relationship between Memphis, Nashville, and New Orleans in *Mojo Triangle*. I have since seen similar models utilized in two CD compilations, *Heart of Southern Soul: From Nashville to Memphis and Muscle Shoals*, Ace Records, 1994 (reissued in 2007), and *Delta Swamp Rock: Sounds of the South*, Soul Jazz Records, 2010. I have also discovered interviews with musician Jim Dickinson and producer Jerry Wexler in which they refer to a "triangle" between Memphis, Muscle Shoals, and Nashville. For Dickinson, see Calemine, "Dixie Fried"; for Wexler, see "Interview." I have not seen anyone refer specifically to a "country-soul triangle."

4. As of yet, no one has analyzed these three cities together, although each has received attention individually. See Fuqua, *Music Fell on Alabama*; Gordon, *It Came from Memphis*; Hemphill, *Nashville Sound*; Kosser, *How Nashville Became Music City, U.S.A.*; McKee and Chisenhall, *Beale Black & Blue*; and Nager, *Memphis Beat*.

5. See Van Deburg, *New Day in Babylon*; Ward, *Just My Soul Responding*; and Werner, *Change Is Gonna Come*.

6. This notion structured the early writing on soul journalism. See Garland, *Sound of Soul*; Haralambos, *Right On*; Haralambos, *Soul Music*; and Shaw, *World of Soul*. The first generation of soul historiography also reflected this tendency. See George, *Death of Rhythm and Blues*, and Hirshey, *Nowhere to Run*. More recently, cultural critic Mark Anthony Neal suggested that soul created a "hypercommunity" among African Americans, a figurative (and sometimes literal) group of shared beliefs and practices that are expressed and interrogated through popular musical forms. See Neal, *What the Music Said*, 39–40. See also Neal, *Songs in the Key of Black Life*, and Neal, *Soul Babies*.

7. By the mid-1970s, even those who did not directly address music felt comfortable using them as metaphors: in 1974, for example, Frank Chin, Jeffrey Paul Chan, Lawson Fusao Inada, and Shawn Wong decried the lack of revolutionary substance in Asian American literature as being "as distinct from the blacks now as country-western is from soul." Chin et al., "Introduction to Chinese- and Japanese-American Literature," 44.

8. Pecknold, *Selling Sound*, 201.

9. See Hughes, "'You're My Soul Song,'" and Pecknold, "Making Country Modern."

10. Nearly every major work on country music has discussed this tension. For discussions of how this process developed in the early days of country music, see Malone, *Don't Get above Your Raisin'*, and Peterson, *Creating Country Music*. For a recent discussion of country's connection to southern identity and conservative politics, see Willman, *Rednecks and Bluenecks*. See also Fox, *Real Country*, and Jenson, *Nashville Sound*.

11. Guralnick, *Sweet Soul Music*, 2. See also Dobkin, *I Never Loved a Man*; George, *Death of Rhythm and Blues*; Gordon, *Respect Yourself*; Hirshey, *Nowhere to Run*; Hoskyns, *Say It One Time*; Jones, *Memphis Boys*; Kempton, *Boogaloo*; Kot, *I'll Take You There*; Ward, *Just My Soul Responding*; and Werner, *Change Is Gonna Come*.

12. Hoskyns, *Say It One Time*, xii. Robert Gordon avoids this tendency in *Respect Yourself*, although he devotes significant attention to the ways white musicians and executives at Stax Records helped transform the racist South through their work.

13. Guralnick, *Sweet Soul Music*, 6.

14. Ware and Back, *Out of Whiteness*, 251.

15. Ward, *Just My Soul Responding*, 223.

16. Another problem with the standard narrative is that it reflects an antiquated understanding of the civil rights movement. The story utilized by Guralnick and his followers has been greatly complicated in recent decades by a new generation of scholars, who have expanded the movement's chronological boundaries and troubled the supposed divisions between the integrationism of the early 1960s and the later ascendance of Black Power. See, for example, Hall, "Long Civil Rights Movement"; Jeffries, *Bloody Lowndes*; Sugrue, *Sweet Land of Liberty*; and Tyson, *Radio Free Dixie*.

17. Some examples of a labor-focused analysis of music include Gilbert, "Product of Our Souls"; Kelley, "Without a Song"; Stahl, *Unfree Masters*; Suisman, *Selling Sounds*; and Weidner, *Black Arts West*.

18. Wald, *Escaping the Delta*, 67. I am particularly inspired by Wald's use of musical professionalism to debunk what he calls the "romantic foolishness"—much of which is grounded in racial stereotype—that surrounds Robert Johnson and early Delta blues players in *Escaping the Delta*. Wald continues this analytical approach in a subsequent book that challenges much of the orthodoxy surrounding rock 'n' roll. See Wald, *How the Beatles Destroyed Rock 'n' Roll*.

19. Kelley analyzes the duality of "performing" in the context of musicians' work in "Without a Song," 124–25. A broad body of literature exists on music's role in the performance of racial, regional, and national identity. Beyond the previously cited works, I have been particularly influenced by McCann, *Hello, Hello Brazil*; Meintjes, *Sound of Africa!*; and Radano, *Lying Up a Nation*.

20. Boyle, "Kiss," 523. For other insightful discussions of interracial workplaces, see Bolster, *Black Jacks*, and Letwin, *Challenge of Interracial Unionism*.

21. Rob Bowman, Robert Gordon, and Roben Jones each get close to this in their studio-based histories of Memphis's Stax Records and American Studios, respectively. All three pay significant attention to the day-to-day activities of musicians, but they each frame their analyses primarily around the civil rights movement. See Bowman, *Soulsville, U.S.A.*; Gordon, *Respect Yourself*; and Jones, *Memphis Boys*.

22. Ward, *Just My Soul Responding*, 222. When he describes the feeling of several black musicians, Craig Werner offers a related insight that southern soul "amounted to a new kind of plantation where the black singers did the work while the white management made the decisions." See Werner, *Change Is Gonna Come*, 75.

23. Strangely, this oversight does not exist in other studies of U.S. musical history. Much of the writing on blues, folk, rock 'n' roll, and other genres has deftly explored the unequal power dynamics of integrated musical spaces and their effects on the music's racial identity. See, for example, Filene, *Romancing the Folk*; and Hamilton, *In Search of the Blues*.

24. Miller, *Segregating Sound*, 3–7. This process accompanied a migration of both black and white out of the rural South and into cities, particularly in the North. Both "hillbilly" and "race," and later country and soul, reflected both the aspirations of these newly migrated southerners and concerns about their interactions in new, urban contexts. For a particularly engrossing discussion of these dynamics, and the way they were expressed through music, see Gregory, *Southern Diaspora*.

25. Miller, *Segregating Sound*, 3–4. For more on the creation of "hillbilly" and "race," particularly as it related to the continued participation of black and white musicians across the "musical color line," see Huber, "Black Hillbillies." Other insightful discussions of this period include Brooks, *Lost Sounds*; and Suisman, *Selling Sounds*.

26. Terry Pace and Robert Palmer, "Pop Hits Rock the World," *Florence (Ala.) Times-Daily*, August 1, 1999, 12.

27. Brian Ward frames his discussion of the music around his notion of a "southern soul paradox," while Craig Werner describes the "contradiction" of such black-identified

music made by an integrated group of musicians. See Ward, *Just My Soul Responding*, 217; and Werner, *Change Is Gonna Come*, 72.

CHAPTER 1

1. Younger, *Get a Shot of Rhythm and Blues*, 37. This narrative structures the 2013 documentary *Muscle Shoals*. See also Guralnick, *Sweet Soul Music*, 6; and Hoskyns, *Say It One Time*, 95–96.

2. See Leftwich, *Two Hundred Years at Muscle Shoals*; and Owen, *Tennessee Valley Authority*.

3. Here, as with most details concerning Alexander's life, I am indebted to Richard Younger's definitive biography, *Get a Shot of Rhythm and Blues*. He discusses the TVA roots of Alexander's music, experiences echoed in a 1999 documentary, *Built for the People*, where Shoals bassist David Hood and FAME owner Rick Hall discuss the TVA's impact on the recording industry.

4. See Malone and Neal, *Country Music, U.S.A.*, 33. The connection between the New Deal and the popular-music industry has not been discussed by scholars who chart the projects' effects, historians who chronicle the cultural and economic changes of the New Deal era in the South, or chroniclers of popular music seeking to determine the roots of modern-day styles and phenomena. The best general works on rural electrification are Brown, *Electricity for Rural America*; and Pence, *Next Greatest Thing*. Recent books on the cultural effects of electrification projects do not extensively discuss the musical consequences. See Craig, *Out of the Dark*; and Kline, *Consumers in the Country*. The most noteworthy example among southern historians may be Pete Daniel, who chronicles the TVA in other work but argues in *Lost Revolutions* that the southern music boom—specifically rock 'n' roll—was rooted in the post–World War II period.

5. Miller explores the ironies of the "authentic" southerner recording in the North, particularly in relation to white singer Vernon Dalhart. See Miller, *Segregating Sound*, 140–42 and 146–47. This process, too, evinced the complex meaning of various southern-identified genres in the early period. Generally speaking, pop and jazz were recorded in studio settings that—in both practice and connotation—reflected their connection to urban modernity. Meanwhile, supposedly "traditional" genres like blues and hillbilly were primarily recorded "in the field" by record producers or folklorists who consciously hoped to capture the "real" sounds of the disappearing American past. Particularly in the case of African American musicians, this resulted in a significant narrowing of repertoire. As Marybeth Hamilton and Elijah Wald demonstrate, for example, white producers and academics prohibited many black blues musicians from recording the numerous pop, vaudeville, and sometimes hillbilly songs that they regularly performed because this music did not conform to the producers' understandings of real southern black identity. This process extended to some white musicians as well, as Barry Mazor and David Whisnant examine, and illustrates how deeply the production of popular music both reflected and influenced broader cultural ideologies in the twentieth century. See Hamilton, *In Search of the Blues*; Mazor, *Meeting Jimmie Rodgers*; Wald, *Escaping the Delta*; and Whisnant, *All That Is Native and Fine*.

6. See Craig, *Out of the Dark*; Havighurst, *Air Castle of the South*; Laird, *Louisiana Hayride*; and Wilkinson, "Hot and Sweet."

7. See Cantor, *Wheelin' on Beale*.

8. Grass, "Totally Unrestricted."

9. See Segrave, *Jukeboxes*, 48–49.

10. For the larger story of the independent record boom of the 1940s through 1960s, see Broven, *Record Makers and Breakers*.

11. See Malone, *Singing Cowboys and Musical Mountaineers*.

12. Quoted in "Rock and Roll Explodes," an episode of the Time/Warner series *The History of Rock and Roll*, 1995.

13. Hoss Allen interview, September 7, 1984, Nashville, PKMC, 2.

14. Callahan and Edwards, "Randy Wood."

15. Hoss Allen interview, September 7, 1984, Nashville, PKMC, 15–16. Ted Jarrett, one of the most prominent black musicians in Nashville from this period, recalls Wood's early association with King Records. See Jarrett, *You Can Make It if You Try*. For more on Wood's relationship to R&B, see Broven, *Record Makers and Breakers*, 97–102.

16. Quoted in Barlow, *Voice Over*, 162.

17. Ibid., 163. For related discussions, see Cantor, *Dewey and Elvis*; and Newman, *Entrepreneurs of Profit and Pride*.

18. Ibid., 162. For radio and civil rights, see Cantor, *Wheelin' on Beale*; Newman, *Entrepreneurs of Profit and Pride*; and Ward, *Radio and the Struggle for Civil Rights in the South*.

19. Hoss Allen interview, September 7, 1984, Nashville, PKMC, 47.

20. Ibid., 15, 18.

21. Broven, *Record Makers and Breakers*, 104.

22. One of the most important examples outside of the country-soul triangle was the Cincinnati-based King Records, which successfully marketed recordings to the country, pop, and R&B audiences and utilized both material and studio personnel that crossed racialized genre lines. For the history of King, see Fox, *King of the Queen City*.

23. See Jarrett, *You Can Make It if You Try*, 93. For more on this period in Nashville's racial history, see Houston, *Nashville Way*.

24. For histories of Sun, see Escott, *Good Rockin' Tonight*; and Floyd, *Sun Records*.

25. Terry Pace and Robert Palmer, "Breaking the Sound Barrier," *Florence (Ala.) Times-Daily*, August 1, 1999, 4–5.

26. Carla Thomas interview, September 5, 1984, Memphis, PKMC, 93.

27. I thank David Gilbert for making me aware of the Memphis Students in connection to his research on black musicians in New York in the early twentieth century. See Gilbert, "Product of Our Souls."

28. Sam Phillips, interview by Pete Daniel and Charlie McGovern, May 22, 1992, Memphis, RSVHPC, series 4, box 7, 112.

29. Sun secretary Marion Keisker appears to be the source of this quote, which she repeated—in various forms—several times, including to Presley biographers Albert Goldman and Jerry Hopkins. See Birnbaum, *Before Elvis*, 1.

30. See Altschuler, *All Shook Up*; Bertrand, *Race, Rock, and Elvis*; and Daniel, *Lost Revolutions*.

31. Larry Birnbaum correctly observes that Presley's earliest Sun recordings do not exhibit the country-R&B blend. See Birnbaum, *Before Elvis*, 1–3.

32. Rufus Thomas, interview by Pete Daniel, David Less, and Charles McGovern. August 5, 1992, Memphis, RSVHPC, series 4, box 9, 12. Both Rufus Thomas and daughter Carla reiterate their bitterness about Sun and its legacy in interviews conducted by historian Portia Maultsby. See Rufus Thomas interview, September 6, 1984, Memphis, PKMC, 10; and Carla Thomas interview, September 5, 1984, Memphis, PKMC, 93. Rufus Thomas, along with African American Sun artists Little Milton Campbell and Roscoe Gordon, also articulates these complaints in Floyd, *Sun Records*, 39–43.

33. Sam Phillips, interview by Pete Daniel and Charlie McGovern, May 22, 1992, Memphis, RSVHPC, series 4, box 7, 114–15. This larger issue of racial appropriation is addressed in nearly every work on race and rock and roll, and in nearly every work on Presley. See Bertrand, *Race, Rock, and Elvis*; and Escott, *Good Rockin' Tonight*; as well as Frith, "Academic Elvis"; and Marcus, *Mystery Train*, 120–75.

34. "Country Music: The Nashville Sound," *Time*, November 27, 1964.

35. Red Foley had Top 10 covers of the Charms' "Hearts of Stone," Faye Adams's "Shake a Hand," and the Soul Stirrers' "Peace in the Valley." For information on these and other hit R&B covers by country artists in the 1950s, see Birnbaum, *Before Elvis*, 233.

36. For the story of Nashville R&B, see Jarrett, *You Can Make It if You Try*; and Staff of the Country Music Hall of Fame and Museum, *Night Train to Nashville*.

37. Killen remarks from "The Men Who Made the Music," held at the University of North Alabama, moderated by Terry Pace, in 1999. Recording in possession of author.

38. Janelle Holley, "Florence's Buddy Killen Moving Up in Music World," *Florence (Ala.) Times*, January 10, 1960, 10.

39. Fuqua, *Music Fell on Alabama*, 21; David Palmer, "Denton on Musical Comeback Trail," *Florence (Ala.) Times*, June 1, 1985, 5A–6A. Fuqua's impressive history of Muscle Shoals music provides clarification and detail for much of the factual information here, as does Younger's *Get a Shot of Rhythm and Blues*.

40. Joiner quote from Younger, *Get a Shot of Rhythm and Blues*, 20.

41. Rick Hall, interview by Richard Younger, 1997, location unknown, 1.

42. Younger, *Get a Shot of Rhythm and Blues*, 21, 24; "Record Firm Opens Office in Sheffield," *Florence (Ala.) Times-Daily*, October 16, 1965, 2.

43. Rick Hall, interview by Richard Younger, 1997, location unknown, 10.

44. Holley, "Local Singing Group Has New Record on Market," *Florence (Ala.) Times*, February 24, 1960, sec. 2, 4. It is likely that the musicians on this recording featured Reggie Young and Bobby Emmons, both of whom later became prominent session players at Memphis's American Studios.

45. The area commonly known as "Muscle Shoals" actually consists of four neighboring communities: Florence, Muscle Shoals, Sheffield, and Tuscumbia. Throughout this text, I use "Muscle Shoals" to refer to the entirety of the locality.

46. Dan Penn, interviews by Richard Younger, 1994–99, location unknown, 3.

47. Dan Penn, telephone interview by author, December 2, 2005. It is worth noting that, later in this interview, Penn admitted that some country singers—he named

George Jones—did sing with "soul." It is also noteworthy that Penn's remarks reflect both a belief in inherent musical difference ("just something in them"), and the argument—made by many in soul's heyday, discussed in detail in chapter 3—that soul music's inherent blackness came from shared historical experience.

48. Dan Penn, interview by David Less, April 6, 2000, Memphis, RSVHPC, series 4, box 7, 29.

49. Ibid.

50. Hoskyns, *Say It One Time*, 96.

51. On the racial politics of the "frat circuit," see Guralnick, *Sweet Soul Music*, 160–62.

52. Guralnick, *Sweet Soul Music*, 187–88.

53. Dan Penn, interviews by Richard Younger, 1994–99, location unknown, 1.

54. Younger, *Get a Shot of Rhythm and Blues*, 24.

55. Dan Penn, interview by David Less, April 6, 2000, Memphis, RSVHPC, series 4, box 7, 22.

56. Arthur Alexander, interview by Richard Younger, 1993, location unknown, 2–3.

57. Hoskyns, *Say It One Time*, 87; Younger, *Get a Shot of Rhythm and Blues*, 29.

58. Guralnick, *Sweet Soul Music*, 197. Spooner Oldham today denies that he ever referred to himself as a "nigger," though he does not rule out the possibility that Donnie Fritts and Dan Penn used the term. Spooner Oldham, telephone interview by author, January 10, 2006.

59. Younger, *Get a Shot of Rhythm and Blues*, 57.

60. Ibid., 37.

61. Dan Penn, interviews by Richard Younger, 1994–99, location unknown, 3.

62. David Briggs, interviews by Richard Younger, 1996–98, location unknown, 2.

63. Younger, *Get a Shot of Rhythm and Blues*, 102, 15.

64. Arthur Alexander, interview by Richard Younger, 1993, location unknown, 8–9, 16.

65. Dan Penn, interviews by Richard Younger, 1994–99, location unknown, 1.

66. Bill Jobe, "This 'n' That," *Florence (Ala.) Times*, August 31, 1960, Sec. 3, 5. Jobe earlier profiled Alexander in "Record Soon by Sheffield Lad on NRC," *Florence (Ala.) Times*, June 16, 1960, sec. 4, 5. Interestingly, this piece does not mention Alexander's race.

67. Arthur Alexander, interview by Richard Younger, 1993, location unknown, 22–23; Rick Hall, interview by Richard Younger, 1997, location unknown, 7.

68. Rick Hall, interview by Richard Younger, 1997, location unknown, 8.

69. Younger, *Get a Shot of Rhythm and Blues*, 42–43. It is unclear why Hall—who previously worked with both Chess and Vee-Jay—did not go to black-oriented labels.

70. Janice Hume, "FAME Mines Gold in Shoals," *Florence (Ala.) Times*, May 21, 1982, 6.

71. When Wood wanted to find good R&B material for Boone to cover, he asked WLAC deejay Gene Nobles. Hoss Allen interview, September 7, 1984, Nashville, PKMC, 24.

72. The company's early output was more stylistically (and racially) diverse than it became by the time of Alexander's releases. See Dot/Paramount Records singles discography, Ray Topping Papers, Rock and Roll Hall of Fame and Museum Library and Archives.

73. Younger, *Get a Shot of Rhythm and Blues*, 48, 74.

74. David Briggs, interviews by Richard Younger, 1996–98, location unknown, 4; Forrest Riley, interview by Richard Younger, date unknown, location unknown, 2.

75. Arthur Alexander, interview by Richard Younger, 1993, location unknown, 11.

76. "Reviews of New Singles," *Billboard*, January 6, 1962, 25; "Nashville Sees Hot 'Move On,'" *Billboard*, January 20, 1962, 1.

77. Terry Pace and Robert Palmer, "Session with 'Queen of Soul' Produces Gold, Turmoil," *Florence (Ala.) Times-Daily*, August 1, 1999, 10–11; Arthur Alexander, interview by Richard Younger, 1993, location unknown, 2.

78. Arthur Alexander, interview by Richard Younger, 1993, location unknown, 24.

79. Quoted in Younger, *Get a Shot of Rhythm and Blues*, 57.

80. Ibid., 79.

81. The Seeburg jukebox company even recommended that Alexander be stocked in country jukeboxes. See "Jukebox Album Releases," *Billboard*, October 27, 1962, 51.

82. MGM ad, *Cashbox*, June 18, 1960, 5.

83. "Pop Absorbs Rhythm & Blues," *Cashbox*, March 12, 1960, 3.

84. "Coming Up! Nashville Country Music Festival," *Cashbox*, October 28, 1961, 3; "The Country Music Sound: Stronger Than Ever," *Cashbox*, July 2, 1960, 3.

85. "Pop Absorbs Rhythm & Blues."

86. Of course, as Diane Pecknold notes, Charles's recording did not initially receive airplay or support from country-oriented radio stations. See Pecknold, "Making Country Modern."

87. "Album Reviews," *Billboard*, May 5, 1962, 24; "Album Reviews," *Cashbox*, May 12, 1962, 30.

88. Younger, *Get a Shot of Rhythm and Blues*, 56–57.

89. Arthur Alexander, interview by Richard Younger, 1997, location unknown, 18.

90. Pianist Spooner Oldham claimed that the Nashville musicians who played on the released version of "Anna" essentially copied the performance of the FAME players. Spooner Oldham, interview by author, January 10, 2006, by telephone.

91. Arthur Alexander, interview by Richard Younger, 1997, location unknown, 11. It is worth noting that the context of this quote is unclear in the interview transcript. Alexander's phrasing suggests that Tom Stafford may have uttered these words, and they may have been directed at both the early recording scene in Muscle Shoals and that in Nashville. Either way, it is clear that Alexander understood his commercial opportunities to be limited by his race.

92. Steve Alaimo's long and fascinating career includes several intersections with the musicians of the country-soul triangle. He cowrote Latimore's "There's a Red-Neck in the Soul Band," and David Whiteis notes that his "resume includes everything from hitting the pop charts as a balladeer (1963's 'Every Day I Have to Cry') and hosting the mid-1960s teen-dance TV show *Where the Action Is* to producing sides on artists ranging from pre-Stax Sam & Dave (1961's 'My Love Belongs to You' on Marlin) and pre–Allman Brothers Duane and Gregg Allman (in a band called the 31st of February) to the pop group Mercy ('Love [Can Make You Happy]' in 1969). Through the years, he's also owned or co-owned some of the most important indie labels in the business." See Whiteis, *Southern Soul-Blues*, 38.

93. Rick Hall, interview by Richard Younger, 1997, location unknown, 11, 13.

94. Ibid., 13. To be fair, Hall has occasionally offered a more pragmatic justification for FAME's shift to black music. See Fuqua, *Music Fell on Alabama*, 31 and 35.

95. In the 2013 documentary *Muscle Shoals*, Hall even suggests that it was he, not Tom Stafford, who discovered Alexander and convinced him to record "You Better Move On."

96. Fuqua, *Music Fell on Alabama*, 36.

97. Dan Penn, telephone interview by author, December 2, 2005.

98. Pace and Palmer, "Leighton's Hughes Turns into a Real Steal," *Florence (Ala.) Times-Daily*, August 1, 1999, 6; Fuqua, *Music Fell on Alabama*, 40. Dan Penn has since suggested that this was not actually the case, and that Hall never wanted to release "Lollipops" as the A-side. Penn comments made at Rhodes College, Memphis, February 28, 2013.

99. One of his earliest recordings was produced by Hoss Allen. See Gary A. Calta, "Diggin' Up Discographies," *Goldmine*, no. 12, n.d., JBR&BC, box 8, folder 19.

100. "Men Who Made the Music"; Killen, *By the Seat of My Pants*, 159–60.

101. "Men Who Made the Music."

102. Foster, *My Country*, 231.

103. Killen, *By the Seat of My Pants*, 162.

104. Ibid., 162, 164.

105. Ibid., 160.

106. See Reggie Young, interview by David Less, January 19, 1998, Nashville, RSVHPC, series 4, box 9, 51; Bobby Wood, telephone interview by author, June 23, 2010.

107. It is noteworthy that, unlike Killen, Tex defines these musicians by the genre they played rather than the color of their skin. Quoted in Hirshey, *Nowhere to Run*, 336.

108. Killen, *By the Seat of My Pants*, 163.

109. Even more striking, no African Americans spoke during any part of the daylong symposium on Muscle Shoals music that climaxed with this event.

CHAPTER 2

1. Gerald Wexler, "The Lost Summer," *Kansas Magazine*, 1947, 55–58, JWP, box 1, folder 8. For more on Wexler's short story, see Zanes, *Dusty in Memphis*, 53–54.

2. Article draft, "Book Brings Wexler Back to the Shoals," undated, JWC, series 1, folder 5.

3. "Atl. Sales up 50% in Biggest Year," *Billboard*, December 22, 1967, 6. Similar articles can be found in the years that immediately precede and follow.

4. For more on Wexler's involvement in the triangle, see Wexler, *Rhythm and the Blues*, 208; *Jerry Wexler: Soul Man*, BBC documentary, 1999, JWC, series 2.

5. Quoted in *Atlantic Soul*, BBC documentary, 2007, JWC, series 2.

6. Wexler, *Rhythm and the Blues*, 192.

7. For example, it remains the primary way the music of the period is discussed in recent scholarship on Memphis. See Dowdy, *Brief History of Memphis*; Green, *Battling the Plantation Mentality*; and Rushing, *Memphis and the Paradox of Place*.

8. Mary Ann Lee, "What Is the Memphis Sound?," *Memphis Press-Scimitar*, December 22, 1972, Showtime 3, *MPS* Collection.

9. Elton Whisenhunt, "Memphis Sound: A Southern View," *Billboard*, June 12, 1965, 6.

10. Pete Hamill, "Saga of a Record Maker," *Cosmopolitan*, 1968, 95–97, 139, JWC, series 1, folder 1.

11. It also helped structure Ben Sidran's recent appraisal of Jewish contributions to U.S. popular music, in which Wexler plays a crucial and liberating role. See Sidran, *There Was a Fire*.

12. Soul star Clarence Carter recalled the importance of this egalitarian style of address in the 2013 documentary *Muscle Shoals*.

13. This phrase is derived from a line in "Soul Man," recorded by Sam & Dave and written by Isaac Hayes and David Porter.

14. Bobby Wood, telephone interview by author, June 23, 2010.

15. See Guralnick, *Sweet Soul Music*, 110–21; and Lauterbach, *Chitlin' Circuit*, 179–201.

16. Nashville's Ted Jarrett recalled in his autobiography that he was particularly fearful of emotional reactions from white women in the audience. "I didn't want any white woman getting me hanged," he noted. See Jarrett, *You Can Make It if You Try*, 81. Relatedly, Fred Ford described his near-lynching following a gig in northern Mississippi. The all-white crowd loved Ford's band, but they reacted with violence after Ford's drummer showed a young white girl how to play the drums. Fred Ford, interview by Pete Daniel, David Less, and Charles McGovern, May 20, 1992, Memphis, RSVHPC, series 4, box 3, 24–28.

17. Guralnick, *Sweet Soul Music*, 301.

18. Steve Cropper, interview by David Less, December 10, 1999, Nashville, RSVHPC, series 4, box 2, 29.

19. For the racially transgressive narrative, see Gordon, *It Came from Memphis*, 50–54; and Guralnick, *Sweet Soul Music*, 108–10, 114.

20. Bobby Manuel, interview by Pete Daniel, David Less, and Charles McGovern, May 15, 1992, Memphis, RSVHPC, series 4, box 5, 7.

21. For information on the construction of blackness as a musical commodity, see Lott, *Love and Theft*; and Radano, "Hot Fantasies."

22. Don Nix, interview by David Less, December 9, 1999, Nashville, RSVHPC, series 4, box 6, 11.

23. Gordon, *Respect Yourself*, 18. Gordon also suggests that it was "society's blunted sensibility," not the racialism of the Spades themselves, that was to blame for the crude moniker.

24. Don Nix, interview by David Less, December 9, 1999, Nashville, RSVHPC, series 4, box 6, 11.

25. As Marybeth Hamilton insightfully notes, these memories—particularly in the case of white southerners in the nineteenth century—were more a product of nostalgic retrospection than actual experience. They reflected a post-Reconstruction attempt to assert the antebellum plantation as a place of harmony and good feeling, as opposed to the hostile chaos of the postemancipation world. See Hamilton, *In Search of the Blues*, 66–70.

26. Quoted in Bowman, *Soulsville, U.S.A.*, 22.

27. See ibid, as well as Guralnick, *Sweet Soul Music*; and Lisle, liner notes to *Late Late Party*. Beyond the previously cited minstrel literature, I also take inspiration on the issue of white racial cross-dressing from Deloria, *Playing Indian*.

28. Fred Ford, interview by Pete Daniel, David Less, and Charles McGovern, May 20, 1992, Memphis, RSVHPC, series 4, box 3, 22.

29. Willie Mitchell, interview by Pete Daniel and Charles McGovern, August 4, 1992, Memphis, RSVHPC, series 4, box 6, 12–13.

30. Any discussion of Stax Records is built on the remarkable and exhaustive work of Rob Bowman and Robert Gordon, whose *Soulsville, U.S.A.*, and *Respect Yourself* (respectively) are the necessary starting point for all scholars interested in Stax. Their works permeate these pages, and—though I have specific references to important sections or quotes from each text—the reader should understand that their influence is heavy throughout.

31. Contemporaneous and subsequent discussions of Stax's history have nearly all described Stewart as a "country fiddler" when talking about his experiences prior to Stax. This designation is usually presented partly as a surprising example of musical cross-pollination and partly as a somewhat condescending dismissal of his pre-Stax musical endeavors. While there is no question that Stewart needed both the practical and conceptual help of his sister, not to mention the active involvement of Memphis's young black community, to launch a successful label, the "country fiddler" trope denies Stewart's many years of involvement in Memphis musical networks. He predates Sun's heyday and represents the roots of Stax in Memphis's fertile musical environment as strongly as any of his collaborators.

32. Jim Stewart, interview by Pete Daniel, Peter Guralnick, David Less, and Charles McGovern, May 19, 1992, Memphis, RSVHPC, series 4, box 8, 11, 3.

33. Bowman, *Soulsville, U.S.A.*, 8.

34. Wayne Jackson, interview by Pete Daniel and David Less, November 9, 1999, Memphis, RSVHPC, series 4, box 4, 36.

35. "Research and development" from Gordon, *Respect Yourself*, 40. Other material from Deanie Parker, interview by David Less, November 7, 1999, Memphis, RSVHPC, series 4, box 6, 87.

36. Carla Thomas, interview by Pete Daniel and David Less, November 10, 1999, Memphis, RSVHPC, series 4, box 9, 11; Marvell Thomas, interview by David Less, November 11, 1999, Memphis, RSVHPC, series 4, box 9, 3–4.

37. Marvell Thomas, interview by David Less, November 11, 1999, Memphis, RSVHPC, series 4, box 9, 15.

38. Ibid., 30–31.

39. Carla Thomas interview, September 5, 1984, Memphis, PKMC, 3.

40. In fact, the rest of her debut album was recorded in Nashville, where Thomas was attending classes at Tennessee State University. Ibid., 13, 15.

41. Rufus Thomas, interview by Pete Daniel, David Less, and Charles McGovern, August 5, 1992, Memphis, RSVHPC, series 4, box 9, 13.

42. Gordon, *Respect Yourself*, 51.

43. Floyd Newman, interview by Pete Daniel and David Less, November 9, 1999, Memphis, RSVHPC, series 4, box 6, 72; Lewie Steinberg, interview by David Less, December 8, 1999, Memphis, RSVHPC, series 4, box 8, 133.

44. See Gordon, *Respect Yourself*, 56.

45. Wayne Jackson, interview by Pete Daniel and David Less, November 9, 1999, Memphis, RSVHPC, series 4, box 4, 47–48.

46. Don Nix, interview by David Less, December 9, 1999, Nashville, RSVHPC, series 4, box 6, 42–43.

47. In 2014, Don Nix told a story about traveling to Texas for some shows with the black vocal group the Astors. When they reached their destination, the Astors were unable to find accommodations. They slept at the YMCA, while Nix stayed at a friend's house. Nix made these remarks at Rhodes College in Memphis on April 13, 2014.

48. Steve Cropper, interview by David Less, December 10, 1999, Nashville, RSVHPC, series 4, box 2, 45.

49. Lewie Steinberg, interview by David Less, December 8, 1999, Memphis, RSVHPC, series 4, box 8, 146.

50. Ibid., 134.

51. Marvell Thomas, interview by David Less, November 11, 1999, Memphis, RSVHPC, series 4, box 9, 77; Andrew Love, interview by Pete Daniel and David Less, November 9, 1999, Memphis, RSVHPC, series 4, box 4, 155.

52. Bowman, *Soulsville, U.S.A.*, 38.

53. For information on the individual biographies of Booker T. and the MGs, see Bowman, *Soulsville, U.S.A.*, 36–38.

54. See Gordon, *Respect Yourself*, 62–63.

55. Steve Cropper, interview by David Less, December 10, 1999, Nashville, RSVHPC, series 4, box 2, 60–61. Cropper's words are very much in keeping with a thesis recently forwarded by Elijah Wald, who suggests that music critics and scholars have underestimated the role and value of social dancing in the creation of popular music. See Wald, *How the Beatles Destroyed Rock 'n' Roll*.

56. Jones, *Memphis Boys*, 3.

57. It is necessary to note here that, while Jones played on all the recordings that were issued under the MGs name, many of the recordings from 1962 to 1966 that were backed by Booker T. and the MGs actually featured Isaac Hayes on keyboards. Jones was attending college during those years.

58. Steve Cropper, interview by David Less, December 10, 1999, Nashville, RSVHPC, series 4, box 2, 81–83; Donald "Duck" Dunn, interview by David Less, February 26, 1998, Robinsonville, Miss., RSVHPC, series 4, box 3, 44. This generational split—Steinberg was two decades older than Dunn—reflected a larger shift in U.S. popular music, as the sounds and techniques that defined the heyday of big-band jazz were supplanted by smaller groups whose style drifted toward harder rhythms and the controlled abandon of rock 'n' roll. For a recent discussion of this, see Zak, *I Don't Sound Like Nobody*.

59. See Gordon, *Respect Yourself*, 51–52.

60. As Rob Bowman notes, the musicians on the earliest Stax hits, including "Gee Whiz," were all African American. See Bowman, *Soulsville, U.S.A.*, 20.

61. One of the most passionate advocates of this idea is Emerson Able, the longtime band director at Memphis's Manassas High School and Isaac Hayes's musical director in the 1970s. See Emerson Able, interview by Preston Lauterbach, May 8, 2012, Memphis, Crossroads to Freedom Digital Archive, Rhodes College. Able made similar comments at a November 15, 2012, event at Rhodes College.

62. Donald "Duck" Dunn, interview by David Less, February 26, 1998, Robinsonville, Miss., RSVHPC, series 4, box 3, 22.

63. These fears were stoked by the fact that many black locals had larger treasuries than the white branches. See Seltzer, *Music Matters*, 110–11; and Howard

Taubman, "Petrillo Quietly Battles Musicians' Segregation." *New York Times*, April 23, 1966, 16.

64. At one point, AFM official O. C. Harmon chastised Shoals musician Spooner Oldham for hiring too many Memphis musicians for a session in Muscle Shoals. Letter from O. C. Harmon to Dewey L. Oldham, March 2, 1967, SOP, box 1, folder 1.

65. Donald "Duck" Dunn, interview by David Less, February 26, 1998, Robinsonville, Miss., RSVHPC, series 4, box 3, 23, 28.

66. Reggie Young, interview by David Less, January 19, 1998, Nashville, RSVHPC, series 4, box 9, 23.

67. Hi is the only major Memphis studio in the 1960s that has not been the subject of a book-long analysis. Roben Jones's *Memphis Boys* contains a wealth of information on Hi's early days.

68. Jones, *Memphis Boys*, 7. Young explained that this technique, in which he bounced a pencil across the strings, mimicked the way jazz drummers used their sticks.

69. Reggie Young, interview by David Less, January 19, 1998, Nashville, RSVHPC, series 4, box 9, 26. See also Willie Mitchell, interview by Pete Daniel and Charles McGovern, August 4, 1992, Memphis, RSVHPC, series 4, box 6, 4. Joe Hall later played keyboards on some recordings at Stax, including Wilson Pickett's hit version of "In the Midnight Hour."

70. Bowman, *Soulsville, U.S.A.*, 61.

71. During this period, Memphis newspapers ran numerous articles that were expressly designed to trace the sound's historical roots and contemporary impacts. They reached the same conclusion: the Memphis sound was black music produced by integrated musicians. See, for example, Robert Johnson, "The Story behind the Memphis Sound," *Memphis Press-Scimitar*, September 29, 1967, 3, 19; Lane Johnston, "Easier to Set Aside Day Than to Explain Its Name," *Memphis Press-Scimitar*, September 27, 1968, page unknown; Mary Ann Lee, "TV News and Views: Just What Is Memphis Sound? Many Memphians Not Too Sure," *Memphis Press-Scimitar*, February 25, 1971, Lee, "What Is the Memphis Sound?"; and Kay Morgan, "Soul of Memphis," *Memphis Press-Scimitar*, May 28, 1969, 97–98. All of these articles are located in the *MPS* Collection.

72. Whisenhunt, "Memphis Sound."

73. James Cortese, "Sounds of Memphis—'Everybody Is Queen of Something,' Says Carla," *Memphis Commercial Appeal*, March 31, 1968, 6, found in Smithsonian Memphis Rock 'n' Soul Exhibit Archives, National Museum of American History, Washington, D.C.

74. Bob Talley, interview by Pete Daniel, David Less, and Charles McGovern, May 22, 1992, Memphis, RSVHPC, series 4, box 9, 52.

75. "Stax Fax: Biography . . . Presenting Booker T. & the M.G.'s" press release, Stax Records, n.d. (1967 or early 1968), JRB&B Collection, box 5, folder 15.

76. Quoted in Sterling Greenwood, "Memphis Sound? 'No Such Thing,'" *Memphis Press-Scimitar*, April 3, 1970, Showtime 9, *MPS* Collection.

77. Quoted in Claude Hall, "Memphis Grabs Ad World as the Happening Sound," *Billboard*, May 3, 1969, 24, 28.

78. David Porter, interview by Pete Daniel and Charles McGovern, August 7, 1992, Memphis, RSVHPC, series 4, box 7, 58.

79. Garland, *Sound of Soul*, 2, 120. For discussion of Memphis and Stax, see ibid., 120–64. Similar treatments exist in Haralambos, *Soul Music*; and Shaw, *World of Soul*.

80. Morgan, "Soul of Memphis."

81. Burt Korall, "How the Memphis Sound Came to Be," *New York Times*, November 23, 1969, M6.

82. Ibid.

83. Marty Bennett, "Black-and-White Duos on Disks Reflect New Interracial Stance," *Variety*, September 4, 1968, JBR&BC, box 5, folder 19; Peter Giraudo, "Review: Soul Limbo," *Rolling Stone*, November 9, 1968, JBR&BC, box 5, folder 15.

84. Glenn D. Kittler, "Can Integration Really Work?," *Coronet*, August 1970, 124–30, JBR&BC, box 5, folder 19.

85. Bowman, *Soulsville, U.S.A.*, 61.

86. Ibid.

87. Garland, *Sound of Soul*, 134.

88. "Stax Fax: Biography . . . Presenting Booker T. & The M.G.'s" press release, n.d. (1967 or early 1968), JBR&BC, box 5, folder 15.

89. James Kingsley, "Fate, Luck, Stewart Combined for Memphis Sound," *Memphis Commercial Appeal*, March 26, 1970, 5. See also James Cortese, "Memphis Sound Sings Cash Tune of Ninety Million as City's Recording Industry Turns to Gold," *Memphis Commercial Appeal*, March 3, 1968, 8; Johnson, "Story behind the Memphis Sound"; and Mary Ann Lee, "Putting the Memphis Sound on Paper: The Free-Form Style of Steve Cropper," *Memphis Press-Scimitar*, May 24, 1968, Showtime 3, all *MPS* Collection.

90. Hoskyns, *Say It One Time*, 210. In discussing this performance, historian Alice Echols suggests that the tepid response to Joplin's performance among Stax's black Memphis audience symbolized larger changes in the nation's racial politics. "The Stax-Volt show signaled a decline of the interracialism that had marked popular music during the mid-1960s and the opening of a divide that would only widen in the years to come as black-and-white music diverged," she wrote. Echols presents Joplin's failed attempt to redeem herself through the power of black music not as problematic but rather as a tragic casualty of the Black Power era. At the very least, Echols's take is questionable, and her conflation of chronology in her discussions of Joplin's attempts at "cultural hybridity" further mars her argument. See Echols, "Little Girl Blue," 59.

91. Jones, *Memphis Boys*, 75.

92. Bobby Wood, telephone interview by author, June 23, 2010.

93. Dan Penn later claimed that Presley's biggest American hit—"Suspicious Minds"—ripped off the beginning of a Penn-written soul hit called "Sweet Inspiration." Penn comments made at Rhodes College, February 28, 2013.

94. The most extensive discussion of Presley's American sessions is in Guralnick, *Careless Love*, 318–40.

95. Letter from Dusty Springfield to Steve [last name unknown], July 1968, JWP, box 1, folder 1.

96. Ibid.; letter from Dusty Springfield to Jerry Wexler, August 31, 19?? [probably 1968], JWP, box 1, folder 1.

97. It has been reissued in a deluxe edition, appears regularly on "best of" lists, and serves as the subject of a book by Warren Zanes, *Dusty in Memphis*.

98. Other examples include jazz flautist Herbie Mann and rock group Paul Revere and the Raiders, who recorded the soul-inflected albums *Memphis Underground* and *Goin' to Memphis* (respectively) at American.

99. Jones, *Memphis Boys*, 17.

100. Paul Bernish, "Memphis Hopes Boom in Recordings Will Aid Local Racial Harmony," *Wall Street Journal*, March 30, 1970, 1. Thank you to Diane Pecknold for bringing this article to my attention.

101. "Memphis Sound Guest of Honor at BMI Party," *Billboard*, April 14, 1968, 14; James D. Kingsley, "From the Music Capitals of the World—Memphis," April 26, 1969, *Billboard*, 26, 28.

102. Lee, "What Is the Memphis Sound?"

103. "Memphis Music to Present Eleven Awards," *Billboard*, April 24, 1971, 3, 70.

104. Thomas Fox, "Sights and Sounds—Country Music Lovers to Unite," *Memphis Commercial Appeal*, June 13, 1971, page unknown, found in Memphis Rock 'n' Soul Exhibit Archives, National Museum of American History, Archives Center, Smithsonian Institution, Washington, D.C. In 1975, Stax cofounder Estelle Axton noted that "country is coming to life here now, and Memphis recording companies are turning more to cosmopolitan country rather than fiddle country." See Jane Sanderson, "Memphis Talent Keeps Music Industry on Upbeat," *Memphis Press-Scimitar*, January 15, 1975, 10, found in *MPS* Collection.

105. Cantwell and Friskics-Warren, *Heartaches by the Number*, 143.

106. Bill Littleton, "Nashville News," *International Musician*, September 1974, 10, 21; Hentoff, "Folk Ferment in American Pop Music," *International Musician*, May 1966, 4; Littleton, "Nashville News," *International Musician*, August 1970, 10; Littleton, "Nashville News," *International Musician*, December 1970, 10; Littleton, "Nashville News," *International Musician*, August 1971, 11 and 16; Littleton, "Nashville News," *International Musician*, November 1970, 8; Littleton, "Charley Pride," *International Musician*, October 1973, 6, 21.

107. John Grissim, "The Nashville Cats," *Rolling Stone*, December 9, 1971, 30–32.

108. Ibid.

109. Lee, "What Is the Memphis Sound?"

110. Garland, *Sound of Soul*, 164.

111. Jim Dickinson, interview by author, August 8, 2003, Memphis. Dickinson offered a similar comment to Robert Gordon, saying that the MGs were "four men who under normal circumstances would not have known each other, much less worked together in ensemble like they did. The American [Studios] rhythm section," by contrast, "are guys who play golf together." Every member of American's rhythm section was white. Quoted in Gordon, *It Came From Memphis*, 169. Both remarks echo the insight of historian Daniel Letwin that, despite interracial work and organizing among coal miners in Alabama, "above ground, black and white went their separate ways." See Letwin, *Challenge of Interracial Unionism*, 7. It is worth acknowledging that Robert Gordon has recently suggested that Cropper and Jones did associate outside of Stax, at least in its earliest days. Citing a 1970s interview with the duo, he suggests that the two "began to hang out together" in the early 1960s, with Cropper picking up Jones after school and driving around Memphis. It was, in fact, on one of these trips that the pair first heard the riff that would eventually develop into "Green Onions." See Gordon, *Respect Yourself*, 62–63.

112. Sam Moore interview, February 24, 1983, Los Angeles, and September 5, 1984, Memphis, PKMC, 23. See also Rufus Thomas interview, September 6, 1984, Memphis, PKMC, 18–19.

113. Wexler, *Rhythm and the Blues*, 194.

114. Quoted in Ware and Back, *Out of Whiteness*, 236.

115. Wexler, *Rhythm and the Blues*, 208.

116. Quoted in Dobkin, *I Never Loved a Man*, 141.

117. Marvell Thomas, interview by David Less, November 11, 1999, Memphis, RSVHPC, series 4, box 9, 74.

118. Wexler, *Rhythm and the Blues*, 210.

119. This version of the story, supported by quoted recollections from bassist/trombonist David Hood and guitarist Jimmy Johnson, is included in Jones, *Memphis Boys*, 56.

120. Ibid.

121. *Jerry Wexler: Soul Man*, BBC documentary, 1999, JWC, series 2.

122. "Black throat" from Palao, liner notes for *The Fame Recordings*; "Tempt the niggers" from Guralnick, *Sweet Soul Music*, 341.

123. Quoted in Werner, *Higher Ground*, 133.

124. Quoted in Dobkin, *I Never Loved a Man*, 138.

125. Quoted in Jones, *Memphis Boys*, 56.

126. Ibid., 57, 61–62.

127. See Dobkin, *I Never Loved a Man*; Guralnick, *Sweet Soul Music*; Jones, *Memphis Boys*; and Werner, *Higher Ground*.

128. Quoted in Dobkin, *I Never Loved a Man*, 6.

129. Chris Porterfield, "Lady Soul: Singing It Like It Is," *Time*, June 28, 1968, 62–66. An extended sidebar offers a list of numerous historical and contemporary figures and tells the reader—with no explanation—which of them does and does not have "soul." To be fair, Porterfield makes a crucial distinction when asserting this binary. He admits that some singers, like Franklin, sound "soulful" no matter what they're singing, even when—as Porterfield and R&B singer Lou Rawls both admit in the article—many artists choose to do "white"-sounding material as a professional choice to attract as wide an audience as possible and diversify their output. While Porterfield does not unpack these contradictions, he nonetheless acknowledges one of the crucial ambiguities of musical "soul" in a piece that too often reifies its ideological underpinnings. Interestingly, writer Roben Jones mentions (but does not cite) a contemporaneous comment by Franklin suggesting that Warwick was "not soulful," and Jones then postulates that this comment led Warwick to record at American Studios in Memphis. See Jones, *Memphis Boys*, 140.

CHAPTER 3

1. "Letters: July 12, 1968." *Time*, July 12, 1968.

2. The best works on this topic are Thomas, *Listen Whitey!*; and Vincent, *Party Music*.

3. Van Deburg, *New Day in Babylon*, 171. See also Joseph, *Waiting 'til the Midnight Hour*; and Woodard, *Nation within a Nation*. Each of these works addresses the importance of soul music for Black Power but devotes little attention to the music's production.

4. See Baraka, *Black Music*; and Baraka (Jones), *Blues People. Black Music* contains Baraka's most extensive work on soul music, "The Changing Same," in which Baraka both questions and celebrates the potential of soul as a means of affecting cultural and political change in the United States. See Baraka, *Black Music*, 205–41.

5. William Van Deburg offers a modified version of these two elements, describing soul music as "the aesthetic property of blacks" that whites threatened to "commercialize and 'whiten,'" but Van Deburg is primarily interested in the performance of soul music by whites, not the behind-the-scenes economics of the music business. See Van Deburg, *New Day in Babylon*, 205. On "black capitalism" of the period, see Hill and Rabig, *Business of Black Power*.

6. In *Respect Yourself*, Robert Gordon uses this framework to deftly analyze the second half of Stax Records' history. Although Gordon falls prey to some aspects of the narrative of decline that has accompanied most studies of southern soul in the Black Power era, he deserves tremendous credit for exploring the ways Stax both deployed and shaped this discourse during the late 1960s and early 1970s.

7. Booker Griffin, "The Way It Is: Osmond Brothers Exemplifying Rape of Black Music," *Los Angeles Sentinel*, February 25, 1971, A7. Over the course of his distinguished career, Griffin hosted a weekly show on KFJG, developed the NAACP Image Awards, and worked for a variety of causes, including the rebuilding of Watts after the 1965 uprising and the presidential campaign of Robert F. Kennedy. For information on Griffin, see John L. Mitchell, "Obituary: Booker Griffin Jr.: Black Radio Talk Show Host," *Los Angeles Times*, July 8, 1993.

8. See Feldstein, "'I Don't Trust You Anymore'"; George, *Death of Rhythm and Blues*; and Ward, *Just My Soul Responding*.

9. This had been a project for black activists since the nineteenth century and formed the basis of two of the most prominent early works of black cultural criticism. See Du Bois, *Souls of Black Folk*; and Trotter, *Music and Some Highly Musical People*. For more recent scholarly appraisals, see Brooks, *Bodies in Dissent*; Lhamon, *Raising Cain*; and Sotiropolous, *Staging Race*.

10. Neal, *What the Music Said*, 40–41. One limitation of Neal's analysis is his relatively ahistorical appraisal of soul-era "blackness" as a concept. In fact, though scholars have interrogated and problematized musical "blackness" in an earlier era, the soul era remains relatively untheorized. There are significant exceptions. In *Dancing in the Street*, her study of Motown Records and African American cultural politics, Suzanne Smith offers a masterful discussion of how the black-owned company deployed changing—and sometimes contradictory—versions of "blackness" in the 1950s and 1960s. Brian Ward offers a larger demonstration of this relationship in *Just My Soul Responding*. For Ward, as for Smith, soul music played a dynamic and historically contingent role in framing the presentation of blackness in the contexts of U.S. politics and commercial culture.

11. Guralnick, *Sweet Soul Music*, 3–4.

12. Penn has repeatedly told this story in live performance. For a recorded example, see *Moments from This Theater*, 1998, Proper Records.

13. Robert Gordon, "Memphis, 1956–74: Rhythm and Blues Heard round the World," *Details*, July 1992, 99.

14. Quoted in Jones, *Memphis Boys*, 144.

15. Gordon, *Respect Yourself*, 199.

16. Most subsequent scholars have followed Guralnick's lead, including Hoskyns and Jones.

17. Guralnick, *Sweet Soul Music*, 3. Guralnick also blames the King assassination for the eventual "resegregation" of the popular music charts in the early 1970s. This suggestion, too, obscures a far more complicated combination of factors.

18. Ibid., 355; Robert Gordon, "Memphis, 1956–74: Rhythm and Blues Heard round the World," *Details*, July 1992; Kemp, *Dixie Lullaby*, 3.

19. Quoted in Gordon, *Respect Yourself*, 184.

20. Quoted in Paul Bernish, "Memphis Hopes Boom in Recordings Will Aid Local Racial Harmony," *Wall Street Journal*, March 30, 1970.

21. Ibid.

22. Deanie Parker, interview by David Less, November 7, 1999, Memphis, RSVHPC, series 4, box 6, 102.

23. Loeb described the Memphis sound as "'an industry that attracts quality and ability and I'm delighted it's here. It is a new sound, and it's a good one.'" See Lane Johnston, "Easier to Set Aside Day Than to Explain Its Name," *Memphis Press-Scimitar*, September 27, 1968, page unknown, found in *MPS* Collection.

24. *Stax Fax*, n.d. (almost certainly 1968 or 1969), JBR&BC, folder 19.

25. "Stax' Al Bell: 'A New Second Major Market,'" *Cashbox*, November 25, 1972, 38.

26. Gordon, *Respect Yourself*, 116.

27. Donald "Duck" Dunn, interview by David Less, February 26, 1998, Robinsonville, Miss., RSVHPC, series 4, box 3, 48.

28. "Black Record Companies Must Be a Part of the Black Community," press release, Richard Gersh Associates, July 22, 1971, JBR&BC, folder 20.

29. Ibid.

30. Gordon, *Respect Yourself*, 202. Gordon offers a poignant analysis of Bell's "diversification" strategy, including the story of his interest in releasing a Scottish teenager named Lena Zavaroni. For Zavaroni, see Gordon, *Respect Yourself*, 335–36.

31. In 1975, when Bell and Stax were sued by financer Union Planters Bank, the Memphis branch of Jackson's Operation PUSH called for a boycott of the institution. Rev. Samuel Kyles, a longtime leader of the Memphis movement, decried the bank for "making some obvious moves to destroy a black giant." See Jess Bunn, "PUSH Group Claims Bank Violated Agreement with Stax," *Memphis Press-Scimitar*, December 27, 1975, page unknown, found in *MPS* Collection.

32. "Black Record Companies Must Be a Part of the Black Community," press release, Richard Gersh Associates, July 22, 1971, JBR&BC, folder 20.

33. Stax's embrace of Black Power far outpaced that of its biggest rival, the other prominent black-controlled soul label, Motown Records. Motown supported numerous black political causes, released recordings by Martin Luther King and others, and even founded a political subsidiary called Black Forum. Still, it discouraged its artists from making explicit political statements and marketed itself as a cross-racial "Sound of Young America." Like at Stax, Motown's artists and executives wrestled with their sometimes conflicting desires to both appeal to white audiences and support black

political causes. This intensified in the Black Power years, as the new politics heightened expectations for black-produced cultural forms. Even though Motown had—in Suzanne Smith's words—"completely transformed popular ideas about what 'black' music was or could do," the label remained unsure of how to embrace soul's racial politics. Stax went much further. See Smith, *Dancing in the Street*, 14.

34. Quoted in Robert Gordon, "Memphis, 1956–74: Rhythm and Blues Heard round the World," *Details*, July 1992, 99.

35. Kemp, *Dixie Lullaby*, 3.

36. See Ward, *Just My Soul Responding*, 393–416.

37. "CORE Director Charges Majors Hold Monopoly," *Cashbox*, August 25, 1973, 9.

38. See Feretti, "White Captivity of Black Radio," 87–89; Ward, "Jazz and Soul, Race and Class."

39. Stax press release, August 24, 1971, *MPS* Collection.

40. For more on NARA/NATRA, see Barlow, *Voice Over*, 219–39; Cashmore, *Black Culture Industry*, 113–14; George, *Death of Rhythm and Blues*, 113–15, 165–67; Guralnick, *Sweet Soul Music*, 181–83; Wade and Picardie, *Music Man*, 170–83; Ward, *Just My Soul Responding*, 432–36; and Ward, *Radio and the Struggle for Civil Rights in the South*, 286–95. Each author references NARA/NATRA in other places, but these sections represent the most extensive and informative descriptions.

41. Quoted in Guralnick, *Sweet Soul Music*, 382.

42. Quoted in Wade and Picardie, *Music Man*, 176. For discussions of the mafia's role in 1960s pop music, see Dannen, *Hit Men*; and James, *Me, the Mob and the Music*.

43. Woodard quoted in Gordon, *Respect Yourself*, 195; George Ware interview, December 6, 1982, Philadelphia, Pa., PKMC, 8–9.

44. Quoted in Wade and Picardie, *Music Man*, 175.

45. George Ware interview, December 6, 1982, Philadelphia, Pa., PKMC, 6.

46. See Gordon, *Respect Yourself*, 200; Guralnick, *Sweet Soul Music*, 383–84; and Wade and Picardie, *Music Man*, 172.

47. Wexler, *Rhythm and the Blues*, 227; Walden quoted in Guralnick, *Sweet Soul Music*, 383.

48. Quoted in Hoskyns, *Say It One Time*, 185.

49. Quoted in Gordon, *Respect Yourself*, 201.

50. Williams quoted in Wade and Picardie, *Music Man*, 179; Banks quoted in Guralnick, *Sweet Soul Music*, 384; Logan Westbrooks, telephone interview by author, March 7, 2011. Brian Ward describes the FPC as the "armed wing of NATRA" in this period, describing its activities in ominous and racially coded terms. He notes, for example, that members "terrorized" NATRA and "darkened the doorways" of radio stations and record labels, for example. "Terrorized" from Ward, *Radio and the Struggle for Civil Rights in the South*, 291; "Darkened the doorways" from Ward, *Just My Soul Responding*, 437.

51. Although NATRA was the most significant of the critics demanding immediate change, it was far from alone. Other organizations arose during this period, including several NATRA offshoots like the New York–based Fraternity of Record Executives (FORE), that participated in much of the same advocacy and charity but never adopted the overtly militant posture of their parent organization. Others sought to address NATRA's deficiencies, like Broadcasters and Musical Artists (BAMA), which

split from NATRA in 1972 over continuing concerns that the organization was not doing enough to address the specific obstacles faced by southern broadcasters.

52. See Barlow, *Voice Over*; Savage, *Broadcasting Freedom*; and Ward, *Radio and the Struggle for Civil Rights in the South*.

53. See Walsh, "Black Oriented Radio"; and Ward, *Radio and the Struggle for Civil Rights in the South*.

54. O'Connor and Cook, "Black Radio." I first became aware of this article in Walsh, "Black-Oriented Radio."

55. Garnett, "How 'Soulful' Is Soul Radio?," 1–2, 18. The activist commented frequently on this issue. Elsewhere he suggested that blacks "need to talk about drug addiction, about slum landlords, about jobs, about education. But the white man gives us twenty-four hours of 'soul' because it pads his already stuffed pockets and keeps black people ignorant." See Feretti, "White Captivity of Black Radio," 92–93. I became aware of Feretti's article in Walsh, "Black-Oriented Radio."

56. Del Shields, "Thoughts on Bill Gavin," *Stax Fax*, n.d. (likely summer of 1968), JBR&BC, folder 19. Gavin and Stax also received tributes in this issue from NATRA officers Lucky Cordell and E. Rodney Jones.

57. Chris Turner, "Do You Have Something to Say?," *Stax Fax*, n.d. (almost certainly 1968 or 1969), JBR&BC, folder 19.

58. Stewart's speech is quoted and discussed in Gordon, *Respect Yourself*, 246.

59. Profile of NARAS meeting, *Stax Fax*, n.d. (1968 or 1969), JBR&BC, folder 19.

60. In the introductory film at the Stax Museum of American Soul Music, Booker T. Jones even claims that the company would still be open today if not for the assassination of Martin Luther King Jr.

61. Brian Ward suggests that they were hired because of intimidation at the 1968 NATRA meeting, and that Baylor and Woodard threatened to break Bell's legs. See Ward, *Just My Soul Responding*, 439.

62. Quoted in Gordon, *Respect Yourself*, 212.

63. Quoted in Wade and Picardie, *Music Man*, 190.

64. Quoted in Gordon, *Respect Yourself*, 152.

65. Dino Woodard mentions this issue briefly in Gordon, *Respect Yourself*, 366. Interestingly, Gordon does not include any other references to the strike.

66. Gordon, *Respect Yourself*, 136; Wade and Picardie, *Music Man*, 189.

67. Marvell Thomas, interview by David Less, November 11, 1999, Memphis, RSVHPC, series 4, box 9, 83.

68. Quoted in Gordon, *Respect Yourself*, 366.

69. Wade and Picardie, *Music Man*, 188; Marvell Thomas, interview by David Less, November 11, 1999, Memphis, RSVHPC, series 4, box 9, 83, 86. Al Bell also told Robert Gordon that he "resist[s] all that gangster talk" when it comes to Baylor, in part because of the racist roots of the NRA and the broader use of violence to repress African Americans and other groups. Bell's comment and others reframe Baylor's tactics around the long history of armed self-reliance among African Americans, which became a crucial component of the Black Power years. For more on this history, see Tyson, *Radio Free Dixie*.

70. It is important to note that some white musicians have a more complex view of Baylor and Woodard. Staff keyboard player Steve "Sandy" Leigh, who joined Stax in

1969, was pistol-whipped by Woodard in the studio, but he also praises Johnny Baylor as "being a very nice guy to me." See Steve Leigh, "Stax Story," http://www.sl-prokeys .com/stax/stax-mclemore.htm.

71. Quoted in Gordon, *Respect Yourself*, 253.

72. "Clark, Other Execs, Get FORE Achievement Nod," *Billboard*, May 3, 1970, 4.

73. Journalist Greg Kot has recently published an engrossing group biography of the Staple Singers. See Kot, *I'll Take You There*.

74. Bowman, *Soulsville, U.S.A.*, 157.

75. Quoted in ibid.

76. Stax Records ad, *Cashbox*, February 19, 1972, 25.

77. "Artist of the Month: The Staple Singers," *Stax Fax*, n.d. (almost certainly 1968 or 1969), JBR&BC, folder 19.

78. Steve Cropper, interview by David Less, December 10, 1999, Nashville, RSVHPC, series 4, box 2, 108–9.

79. Quoted in Bowman, *Soulsville, U.S.A.*, 211.

80. Quoted in ibid., 111.

81. After laying down the rhythm tracks in Muscle Shoals, Bell took the songs to Memphis's Ardent Studios, where overdubs were added and mixing was completed.

82. Chris Porterfield, "Lady Soul: Singing It Like It Is," *Time*, June 28, 1968, 62–66.

83. Katz, *Solid Foundation*, 4.

84. Bell and Mavis Staples still disagree as to who wrote which share of the lyrics, but both acknowledge the other's involvement.

85. See Gordon, *Respect Yourself*, 271.

CHAPTER 4

1. Paul Ackermann, "Gortikov Scorches Whitey Trade in NATRA Speech," *Billboard*, August 23, 1969, 1, 102; Dan Knapp, "Black Craftsmen's Talents Untapped on Entertainment Scene," *Los Angeles Times*, October 5, 1969, T1, T22.

2. "Capitol Elects Lavong R&B Marketing VP," *New York Amsterdam News*, November 22, 1969, 20; Eliot Tiegel, "Black Jobs, Culture Gain Capitol Boost," *Billboard*, April 26, 1969, 1.

3. Tiegel, "Black Jobs," 4.

4. Richard Robinson, "Small Soul Labels Have an Advantage," *Billboard*, August 16, 1969 S14, S24.

5. Terry Pace and Robert Palmer, "Pop Hits Rock the World," *Florence (Ala.) Times-Daily*, August 1, 1999, 12.

6. Logan Westbrooks, telephone interview by author, March 7, 2011.

7. Eliot Tiegel, "Cap Meet 4-Point Plan to Advance Promotional Power," *Billboard*, September 16, 1969, 113.

8. Quoted in "Miller Appointed Fame Veep," *Florence (Ala.) Times-Daily*, January 27, 1970, 16. This quote and article appeared in several other publications.

9. Fame Records advertisement, *Billboard*, May 17, 1969, 30–31.

10. "Candi Staton Biography," Capitol Records press release, July 1969, *MPS* Collection.

11. Capitol ad, *Cashbox*, April 25, 1970, 37.

12. For more on Gentry, including her work at FAME, see George-Warren, "Mystery Girl."

13. Lavette, *Woman Like Me*, 227.

14. James D. Kingsley, "'Fame' Credited to Memphis Sound," *Memphis Commercial Appeal*, May 9, 1969, in *MPS* Collection.

15. Quoted in Fuqua, *Music Fell on Alabama*, 56.

16. Quoted in Daisann McLane, "Muscle Shoals' Southern Hospitality," *Rolling Stone*, March 8, 1979, 24–25.

17. Richards, *Life*, 274.

18. This story is repeated in several places, most recently in the 2013 *Muscle Shoals* documentary.

19. Contemporary Shoals artist Jason Isbell, who has known Hood for years, told this story at the Experience Music Project Pop Music Conference at Tulane University, New Orleans, April 20, 2013.

20. Quoted in Ware and Back, *Out of Whiteness*, 232–33. Dia's statement exemplifies the irony of Motown's perceived musical "bleaching" and its essentially all-black studio band.

21. Ibid.

22. Letter from Idrissa Dia to Jerry Wexler, July 5, 1993, JWP, box 1, folder 3.

23. Ibid. For my knowledge of Senghor, I am indebted to conversations with ethnomusicologist Melissa Reiser.

24. Ware and Back, *Out of Whiteness*, 254–55.

25. Jim Dickinson argued that Eddie Hinton loved Mavis Staples even more than he loved Otis Redding, and Patterson Hood, the son of Shoals bassist David Hood, relates a story of Hinton shouting for three days to try to get a Mavis Staples–style rasp before he recorded a Staples cover. Dickinson quoted in Calemine, "Dixie Fried." Hood's remarks come from the short film *Mighty Field of Vision*.

26. Quoted in Hoskyns, *Say It One Time*, 216.

27. Dickinson quoted in Calemine, "Dixie Fried," and Smith, "Johnny Sandlin."

28. Calemine, "Dixie Fried."

29. George Soule, telephone interview by author, March 3, 2011.

30. Ibid.

31. Ibid.

32. Quoted in Rounce, liner notes to *Something New to Do*. See also "Phillip Mitchell Interview, 2001."

33. Bill Williams, "Muscle Shoals Sound: Sort of a Commune," *Billboard*, December 5, 1970, 46.

34. Quote from Rounce, liner notes to *Something New to Do*. Rounce's liner notes, like the compilation they accompany, foreground Mitchell's status as a "cult hero."

35. Osmond, *Life Is Just What You Make It*, 78.

36. Nancy Hamelin, telephone interview by author, June 22, 2010.

37. Osmond, *Life Is Just What You Make It*, 79.

38. Quoted in "JET Readers Defend White Group Called 'Copycats' of the Jackson Five," *Jet*, March 18, 1971, 59.

39. Robert Christgau linked the Osmonds to white singer Georgia Gibbs, who scored several hits with R&B covers in the late 1950s, while Richard Pryor mentioned the Osmonds and the Jacksons as an example of the racial double-standard in American culture. See Christgau, "Review." Pryor's remarks are on his 1971 Laff Records album *Craps (After Hours)*.

40. Bill Lane, "People, Places 'n' Situwayshuns: Jackson 5 Call Osmonds' 'One Bad Apple' a Commendable Form of Flattery," *Los Angeles Sentinel*, February 25, 1971, B3A.

41. Kathy Orloff, "Osmonds Populating the Clean, Wholesome Side of Pop Fence," *Los Angeles Times*, March 5, 1972, O8.

42. Kathy Orloff, "No Star Trip for Teen Idol Michael Jackson," *Los Angeles Times*, August 20, 1972, X14.

43. Booker Griffin, "The Way It Is: Osmond Brothers Exemplifying Rape of Black Music," *Los Angeles Sentinel*, February 25, 1971, A7.

44. Booker Griffin, "The Way It Is: Black Radio, NATRA and Exploitation," *Los Angeles Sentinel*, A7.

45. Osmond, *Life Is Just What You Make It*, 92, 78.

46. "Rick Hall Started the Muscle Shoals Sound," *Florence (Ala.) Times-Daily*, April 29, 1973, B1.

47. Quoted in Pace and Palmer, "Pop Hits Rock the World," *Florence (Ala.) Times-Daily*, August 1, 1999, 12.

48. Quoted in Hoskyns, *Say It One Time*, 197.

49. Quoted in Younger, *Get a Shot of Rhythm and Blues*, 111.

50. Quoted in Hoskyns, *Say It One Time*, 91, 193–94.

51. "Joe Tex Here," *Milwaukee Star-Times*, February 1, 1973, p. 2; Faith C. Christmas, "Help Muslim Hospital," *Chicago Defender*, June 6, 1972, 1; Greg Mims, "Pittsburghers Pledge Support in Black Muslim Hospital Drive," *Pittsburgh Courier*, June 1, 1974, 3.

52. Ward, *Just My Soul Responding*, 401.

53. Clowning quote from "'Clowning for Whites' Ends for Ex–Joe Tex," *Milwaukee Star* (published as *Milwaukee Star-Times*), February 15, 1973, 1. Other quote from Alan Wilson, "Joe Tex Has an Endless Reservoir," *Hendersonville (N.C.) Times-News*, June 6, 1972, 6. The Wilson story was an Associated Press article, and was thus reprinted throughout the country.

54. Several other soul musicians also joined the Nation during this period, including Lee Jones, the singer from the Masqueraders who called white producer Gene Chrisman "massa" at a Memphis session soon after the King assassination.

CHAPTER 5

1. Lyrics from "I'm a White Boy," written by Merle Haggard. The song is rarely mentioned in discussions of Haggard's career or the rise of conservative country. The best discussion is in Cantwell, *Merle Haggard*, 194–98. Barbara Ching briefly mentions the song's racial implications in *Wrong's What I Do Best*, 34. Guralnick mentions it but does not discuss its meaning, though he does call it "the ultimate redneck song (in both good and bad senses)" in an annotated discography. See Guralnick, *Lost Highway*, 244, 349. The song has also been mentioned in some reviews of the 1978 album on which it appeared.

2. Interestingly, Stax soul artist Johnnie Taylor performed at Nixon's 1969 inaugural ball. See Gordon, *Respect Yourself*, 221.

3. "Country Singles Reviews," *Cashbox*, December 27, 1975, 29.

4. "Irma Jackson" has become a favorite counterexample for writers who wish to claim Haggard, or country more generally, as more racially progressive. Journalists Don Cusic, Bill Friskics-Warren, and Nick Tosches all celebrate the song in their texts. The historian Jefferson Cowie, writing about working-class culture in the 1970s, heralds "Irma Jackson" as a counterweight to the reactionary politics of "Okie" and "Fightin' Side." But David Cantwell has recently noted that the song's tragic narrative "strongly implies that [black-white] relationships are bound to fail," making it less progressive than it initially seems. See Cantwell, *Merle Haggard*, 161; Cantwell and Friskics-Warren, *Heartaches by the Number*, 15; Cowie, *Stayin' Alive*, 180; Cusic, *Discovering Country Music*, 98; and Tosches, *Country*, 214–15.

5. Of course, color-blind rhetoric was a crucial part of the era's conservatism. New Right politicians used the rhetoric to simultaneously oppose civil rights interventions and refute charges of white supremacy. See Lassiter, *Silent Majority*, 148–49; and MacLean, *Freedom Is Not Enough*, 225–27.

6. See Malone, *Country Music, U.S.A.*; Malone, *Don't Get above Your Raisin'*; and Peterson, *Creating Country Music*.

7. Pecknold, *Selling Sound*, 218.

8. Hemphill, *Nashville Sound*, 91, 263. He describes "Music Row" as "a battlefield command post for George Wallace."

9. Ibid., 257–58.

10. Ibid., 260.

11. Werner, *Change Is Gonna Come*, 162. Werner also notes the whiteness of country's artist and fan base.

12. Cantwell and Friskics-Warren, *Heartaches by the Number*, 63.

13. See Pecknold, "Making Country Modern."

14. Quoted in Hemphill, *Nashville Sound*, 163.

15. Pride, *Pride*, 254.

16. "They Call Him Country Charley," *Ebony*, March 1967, 61.

17. Ralph H. Metcalfe Jr., "Charley Pride: Sweet Sound of $ucce$$," *Jet*, April 29, 1971, 56.

18. Bill Littleton, "Charley Pride," *International Musician*, October 1973, 6, 21. Littleton also used this tone in an earlier piece on Ray Charles; see Littleton, "Nashville News," *International Musician*, November 1970, 8.

19. Littleton used the phrase "cross-culturation" in multiple *International Musician* columns in 1970 and 1971.

20. Wallace Huff, "Letters: The Scholar's Choice," *Jet*, July 15, 1971, 4.

21. Egerton, *Americanization of Dixie*, 205.

22. Metcalfe, "Charley Pride," 60. Interestingly, Pride believed that this separation was disappearing by the mid-1970s. "It used to be you'd hear rhythm and blues, or soul, or hillbilly," he said in 1973. "Now there's a dissolving factor of acceptance—accepting without letting sort of idiosyncrasy jeopardize the color or style. It's a matter of relating and listening to it objectively." "Charley Pride Sees New Day in Music," *Jet*, December 13, 1973, 97.

23. "They Call Him Country Charley," 62; "Don't Call Charley Pride a Black Country Singer," *Jet*, December 7, 1978, 56.

24. Pride related the "you sound like them" anecdote in multiple places; see "Charley Pride Sees New Day." For "brothers" story, see Pride, *Pride*, 155–56.

25. "Don't Call Charley Pride a Black Country Singer," 56.

26. "Studio Veteran Builds Country Roster as Popularity Increases," *Memphis Commercial Appeal*, September 25, 1974, page unknown, found in Memphis Information File, Memphis and Shelby County Room, Memphis Public Library and Information Center.

27. Lyric from "Black Speck," written by O. B. McClinton.

28. Quoted in Haralambos, *Right On*, 167. Similarly, Memphis-based star Bobby "Blue" Bland said that he decided to sing R&B instead of country when he started his recording career because "it was the wrong time and the wrong place for a black singer to make it singing white country blues." Quoted in Wald, *Escaping the Delta*, 97.

29. For other discussions of the complex racial politics embedded in the covers of country songs by soul artists, see Awkward, "'South's Gonna Do It Again'"; Awkward, *Soul Covers*; and Pecknold, "Travel with Me."

30. Quoted in Grass, "Totally Unrestricted."

31. Quoted in Dave Hoekstra, "Soul Queen Known for Less-Than-Regal Throne," *Chicago Sun-Times*, July 14, 2006.

32. Womack has recounted this story in numerous places. See, for example, Tyler, "Bobby Womack."

33. "Whirling Busily, Shelby Singleton Spreads Gospel of Country Music," *Billboard*, June 23, 1962, 6.

34. "Singleton Pushing Nashville as Int'l Tourist Attraction," *Cashbox*, April 8, 1967, 56.

35. Paul Hemphill quotes Tex Ritter, who worried that the "suggestive" qualities in Riley's record might lead to the recording of more objectionable material in Nashville. See Hemphill, *Nashville Sound*, 149.

36. Ibid., 44–45.

37. "Shelby Singleton: Making Nashville a Multi-market Threat," *Cashbox*, October 19, 1968, CW 72, CW 74.

38. Lyrics from "The School Bus," written by Paul Allen and Ed Pinkett.

39. For information on this controversy in Memphis, see Pohlmann, *Opportunity Lost*, 70–77.

40. See Self, *All in the Family*, 59–64.

41. Lyrics from "The Battle Hymn of Lt. Calley," written by Jim Smith and Julian Wilson.

42. SSS ad, *Cashbox*, April 10, 1971, 23.

43. "Calley Verdict Spurs Disk Interest," *Cashbox*, April 12, 1971, 9.

44. An ROTC chapter in North Carolina even sold the record to raise money. "Use 'Calley' as Fund-Raiser," *Billboard*, May 8, 1971, 38.

45. Earl Paige, "Jukebox Programmers Putting 'Calley' on Request-Only Basis," *Billboard*, April 24, 1971, 36.

46. Quoted in Bob Bates, "Wayne Newton Set to Appear June 5," *Florence (Ala.) Times-Daily*, May 19, 1971, 1.

47. Quoted in Bob Bates, "Calley Balladeer's Life Hectic," *Florence (Ala.) Times-Daily*, April 12, 1971, 5.

48. For an excellent recent discussion of this, see Kramer, *Republic of Rock*.

49. Quoted in ibid., 150.

50. Terry, *Bloods*, 25.

51. Williams made these remarks in a lecture at the University of Wisconsin–Madison on November 8, 2011.

52. See Kramer, *Republic of Rock*, 183; and Van Deburg, *New Day in Babylon*, 101.

53. Quoted in Fred Farrar, "Marine Chief Orders End to Race Barriers: Afro Hair Styles and Black Salutes OK'd," *Chicago Tribune*, September 4, 1969, 16.

54. See, for example, John T. Wheeler, "Black Power Threat Invades Vietnam," *Tuscaloosa (Ala.) News*, April 20, 1969, 5. This Associated Press story appeared throughout the country.

55. A1/C LeRoy Edwards, "Letter to the Editor," *Ebony*, December 1968, 19.

56. Much of my initial knowledge of Swamp Dogg came from Friskics-Warren, "Swamp Dogg."

57. Jerry Williams, telephone interview by author, June 14, 2007.

58. Ibid.

59. Friskics-Warren, "Swamp Dogg," 38.

60. Ibid., 40. A 1966 Atlantic Records demo reel reveals that Williams's previous stabs at politically oriented songwriting were as ambivalent as those of many of his country counterparts. The unreleased song "Whatever Happened to Love?" is simultaneously a plea for social change and a critique of protestors, whom Williams calls "unemployed [and] unimportant clowns." See Jerry Williams, demo session, November 29, 1966, Atlantic Records Audiotapes, Rock and Roll Hall of Fame and Museum Library and Archives, Cleveland, Ohio.

61. "Swamp Dog's [*sic*] 'Stone' 45 Spurs Anti-Drug Drive," *Billboard*, September 9, 1972, 16; Cream Records ad, *Billboard*, September 9, 1972, 17.

62. Jerry Williams, telephone interview by author, June 14, 2007.

63. Ibid.

64. Ibid.

65. David Johnson, interview by author, January 12, 2010, Muscle Shoals.

66. George Soule, telephone interview by author, March 3, 2011.

67. Williams cowrote the song with Gary Anderson, an African American singer who, under the stage name Gary "U.S." Bonds, had several R&B and pop hits in the early 1960s.

68. Jerry Williams, telephone interview by author, June 14, 2007. This story is strikingly similar to an incident involving Ted Jarrett, one of Nashville's most prominent and successful black musicians. In 1963 Jarrett was honored by BMI for his "Love, Love, Love," a hit for country singer Webb Pierce. When Jarrett arrived at the awards banquet in Nashville, he was initially prevented from entering by a white police officer. "When he saw me, a black man, at this 'white' affair, and recognized me from that dive on Cedar Street, he reasoned that I was trying to crash the party since I couldn't have any good reason for being there. . . . I tried to tell him I was there to accept an award," Jarrett recalled in his autobiography, "but he just couldn't conceive that any black man

he had seen in low places could be the same man to win a national award in country music." See Jarrett, *You Can Make It if You Try*, 65–66.

69. Jerry Williams, telephone interview by author, June 14, 2007.

70. *Rolling Stone*'s John Grissim and Jerry Hopkins each cited South's work with Dylan as a pivotal moment in the national perception of "Music City's" musical possibilities. John Grissim, "The Nashville Cats," *Rolling Stone*, December 9, 1971, 30; Jerry Hopkins, "Joe South: 'Country Music Is Shit,'" *Rolling Stone*, June 14, 1969, 8.

71. Later in his Capitol tenure, his productions were supervised by Sidney Miller, a friend who became an A&R producer after the FAME project ended in 1972.

72. Friskics-Warren, "Swamp Dogg," 43.

73. Capitol Records ad, *Billboard*, December 27, 1969, back cover.

CHAPTER 6

1. "Front Cover," *Cashbox*, March 14, 1970, 7.

2. Lyric from "The South's Gonna Do It Again," written by Charlie Daniels.

3. Country singer Tanya Tucker adopted a similar rhetoric in her recording of "I Believe the South Is Gonna Rise Again." While Tucker did not mention musicians in the manner of Daniels or Williams, she did propose that the post–Civil Rights South would transcend racial divisions. On the politics and economics of the New South from the 1940s to the 1970s, see Carter, *Politics of Rage*; Frederickson, *Dixiecrat Revolt*; and Perlstein, *Nixonland*.

4. Jerry Hopkins, "Joe South: 'Country Music Is Shit,'" *Rolling Stone*, June 14, 1969.

5. Gaillard, *Watermelon Wine*; Reid, *Improbable Rise of Redneck Rock*.

6. Kemp, *Dixie Lullaby*, xii; See also Cobb, "From Muskogee to Luckenbach." Oddly, Jason Sokol's *There Goes My Everything* takes its title from a country song, but Sokol does not discuss country—or any popular music—at all.

7. Another recent example is the 2012 BBC documentary *Sweet Home Alabama*.

8. I reached this conclusion after helpful discussions with David Cantwell, Barry Mazor, and Phoebe Strom. For further discussion of country's long and complicated relationship with Confederate imagery and iconography, see Strom, "Defining Dixie."

9. Jon Landau, "Soul Men," *Rolling Stone*, January 20, 1968, 18.

10. Gillett, *Sound of the City*, 261-262.

11. For information on Carter, see Cobb, *Away down South*, 84–85.

12. Eliot Tiegel, "B.B.'s Travels Bridge the Past with the Present," *Billboard*, January 29, 1972, 49.

13. Wexler, *Rhythm and the Blues*, 252.

14. Sam Sutherland, "Studio Track," *Billboard*, April 14, 1973, 18.

15. Don Nix, interview by David Less, December 9, 1999, Nashville, RSVHPC, series 4, box 6, 88.

16. Quoted in Reid, *Improbable Rise of Redneck Rock*, 231.

17. Lyric from "Willie and Laura Mae Jones," written by Tony Joe White.

18. Merle Haggard sounded a similar note of musical fetishization in his "White Man Singing the Blues," where he is happy to learn that a black bluesman considers him a "soul brother." See Cantwell, *Merle Haggard*, 196.

19. For a valuable recent history of Outlaw, see Streissguth, *Outlaw*.

20. For the best treatments of the Austin country scene, see Reid, *Improbable Rise of Redneck Rock*; and Stimeling, *Cosmic Cowboys and New Hicks*.

21. Perhaps the most famous was Nelson's massive 1980 hit "Always on My Mind," written by Memphis's Mark James and previously recorded by Elvis Presley.

22. One of the group's most prominent Nashville sessions was on Dobie Gray's country-soul hit "Drift Away," as well as other sessions by the black singer.

23. Alexander's singles, like those of Joe Simon, were released on Monument's R&B subsidiary, which was overseen by WLAC's John "John R." Richbourg. Despite Richbourg's track record, Alexander's recordings were produced by Monument's president, Fred Foster. Foster may have paid such close attention because of his expressed interest in making Alexander the centerpiece of Monument's black catalog. See Younger, *Get a Shot of Rhythm and Blues*, 108.

24. Kristofferson told journalist Peter Cooper that his record company once forced him to change a lyric to avoid racial controversy. "I wrote . . . 'If that's against the law, tell me why I never saw a man locked in that jail of yours that wasn't either black or poor as me.' They wouldn't let me say 'black.' I changed it to 'low-down poor.'" Quoted in Streissguth, *Outlaw*, 47.

25. Quoted in Younger, *Get a Shot of Rhythm and Blues*, 126.

26. Ibid.

27. Robert Hilburn, "Iconoclast of the Nashville Sound," *Los Angeles Times*, November 2, 1974, A5.

28. Al Reinert, "King of Country," *New York Times*, March 26, 1978, SM6.

29. Ibid.

30. Reid, *Improbable Rise of Redneck Rock*, 220.

31. Reinert, "King of Country."

32. Stimeling, *Cosmic Cowboys and New Hicks*, 26.

33. Jaimoe Johnson, one of the Allman Brothers' two drummers (with Butch Trucks), is the only African American who was regularly discussed as part of any of the new southern scenes. Though Johnson's involvement in the ensemble is crucial, press discussions of the group mostly centered on white group leaders Duane and Gregg Allman, as well as white guitarist/singer Dickey Betts.

34. "Sweet Home Alabama" is also the song in which Skynyrd gives a shout-out to the Muscle Shoals Rhythm Section, nicknamed "The Swampers."

35. Carlos Greer, "Confessions of a Backup Singer," *People*, June 24, 2013, 34. The documentary *Twenty Feet from Stardom* places Clayton's career—and lack of solo success—directly in the context of the white-centered rock scene of the 1970s.

36. This story is repeated throughout the literature, often quoting work by music journalists Robert Christgau and Dave Marsh. For a recent example, see Cowie, *Stayin' Alive*, 175.

37. In 2012 Skynyrd guitarist Gary Rossington—the last original member of the group—said that they would soon abandon the flag because of its hateful connotations. A day later, after an outcry from fans, the band backed off and said that they would continue to use the stars-and-bars in their shows because it represented "heritage, not hate." See Gupta, "Lynyrd Skynyrd Won't Abandon the Confederate Flag."

38. Quoted in Kemp, *Dixie Lullaby*, 13.

39. Egerton, *Americanization of Dixie*, 202, 208.

40. See Gregory, "Southernizing the American Working Class."

41. It is worth nothing that producers and session leaders in both Memphis and Muscle Shoals were famous for fudging the details on particular sessions in order to avoid overtime payments. See, for example, Atlantic Records document, May 24, 1966, and Phonograph Recording Contract between Atlantic Records and AFM, May 11, 1966, both in SOP, box 1, folder 1.

42. Quoted in Hopkins, "Joe South."

43. In a somewhat fitting irony, ZZ Top recorded many of its most popular recordings in Memphis, at Ardent Studios.

44. Wayne King, "Rock Goes Back South to Where It All Began," *New York Times*, June 20, 1976, 49.

45. See, for example, "Capricorn Records: Shakin' Macon and Making the World Take Notice," *Cashbox*, August 17, 1974, 27.

46. Capricorn ad, *Cashbox*, July 30, 1977, 5.

47. Quoted in Hoskyns, *Say It One Time*, 197.

CHAPTER 7

1. Killen, *By the Seat of My Pants*, 248.

2. Bob Campbell, "Disco-Country Record Was a Natural Says Bill Anderson," *Cashbox*, July 1, 1978, 47. See also Roman Kozak, "Country Talent Linking Up with Rockers on Bookings," *Billboard*, September 23, 1978, 1.

3. Killen, *By the Seat of My Pants*, 247–48.

4. Ibid., 248.

5. The best appraisal of contemporary southern soul is Whiteis, *Southern Soul-Blues*.

6. For histories of disco, see Echols, *Hot Stuff*; and Shapiro, *Turn the Beat Around*.

7. Quoted in Echols, *Hot Stuff*, xxv. Echols's text does not clearly state where this quote came from.

8. This metaphor structures Echols's entire analysis in *Hot Stuff*, but she articulates it most clearly—and mentions the Jackson campaign specifically—on xxiv–xxv.

9. Davis, *Southscapes*, 29. Davis astutely observes this trend in both popular and scholarly understandings. For example, she notes that "those who study the roots of blues and jazz work in black musicology, while those who study the roots of country and bluegrass work in southern musicology."

10. See Frey, "New Great Migration"; and Gregory, *Southern Diaspora*, 321–28.

11. See Minchin and Salmond, *After the Dream*; and Sokol, *There Goes My Everything*.

12. Davis, *Southscapes*, 28.

13. Dick Fricker, "3 Tulsa Stations Vie for Country Listeners," *Billboard*, February 19, 1972, 18; Mary Campbell, "The 'Sophisti-country' Sound," *Baltimore Sun*, April 3, 1967, B4.

14. Younger, *Get a Shot of Rhythm and Blues*, 30–31.

15. Barry Mazor, "Billy Sherrill: Icon and Iconoclast," *Wall Street Journal*, November 9, 2010.

16. Daniel, *Lost Revolutions*, 33.

17. Charlie Rich, interview by Pete Daniel, David Less, and Charles McGovern, August 12, 1992, Memphis, RSVHPC, series 4, box 8, 2–3, 9–10. See also Guralnick, *Feel Like Goin' Home*, 205–7.

18. Bill Williams, "Rosenberg: 'There Was Never Any Question about What the Man's Capabilities Were,'" *Billboard*, September 14, 1974, CR2.

19. "White Ray Charles" from ibid.

20. Quoted in Nat Hentoff, "The Silver Fox Is Off and Running at the Big A," *New York Magazine*, May 27, 1974, 101–3.

21. Ibid. Hentoff's article presents Rich's success as a triumph for this open-minded thinking, and he suggests that Rich represents a loosening of previously rigid cultural values among the country audience.

22. "Opry Hears Soul," *Deseret (Utah) News*, September 10, 1979, A3.

23. "Barbara Mandrell New Country Sweetheart," *Ocala (Fla.) Star-Banner* (AP), August 26, 1979, 14B.

24. "Country Music: '74 to Continue Boom in Crossovers," *Cashbox*, January 26, 1974, 3.

25. Malone, *Country Music, U.S.A.*, 267.

26. Egerton, *Americanization of Dixie*, 207.

27. See Jackson, *House on Fire*.

28. "Billboard's Top Album Picks," *Billboard*, July 14, 1979, 88.

29. Echols, *Hot Stuff*, 23–25, 82, 87.

30. Hoskyns, *Say It One Time*, 208, 217. This moment possesses striking similarities to the rise of folklore and song collecting in the early twentieth century. As Marybeth Hamilton notes, early folklorists believed that the older black songs they collected in the South were a truer representation of both musical integrity and cultural virtue than the new, "canned music" that newly urbanized blacks were making in the North. "In the modern world," Hamilton writes, "[the folklorists] believed, genuine black melodies were fast disappearing, as those 'loved black faces' [of the South] gave way to anonymous new ones who . . . had fully succumbed to the lure of what [they] could only regard as 'canned music.'" See Hamilton, *In Search of the Blues*, 69.

31. Hirshey, *Nowhere to Run*, xv; George, *Death of Rhythm and Blues*, xii–xv.

32. In *Hot Stuff*, Alice Echols briefly mentions some southern-based artists, but she never challenges the idea that disco represented a fundamental shift away from the classic southern sound. See also Werner, *Change Is Gonna Come*.

33. Sylvia's "Drifter" hit number one on the country charts in 1982, while the Bellamy Brothers' "Let Your Love Flow" hit number one on the pop listings.

34. For more on Parton, see Wilson, "Mountains of Contradictions."

35. Blair Sabol, "A Yankee Pilgrim in the Old South," *New York Times*, April 24, 1977, SM10.

36. See Cantwell, *Merle Haggard*, 109.

37. Randy Lewis and Jeff Crossan, "Homogenized Music Leads Retail to Greater Sales; Radio Views It as a Mixed Blessing," *Cashbox*, December 30, 1978, C5.

38. Robert Roth, "N.Y. Club 54 a 'Farm' for Dolly Parton," *Billboard*, September 9, 1978, 43.

39. It helped that the film was directly inspired by the activities of the National Association of Working Women, which was also known as 9to5.

40. Steptoe, "Ode to Country Music." See also Malone, *Don't Get above Your Raisin'*, 168–69; and Millard, "Urban Cowboy," 561.

41. The phenomenon also convinced soul musician Millie Jackson that the country audience would be more accepting of her *Just a Lil' Bit Country* album. "I had to get the OK from my record company," she told a reporter, "but 'Urban Cowboy' was so big there was no flack." See "Millie Jackson Cuts Country Music Album," *Spartanburg (S.C.) Herald Journal*, October 30, 1981, D2.

42. Mark Hunter, "Hitching Discs to Flicks," *Mother Jones*, May 1981, 56.

43. Anthony Haden-Guest, "Jewel of a Nile," *New York Magazine*, February 24, 1986, 46–50, 48.

44. His best example of this is Chuck Wagon & the Wheels' album *Disco Sucks*, which—while certainly blunt—was not a commercial hit, making it an unsatisfying choice for Shapiro's larger argument. For an engaging, if incomplete, history of this recording, see the singer/songwriter's account: Maultsby, "Story of Disco Sucks."

45. Shapiro, *Turn the Beat Around*, 239–40. To be fair, Shapiro does astutely note that Southern rock star Charlie Daniels's 1979 hit "The Devil Went Down to Georgia"—pitting a heroic white southerner against the Devil in a fiddling contest—gives Satan's solo a dance arrangement, making disco literally the "Devil's music." Shapiro also notes that 1970s country represented the South's changing socioeconomics, and he contrasts disco's futurism with country's traditionalism, but he makes little effort to contextualize disco within either country or its larger contexts. Alice Echols barely discusses country in *Hot Stuff*, though she notes Parton as an important example of both country's and disco's sexual politics.

46. "Changing with the Times," *Cashbox*, November 4, 1978, 3.

47. George Soule, telephone interview by author, March 3, 2011.

48. Malaco has been discussed in nearly every work on southern soul, but by far the best source for information on the label is Bowman, "Malaco Records."

49. Hoskyns, *Say It One Time*, 162.

50. Bowman, "Malaco Records," 4.

51. George Soule, telephone interview by author, March 3, 2011.

52. Quoted in Bowman, "Malaco Records," 56.

53. "New Companies," *Billboard*, February 3, 1979, 65.

54. Dahl, "Z. Z. Hill."

55. Lyrics from "Old Time Rock and Roll," written by George Jackson and Thomas Jones.

56. Lyrics from "Down Home Blues," written by George Jackson.

57. Bowman, "Malaco Records," 55.

58. Ibid.

59. Minutaglio, *In Search of the Blues*, 118; Govenar, *Meeting the Blues*, 184. Also, Stephen A. King—in his compelling recent study of blues tourism in the Mississippi Delta—names Malaco as one of the key factors in promoting a broader appreciation (and exploitation) of blues culture in the region. See King, *I'm Feeling the Blue*.

60. Whiteis, *Southern Soul-Blues*, 1.

61. George, *Death of Rhythm and Blues*, 196–97.

62. This became particularly complicated in the way some black nationalists discussed the blues, which they understood as a root for soul music but also derided as "slave music." The most prominent example is Karenga, "Black Art." Of course, Maulana Karenga's dismissal of the blues by no means represented the consensus (or even majority) opinion among Black Power advocates. Most prominently, Leroi Jones's *Blues People* posited blues as the political root of African American expression. For more on this debate, see King, *I'm Feeling the Blues*, 49–51.

63. See Grossman, *Land of Hope*.

64. Numerous national press outlets covered this phenomenon in detail during the 1980s and 1990s. For perhaps the most detailed discussion, see Kevin Chappell, "The New Great Migration to the South," *Ebony*, September 1998, 58. Thadious Davis goes even further, arguing that the reverse migration is "also a claim to a culture and to a region that, though fraught with difficulty and the memory of pain, provides a major grounding for identity. . . . The return to the South is, as well, a form of subversion—a preconscious political activity or a subconscious counteraction to the racially and culturally homogeneous construction of the 'Sunbelt' as a way of occluding black presence in the South." See Davis, *Southscapes*, 35. Sociologist Zandria F. Robinson has recently framed a fascinating discussion of the effects of the "reverse Great Migration" and the larger contours of contemporary black life in what she terms the "post-soul South," around the experiences of African Americans in Memphis. See Robinson, *This Ain't Chicago*.

65. "Letters: Migrating South," *Ebony*, November 1998, 14.

66. Woods, *Development Arrested*, 212.

67. See Whiteis, *Southern Soul-Blues*, 23–25, 120.

68. See Younger, *Get a Shot of Rhythm and Blues*, 170–85.

CODA

1. Beyond the previously cited books and documentaries, two Memphis-based works are worth mentioning: the musical *Memphis* (2003), which posits the interracial friendship (and ultimately romance) between a white deejay and a black singer as a symbol of the breakdown of segregation, and the film *Hustle and Flow* (2005), which centers on the partnership between an African American rapper and a white producer.

2. For example, exhibits at the Country Music Hall of Fame, the Memphis Rock 'n' Soul Museum, and the Stax Museum of American Soul Music all centralize interracial collaborations in their presentations, and each of them presents a simplified version of the stories they present as images of integration's successes.

3. Perhaps the most notable examples are the numerous compilations of African American singers performing country music, which are explicitly framed as a demonstration of the South's musical blends. See the Ace compilations *Behind Closed Doors* (2012) and *Sweet Dreams* (2013) and the Trikont compilations *Dirty Laundry* (2007) and *More Dirty Laundry* (2009).

4. This notion has been central to the curriculum and promotion of the Stax Music Academy and the Soulsville Charter School in Memphis, both of which—it should be noted—have a predominantly black student body.

5. Bush shared a stage with B. B. King, Sam Moore, and other blues and soul stars in 1989, at the urging of strategist Lee Atwater, an enthusiastic fan of black music who also explicitly used white-supremacist stereotypes as part of his work for Bush and others. In 2008 Barack Obama's use of a song by conservative country stars Brooks & Dunn inspired a wave of reportage and commentary, as did the appearance of Nashville heavyweights Garth Brooks and Sugarland at his inaugural celebration. Obama has also hosted an event honoring country music at the White House. See, for example, Willman, "'Only in America.'"

6. Richie's success is part of a larger wellspring of African American country artists that is most obviously embodied by Darius Rucker, who has become the first legitimate black country superstar since Charley Pride. See Wiltz, "Yee Haw!."

7. Quoted in Sullivan, "White House Rocks to Sounds of Memphis."

8. In 2006 I wrote a series of articles on Muscle Shoals for Soul-Sides.com that followed this pattern. See Hughes, "Muscle Shoals Sound."

9. DeMott, *Trouble with Friendship*. I first became aware of DeMott's work in Werner, *Change Is Gonna Come*, 271–72.

10. Rufus Thomas, interview by Pete Daniel, David Less, and Charles McGovern, August 5, 1992, Memphis, RSVHPC, series 4, box 9, 14.

Bibliography

MANUSCRIPT SOURCES

Bloomington, Ind.
    Archives of African American Music and Culture, Indiana University
        Portia K. Maultsby Collection, SC 18
Chapel Hill, N.C.
    Southern Folklife Collection
        Jerry Wexler Collection
Cleveland, Ohio
    Rock and Roll Hall of Fame and Museum Library and Archives
        Atlantic Records Audiotapes
        Spooner Oldham Papers
        Ray Topping Papers
        Jerry Wexler Papers
Memphis, Tenn.
    Memphis Public Library and Information Center
        Memphis Information File
    Rhodes College
        Crossroads to Freedom Digital Archive
    University of Memphis Libraries, Preservation and Special Collections
        Memphis Press-Scimitar Collection
Washington, D.C.
    National Museum of American History, Archives Center, Smithsonian Institution
        Jonas Bernholm Rhythm & Blues Collection
        Memphis Rock 'n' Soul Exhibit Archives
        Rock 'n' Soul Video History Project Collection

INTERVIEWS

All interview transcripts are in possession of the author.

Arthur Alexander, interview by Richard Younger, 1993, location unknown
David Briggs, interviews by Richard Younger, 1996–98, location unknown
Jim Dickinson, interview by author, August 8, 2003, Memphis, Tenn.
Rick Hall, interview by Richard Younger, 1997, location unknown
Nancy Hamelin, telephone interview by author, June 22, 2010
David Johnson, interview by author, January 12, 2010, Muscle Shoals, Ala.
Spooner Oldham, telephone interview by author, January 10, 2006
Dan Penn, telephone interview by author, December 2, 2005

Dan Penn, interviews by Richard Younger, 1994–99, location unknown
Forrest Riley, interview by Richard Younger, date unknown, location unknown
George Soule, telephone interview by author, March 3, 2011
Logan Westbrooks, telephone interview by author, March 7, 2011
Jerry Williams, telephone interview by author, June 14, 2007
Bobby Wood, telephone interview by author, June 23, 2010

NEWSPAPERS AND PERIODICALS

Baltimore Sun
Billboard
Cashbox
Chicago Defender
Chicago Sun-Times
Chicago Tribune
Coronet
Cosmopolitan
Deseret (Utah) News
Details
Ebony
Entertainment Weekly
Florence (Ala.) Times
Florence (Ala.) Times-Daily
Goldmine
Hendersonville (N.C.) Times-News
International Musician
Jet
Kansas Magazine
Los Angeles Sentinel
Los Angeles Times
Memphis Commercial Appeal
Memphis Press-Scimitar
Milwaukee Star-Times
Mother Jones
New York Amsterdam News
New York Magazine
New York Times
Ocala (Fla.) Star-Banner
People
Pittsburgh Courier
Rolling Stone
Spartanburg (S.C.) Herald-Journal
Time
Tuscaloosa (Ala.) News
Variety
Wall Street Journal

BOOKS, ARTICLES, AND DISSERTATIONS

Altschuler, Glenn C. *All Shook Up: How Rock 'n' Roll Changed America*. Pivotal Moments in American History. New York: Oxford University Press, 2004.
Awkward, Michael. *Soul Covers: Rhythm and Blues Remakes and the Struggle for Artistic Identity*. Refiguring American Music. Durham, N.C.: Duke University Press, 2007.
———. "'The South's Gonna Do It Again': Changing Conceptions of the Use of 'Country' Music in the Albums of Al Green." In *Hidden in the Mix: The African-American Presence in Country Music*, edited by Diane Pecknold, 191–203. Durham, N.C.: Duke University Press, 2013.
Baraka, Amiri. *Black Music*. Rpt. New York: Akashi Classics, 2010.
——— (as Leroi Jones). *Blues People: Negro Music in White America*. Rpt. New York: Harper Perennial, 1999.
Barlow, William. *Voice Over: The Making of Black Radio*. Philadelphia: Temple University Press, 1998.

Bertrand, Michael. *Race, Rock, and Elvis*. Music in American Life. Urbana: University of Illinois Press, 2000.

Birnbaum, Larry. *Before Elvis: The Prehistory of Rock 'n' Roll*. Lanham, Md.: Scarecrow, 2013.

Bolster, W. Jeffrey. *Black Jacks: African American Seaman in the Age of Sail*. Cambridge, Mass.: Harvard University Press, 1998.

Bowman, Rob. "Malaco Records: The Last Soul Company." Liner notes to Various Artists, *The Last Soul Company*. Malaco Records, 1999.

———. *Soulsville, U.S.A.: The Story of Stax Records*. New York: Schirmer, 1997.

Boyle, Kevin. "The Kiss: Racial and Gender Conflict in a 1950s Automobile Factory." *Journal of American History* 84, no. 2 (September 1997): 496–523.

Brooks, Daphne. *Bodies in Dissent: Spectacular Performances of Race and Freedom, 1850–1910*. Durham, N.C.: Duke University Press, 2006.

Brooks, Tim. *Lost Sounds: Blacks and the Birth of the Recording Industry, 1890–1919*. Music in American Life. Urbana: University of Illinois Press, 2005.

Broven, John. *Record Makers and Breakers: Voices of the Independent Rock 'n' Roll Pioneers*. Music in American Life. Urbana: University of Illinois Press, 2009.

Brown, D. Clayton. *Electricity for Rural America: The Fight for the REA*. Westport, Conn.: Greenwood, 1980.

Calemine, James. "Dixie Fried with the High Priest of Memphis Mojo," n.d., http://swampland.com/articles/view/title:dixie_fried_with_the_high_priest_of_memphis_mojo_jim_dickinson.

Callahan, Mike, and David Edwards. "Randy Wood: The Dot Records Story," n.d., http://www.bsnpubs.com/dot/dotstory.html.

Cantor, Louis. *Dewey and Elvis: The Life and Times of a Rock 'n' Roll Deejay*. Music in American Life. Urbana: University of Illinois Press, 2005.

———. *Wheelin' on Beale: How WDIA-Memphis Became the Nation's First All-Black Radio Station and Created the Sound That Changed America*. New York: Pharos, 1992.

Cantwell, David. *Merle Haggard: The Running Kind*. American Music Series. Austin: University of Texas Press, 2013.

Cantwell, David, and Bill Friskics-Warren. *Heartaches by the Number: Country Music's 500 Greatest Singles*. Nashville: Vanderbilt University Press/Country Music Foundation Press, 2003.

Carter, Dan T. *The Politics of Rage: George Wallace, the Origins of the New Conservatism, and the Transformation of American Politics*. Baton Rouge: Louisiana State University Press, 1995.

Cashmore, Ellis. *The Black Culture Industry*. London: Routledge, 1997.

Chin, Frank, Jeffrey Paul Chan, Lawson Fusao Inada, and Shawn Wong. "An Introduction to Chinese- and Japanese-American Literature." In *Aiiieeeee! An Anthology of Asian-American Writers*, edited by Frank Chin, Jeffrey Paul Chan, Lawson Fusao Inada, and Shawn Wong, 37–56. Washington, D.C.: Howard University Press, 1974.

Ching, Barbara. *Wrong's What I Do Best: Hard Country Music and Contemporary Culture*. Pivotal Moments in American History. New York: Oxford University Press, 2001.

Christgau, Robert. "Review: The Osmonds," 1971, http://www.robertchristgau.com/get_artist.php?id=3454&name=The+Osmonds.

Cobb, James C. *Away down South: A History of Southern Identity*. New York: Oxford University Press, 2007.

———. "From Muskogee to Luckenbach." In *Redefining Southern Culture: Mind and Identity in the Modern South*, edited by James C. Cobb, 78–92. Athens: University of Georgia Press, 1999.

Cowie, Jefferson. *Stayin' Alive: The 1970s and the Last Days of the Working Class*. New York: New Press, 2010.

Craig, Steve. *Out of the Dark: A History of Radio and Rural America*. Tuscaloosa: University of Alabama Press, 2009.

Cusic, Don. *Discovering Country Music*. New York: Praeger, 2008.

Dahl, Bill. "Z. Z. Hill," n.d., http://www.allmusic.com/artist/p366/biography.

Daniel, Pete. *Lost Revolutions: The South in the 1950s*. Chapel Hill: University of North Carolina Press, 2000.

Dannen, Fredric. *Hit Men: Power Brokers and Fast Money inside the Music Business*. New York: Vintage, 1991.

Davis, Thadious M. *Southscapes: Geographies of Race, Region, and Literature*. Chapel Hill: University of North Carolina Press, 2011.

Deloria, Philip. *Playing Indian*. Yale Historical Publications Series. New Haven, Conn.: Yale University Press, 1999.

DeMott, Benjamin. *The Trouble with Friendship: Why Americans Can't Think Straight about Race*. New York: Atlantic Monthly Press, 1996.

Dickerson, James. *Mojo Triangle: Birthplace of Country, Blues, Jazz and Rock 'n' Roll*. Rev. ed. New York: Schirmer Trade, 2005.

Dobkin, Matt. *I Never Loved a Man the Way I Love You: Aretha Franklin, Respect and the Making of a Soul Music Masterpiece*. New York: St. Martin's, 2004.

Dowdy, G. Wayne. *A Brief History of Memphis*. Charleston, S.C.: History, 2011.

Du Bois, W. E. B. *The Souls of Black Folk*. Rpt. Boston: Bedford, 1997.

Echols, Alice. *Hot Stuff: Disco and the Remaking of American Culture*. New York: W. W. Norton, 2010.

———. "Little Girl Blue." In *The Popular Music Studies Reader*, edited by Andy Bennett, Barry Shank, and Jason Toynbee, 57–63. Abingdon, UK: Routledge, 2006.

Egerton, John. *The Americanization of Dixie: The Southernization of America*. New York: Harper's Magazine Press, 1974.

Escott, Colin. *Good Rockin' Tonight: Sun Records and the Birth of Rock 'n' Roll*. New York: St. Martin's, 1992.

Feldstein, Ruth. "'I Don't Trust You Anymore': Nina Simone, Culture, and Black Activism in the 1960s." *Journal of American History* 91, no. 4 (March 2005): 1349–79.

Feretti, Fred. "The White Captivity of Black Radio." In *Our Troubled Press: Ten Years of the Columbia Journalism Review*, edited by Alfred Balk and James Boylan,

87–95. Boston: Little, Brown, 1971. (Originally published in *Columbia Journalism Review*, Summer 1970.)

Filene, Benjamin. *Romancing the Folk: Public Memory and American Roots Music.* Chapel Hill: University of North Carolina Press, 2000.

Floyd, John. *Sun Records: An Oral History.* Edited by Dave Marsh. For the Record Series. New York: Avon, 1998.

Foster, Pamela E. *My Country: The African Diaspora's Country Music Heritage.* Nashville: Pamela E. Foster, 1998.

Fox, Aaron. *Real Country: Music and Language in Working-Class Culture.* Durham, N.C.: Duke University Press, 2004.

Fox, Jon Hartley. *King of the Queen City: The Story of King Records.* Music in American Life. Urbana: University of Illinois Press, 2009.

Frederickson, Kari. *The Dixiecrat Revolt and the End of the Solid South, 1932–1968.* Chapel Hill: University of North Carolina Press, 2000.

Frey, William H. "The New Great Migration: Black Americans' Return to the South, 1965–2000." In *Redefining Urban and Suburban America: Evidence from Census 2000*, vol. 2, edited by Allan Berube, Bruce Lang, and Robert E. Lang, 53–110. Washington, D.C.: Brookings Institution Press, 2005.

Friskics-Warren, Bill. "Swamp Dogg: Up from the Dirty South." *Oxford American*, no. 45 (Spring 2003): 38–43.

Frith, Simon. "The Academic Elvis." In *Dixie Debates: Perspectives on Southern Cultures*, edited by Richard H. King and Helen Taylor, 99–115. New York: NYU Press, 1996.

Fuqua, C. S. *Music Fell on Alabama.* Montgomery, Ala.: New South, 2008.

Gaillard, Frye. *Watermelon Wine: The Spirit of Country Music.* New York: St. Martin's, 1978.

Garland, Phyl. *The Sound of Soul.* New York: Regenery, 1969.

Garnett, Bernard E. "How 'Soulful' Is Soul Radio?" Nashville: Race Relations Information Center, 1970.

George, Nelson. *The Death of Rhythm and Blues.* New York: Pantheon, 1988.

George-Warren, Holly. "Mystery Girl: The Forgotten Artistry of Bobbie Gentry." In *Listen Again: A Momentary History of Pop Music*, edited by Eric Weisbard, 120–36. Durham, N.C.: Duke University Press, 2007.

Gilbert, David. *The Product of Our Souls: Ragtime, Race, and the Birth of the Manhattan Musical Marketplace.* Chapel Hill: University of North Carolina Press, 2015.

Gillett, Charlie. *The Sound of the City: The Rise of Rock 'n' Roll.* 1st Laurel ed. New York: Dell, 1972.

Gordon, Robert. *It Came from Memphis.* New York: Faber and Faber, 1995.

———. *Respect Yourself: Stax Records and the Soul Explosion.* New York: Bloomsbury, 2013.

Govenar, Alan B. *Meeting the Blues.* New York: Da Capo, 1985.

Grass, Randall. "Totally Unrestricted." Liner notes to Millie Jackson, *Totally Unrestricted! The Millie Jackson Anthology.* Rhino Records, 1997.

Green, Laurie B. *Battling the Plantation Mentality: Memphis and the Black Freedom Struggle.* John Hope Franklin Series in African American History and Culture. Chapel Hill: University of North Carolina Press, 2007.

Gregory, James. *The Southern Diaspora: How the Great Migrations of Black and White Southerners Transformed America*. Chapel Hill: University of North Carolina Press, 2005.

———. "Southernizing the American Working Class: Post-war Episodes of Regional and Class Transformation." *Labor History* 39, no. 2 (1988): 135–54.

Grossman, James. *Land of Hope: Chicago, Black Southerners and the Great Migration*. Chicago: University of Chicago Press, 1991.

Gupta, Prachi. "Lynyrd Skynyrd Won't Abandon the Confederate Flag," September 23, 2012, http://www.salon.com/2012/09/23/lynyrd_skynyrd_wont_abandon_the_confederate_flag/.

Guralnick, Peter. *Careless Love: The Unmaking of Elvis Presley*. New York: Back Bay, 1999.

———. *Feel Like Goin' Home: Portraits in Blues and Rock 'n' Roll*. New York: Vintage, 1971.

———. *Lost Highway: Journeys and Arrivals of American Musicians*. 2nd ed. New York: Back Bay, 1999.

———. *Sweet Soul Music: Rhythm & Blues and the Southern Dream of Freedom*. Boston: Back Bay, 1986.

Hall, Jacqueline Dowd. "The Long Civil Rights Movement and the Political Uses of the Past." *Journal of American History* 91 (March 2005): 1233–63.

Hamilton, Marybeth. *In Search of the Blues*. New York: Basic Books, 1998.

Haralambos, Michael. *Right On: From Blues to Soul in Black America*. New York: Drake, 1975.

———. *Soul Music*. New York: Da Capo, 1995.

Havighurst, Craig. *Air Castle of the South: WSM and the Making of Music City*. Music in American Life. Urbana: University of Illinois Press, 2007.

Hemphill, Paul. *The Nashville Sound*. New York: Simon & Schuster, 1970.

Hill, Laura Warren, and Julie Rabig, eds. *The Business of Black Power: Community Development, Capitalism and Corporate Responsibility in Postwar America*. Rochester, N.Y.: University of Rochester Press, 2012.

Hirshey, Gerri. *Nowhere to Run: The Story of Soul Music*. New York: Times Books, 1984.

Hoskyns, Barney. *Say It One Time for the Broken-Hearted: Country Soul in the American South*. New York: Harper-Collins, 1987.

Houston, Benjamin. *The Nashville Way: Racial Etiquette and the Struggle for Social Justice in a Southern City*. Politics and Culture in the Twentieth-Century South. Athens: University of Georgia Press, 2012.

Huber, Patrick. "Black Hillbillies: African-American Musicians on Old-Time Records, 1924–1932." In *Hidden in the Mix: The African-American Presence in Country Music*, edited by Diane Pecknold, 19–81. Durham, N.C.: Duke University Press, 2013.

Hughes, Charles L. "The Muscle Shoals Sound, Parts 1, 2 and 3," January 2006, http://www.soul-sides.com.

———. "'You're My Soul Song': How Southern Soul Changed Country Music." In *Hidden in the Mix: The African-American Presence in Country Music*, edited by Diane Pecknold, 283–305. Durham, N.C.: Duke University Press, 2013.

"Interview with Jerry Wexler [Part 3 of 4]," WGBH Open Vault, http://openvault
.wgbh.org/catalog/8f646d-interview-with-jerry-wexler-part-3-of-4.

Jackson, John. *A House on Fire: The Rise and Fall of Philadelphia Soul.* New York:
Oxford University Press, 2004.

James, Tommy. *Me, the Mob and the Music: One Helluva Ride with Tommy James &
the Shondells.* New York: Scribner, 2010.

Jarrett, Ted. *You Can Make It if You Try: The Ted Jarrett Story of R&B in Nashville.*
New York: Hillsboro, 2005.

Jeffries, Hasan Kwame. *Bloody Lowndes: Civil Rights and Black Power in Alabama's
Black Belt.* New York: NYU Press, 2010.

Jenson, Joli. *The Nashville Sound: Authenticity, Commercialization and Country
Music.* Nashville: Country Music Foundation Press, 1998.

Jones, Roben. *Memphis Boys: The Story of American Studios.* American Made Music
Series. Oxford: University Press of Mississippi, 2010.

Joseph, Peniel. *Waiting 'til the Midnight Hour: A Narrative History of Black Power in
America.* New York: Henry Holt, 2006.

Karenga, Maulana (Ron). "Black Art: Mute Matter Given Force and Function." In *The
Norton Anthology of African American Literature*, edited by Henry Louis Gates
and Nellie Y. McKay, 1972–77. New York: W. W. Norton, 1997.

Katz, David. *Solid Foundation: An Oral History of Reggae.* New York: Bloomsbury,
2003.

Kelley, Robin D. G. "Without a Song: New York Musicians Strike Out against
Technology." In *Three Strikes*, edited by Howard Zinn, Dana Frank, and Robin D.
G. Kelley, 124–59. Boston: Beacon, 2001.

Kemp, Mark. *Dixie Lullaby: A Story of Music, Race and New Beginnings in a New
South.* New York: Free Press, 2004.

Kempton, Arthur. *Boogaloo: The Quintessence of American Popular Music.* New York:
Pantheon, 2003.

Killen, Buddy, with Tom Carter. *By the Seat of My Pants: A Life in Country Music.*
New York: Simon and Schuster, 1993.

King, Stephen A. *I'm Feeling the Blues Right Now: Blues Tourism and the Mississippi
Delta.* American Made Music Series. Oxford: University of Mississippi Press, 2011.

Kline, Ronald D. *Consumers in the Country: Technology and Social Change in Rural
America.* Baltimore: Johns Hopkins University Press, 2000.

Kosser, Michael. *How Nashville Became Music City, U.S.A.: 50 Years of Music Row.*
Milwaukee: Hal Leonard, 2006.

Kot, Greg. *I'll Take You There: Mavis Staples, the Staple Singers and the March Up
Freedom's Highway.* New York: Scribner, 2014.

Kramer, Michael J. *The Republic of Rock: Music and Citizenship in the Sixties
Counterculture.* New York: Oxford University Press, 2013.

Laird, Tracey E. W. *Louisiana Hayride: Radio and Roots Music along the Red River.*
American Musicspheres. New York: Oxford University Press, 2005.

Lassiter, Matthew. *The Silent Majority: Suburban Politics in the Sunbelt South.*
Politics and Society in Twentieth-Century America. Princeton, N.J.: Princeton
University Press, 2006.

Lauterbach, Preston. *The Chitlin' Circuit and the Road to Rock and Roll*. New York: W. W. Norton, 2011.

Lavette, Bettye, with David Ritz. *A Woman Like Me*. New York: Blue Rider, 2012.

Leftwich, Nina. *Two Hundred Years at Muscle Shoals: An Authentic History of Colbert County, 1700–1900*. Tuscumbia, Ala.: Nina Leftwich, 1935.

Leigh, Steve. "Stax Story," 2007, http://www.sl-prokeys.com/stax/stax-mclemore.htm.

Letwin, Daniel. *The Challenge of Interracial Unionism: Alabama Coal Miners, 1878–1921*. Chapel Hill: University of North Carolina Press, 1998.

Lewis, George H. "The Commercial Art World of Country Music." In *All That Glitters: Country Music in America*, edited by George H. Lewis, 161–73. Bowling Green, Ohio: Bowling Green University Popular Press, 1993.

Lhamon, W. T. *Raising Cain: Blackface Performance from Jim Crow to Hip-Hop*. Cambridge: Harvard University Press, 1998.

Lisle, Andria. "Late Late Party." Liner notes to Charles Axton, *Late Late Party*. Light in the Attic Records, 2011.

Lott, Eric. *Love and Theft: Blackface Minstrelsy and the American Working Class*. Race and American Culture. New York: Oxford University Press, 1995.

MacLean, Nancy. *Freedom Is Not Enough: The Opening of the American Workplace*. Russell Sage Foundation Books. Cambridge, Mass.: Harvard University Press, 2006.

Malone, Bill C., and Jocelyn Neal. *Country Music, U.S.A.* 3rd rev. ed. Austin: University of Texas Press, 2004.

Malone, Bill C. *Don't Get above Your Raisin': Country Music and the Southern Working Class*. Music in American Life. Urbana: University of Illinois Press, 2002.

———. *Singing Cowboys and Musical Mountaineers: Southern Culture and the Roots of Country Music*. Mercer University Lamar Memorial Lectures. Rpt. Athens: University of Georgia Press, 2003.

Marcus, Greil. *Mystery Train: Images of America in Rock 'n' Roll Music*. Rpt. New York: Plume, 2008.

Maultsby, Chuck. "The Story of Disco Sucks." August 2006, http://chuckmaultsby.net/id11.html.

Mazor, Barry. *Meeting Jimmie Rodgers: How America's Original Roots Music Hero Changed the Pop Music Sounds of a Century*. New York: Oxford University Press, 2009.

McCann, Bryan. *Hello, Hello Brazil: Popular Music in the Making of Modern Brazil*. Durham, N.C.: Duke University Press, 2004.

McKee, Margaret, and Fred Chisenhall, *Beale Black & Blue: Life and Music on Black America's Main Street*. Baton Rouge: Louisiana State University Press, 1993.

Meintjes, Louise. *Sound of Africa! Making Music Zulu in a South African Studio*. Durham, N.C.: Duke University Press, 2003.

Millard, Bill. "Urban Cowboy." In *The Encyclopedia of Country Music*, edited by Paul Kingsbury, 561. New York: Oxford University Press, 1998.

Miller, Karl Hagstrom. *Segregating Sound: Inventing Folk and Pop Music in the Age of Jim Crow*. Refiguring American Music. Durham, N.C.: Duke University Press, 2010.

Minchin, Timothy, and John A. Salmond. *After the Dream: Black and White Southerners since 1865*. Civil Rights and the Struggle for Black Equality in the Twentieth Century. Lexington: University of Kentucky Press, 2011.

Minutaglio, Bill. *In Search of the Blues: A Journey to the Soul of Black Texas*. Southwestern Writers Collection Series/Wittliff Collections. Austin: University of Texas Press, 2010.

Nager, Larry. *Memphis Beat: The Lives and Times of America's Musical Crossroads*. New York: St. Martin's, 1998.

Neal, Mark Anthony. *Songs in the Key of Black Life: A Rhythm and Blues Nation*. New York: Routledge, 2003.

———. *Soul Babies: Black Popular Culture and the Post-soul Aesthetic*. New York: Routledge, 2002.

———. *What the Music Said: Black Popular Culture and Black Life*. New York: Routledge, 1999.

Newman, Mark. *Entrepreneurs of Profit and Pride: From Black-Appeal to Radio Soul*. New York: Praeger, 1988.

O'Connor, Douglas, and Gayla Cook. "Black Radio: The 'Soul' Sellout." In *Issues and Trends in Afro-American Journalism*, edited by James S. Tinney and Justine J. Rector, 233–46, Lanham, Md.: University Press of America, 1980. (Originally published in *Progressive*, August 1973.)

Osmond, Donny, with Patricia Romanowski. *Life Is Just What You Make It: My Story So Far*. New York: Hyperion, 1999.

Owen, Marguerite. *The Tennessee Valley Authority*. New York: Praeger, 1973.

Palao, Alec. Untitled liner notes to Dan Penn, *The Fame Recordings*. Ace Records, 2012.

Pecknold, Diane, ed. *Hidden in the Mix: The African-American Presence in Country Music*. Durham, N.C.: Duke University Press, 2013.

———. "Making Country Modern: The Legacy of Modern Sounds in Country and Western Music." In *Hidden in the Mix: The African-American Presence in Country Music*, edited by Diane Pecknold, 82–99. Durham, N.C.: Duke University Press, 2013.

———. *The Selling Sound: The Rise of the Country Music Industry*. Refiguring American Music. Durham, N.C.: Duke University Press, 2007.

———. "Travel with Me: Country Music, Race and Remembrance," In *Pop When the World Falls Apart*, edited by Eric Weisbard, 185–200. Durham, N.C.: Duke University Press, 2012.

Pence, Richard, ed. *The Next Greatest Thing*. Washington, D.C.: National Rural Electric Cooperative Association, 1984.

Perlstein, Rick. *Nixonland: The Rise of a President and the Fracturing of America*. New York: Scribner, 2009.

Peterson, Richard. *Creating Country Music: Fabricating Authenticity*. Chicago: University of Chicago Press, 1999.

"Phillip Mitchell Interview, 2001." Interviewer unknown. http://www.soulcellar.co.uk/phillip/PhillipInterview2001.htm.

Pohlmann, Marcus. *Opportunity Lost: Race and Poverty in the Memphis City Schools*. Knoxville: University of Tennessee Press, 2008.

Pride, Charley, with Jim Henderson. *Pride: The Charley Pride Story*. New York: W. W. Morrow, 1994.

Radano, Ronald. "Hot Fantasies: American Modernism and the Idea of Black Rhythm." In *Music and the Racial Imagination*, edited by Ronald Radano and Phillip V. Bohlman, 459–80. Chicago Studies in Ethnomusicology. Chicago: University of Chicago Press, 2003.

———. *Lying Up a Nation: Race and Black Music*. Chicago: University of Chicago Press, 2003.

Reid, Jan. *The Improbable Rise of Redneck Rock*. New ed. Jack and Doris Smothers Series in Texas Life, History and Culture. Austin: University of Texas Press, 2004.

Richards, Keith. *Life*. New York: Little, Brown, 2010.

Robinson, Zandria F. *This Ain't Chicago: Race, Class and Regional Identity in the Post-soul South*. New Directions in Southern Studies. Chapel Hill: University of North Carolina Press, 2014.

Rounce, Tony. Untitled liner notes to *Something New to Do: The Phillip Mitchell Songbook*. Kent Records, 2013.

Rushing, Wanda. *Memphis and the Paradox of Place: Globalization and the American South*. New Directions in Southern Studies. Chapel Hill: University of North Carolina Press, 2009.

Savage, Barbara Dianne. *Broadcasting Freedom: Radio, War and the Politics of Race, 1938-1948*. John Hope Franklin Series in African American History and Culture. Chapel Hill: University of North Carolina Press, 2009.

Segrave, Kerry. *Jukeboxes: An American Social History*. Jefferson, N.C.: McFarland, 2002.

Self, Robert O. *All in the Family: The Realignment of American Democracy since the 1960s*. New York: Hill & Wang, 2013.

Seltzer, George. *Music Matters: The Performer and the American Federation of Musicians*. Metuchen, N.J.: Scarecrow, 1989.

Shapiro, Peter. *Turn the Beat Around: The Secret History of Disco*. New York: Faber & Faber, 1995.

Shaw, Arnold. *The World of Soul: Black America's Contribution to the Pop Music Scene*. New York: NTC/Contemporary, 1970.

Sidran, Ben. *There Was a Fire: Jews, Music and the American Dream*. New York: Nardis, 2012.

Smith, Michael Buffalo. "Johnny Sandlin: Southern Producer, Engineer and Musician," spring 2004, http://swampland.co/articles/view/title:johnny_sandlin.

Smith, Suzanne E. *Dancing in the Street: Motown and the Cultural Politics of Detroit*. Cambridge, Mass.: Harvard University Press, 1999.

Sokol, Jason. *There Goes My Everything: White Southerners in the Age of Civil Rights, 1945-1975*. New York: Vintage, 2007.

Sotiropolous, Karen. *Staging Race: Black Performers in Turn of the Century America*. Cambridge, Mass.: Harvard University Press, 2008.

Southern, Eileen. *The Music of Black Americans: A History*. 3rd ed. New York: W. W. Norton, 1997.

Staff of the Country Music Hall of Fame and Museum. *Night Train to Nashville: Music City Rhythm & Blues, 1945–1970*. Nashville: CMF Press, 2004.

Stahl, Matt. *Unfree Masters: Popular Music and the Politics of Work*. Refiguring American Music. Durham, N.C.: Duke University Press, 2012.

Steptoe, Tyina. "An Ode to Country Music from a Black Dixie Chick." *Oxford American*, no. 54 (Spring 2006): 26–27.

Stimeling, Travis. *Cosmic Cowboys and New Hicks: The Countercultural Sounds of Austin's Progressive Country Music Scene*. New York: Oxford University Press, 2011.

Streissguth, Michael. *Outlaw: Waylon, Willie, Kris and the Renegades of Nashville*. New York: IT Press, 2013.

Strom, Phoebe. "Defining Dixie: Country Music's Evolution of Identity." *Rhodes Historical Review* 16 (Spring 2014): 33–64.

Sugrue, Thomas. *Sweet Land of Liberty: The Forgotten Struggle for Civil Rights in the North*. New York: Random House, 2008.

Suisman, David. *Selling Sounds: The Commercial Revolution in American Music*. Cambridge, Mass.: Harvard University Press, 2009.

Sullivan, Bartholomew. "White House Rocks to Sounds of Memphis." *Memphis Commercial Appeal*, April 9, 2013, http://www.commercialappeal.com/news/2013/apr/09/white-house-rocks-to-sounds-of-memphis-soul/.

Terry, Wallace. *Bloods: Black Veterans of the Vietnam War: An Oral History*. New York: Ballantine, 1984.

Thomas, Pat. *Listen Whitey! The Sounds of Black Power, 1965–1975*. San Francisco: Fantagraphics, 2012.

Tosches, Nick. *Country: The Twisted Roots of Rock and Roll*. Rpt. New York: Da Capo, 1985.

Trotter, James M. *Music and Some Highly Musical People*. Rpt. New York: Johnson Reprint Corporation, 1968.

Tyler, Kieron. "Bobby Womack: Across 110th Street, BBC Four," June 8, 2013, http://www.theartsdesk.com/new-music/bobby-womack-across-110th-street-bbc-four.

Tyson, Timothy B. *Radio Free Dixie: Robert F. Williams and the Roots of Black Power*. Chapel Hill: University of North Carolina Press, 1999.

Van Deburg, William L. *New Day in Babylon: The Black Power Movement and American Culture, 1965–1975*. Chicago: University of Chicago Press, 1992.

Vincent, Rickey. *Party Music: The Inside Story of the Black Panthers' Band and How Black Power Transformed Soul Music*. Chicago: Lawrence Hill, 2013.

Wade, Dorothy, and Justine Picardie. *Music Man: Ahmet Ertegun, Atlantic Records and the Triumph of Rock 'n' Roll*. New York: W. W. Norton, 1990.

Wald, Elijah. *Escaping the Delta: Robert Johnson and the Invention of the Blues*. New York: Amistad, 2004.

———. *How the Beatles Destroyed Rock 'n' Roll: An Alternate History of American Popular Music*. New York: Oxford University Press, 2009.

Walsh, Stephen. "Black-Oriented Radio and the Civil Rights Movement." In *Media, Culture and the Modern African American Freedom Struggle*, edited by Brian Ward, 67–81. Gainesville: University of Florida Press, 2001.

Ward, Brian. "Jazz and Soul, Race and Class, Cultural Nationalists and Black Panthers: A Black Power Debate Revisited." In *Media, Culture and the African American Freedom Struggle*, edited by Brian Ward, 161–96. Gainesville: University of Florida Press, 2001.

———. *Just My Soul Responding: Rhythm and Blues, Black Consciousness and Race Relations*. Berkeley: University of California Press, 1998.

———. *Radio and the Struggle for Civil Rights in the South*. New Perspectives on the History of the South. Gainesville: University of Florida Press, 2006.

Ware, Vron, and Les Back. *Out of Whiteness: Color, Politics and Culture*. Chicago: University of Chicago Press, 2002.

Weidner, Daniel. *Black Arts West: Culture and Struggle in Postwar Los Angeles*. Durham, N.C.: Duke University Press, 2010.

Werner, Craig. *A Change Is Gonna Come: Music, Race and the Soul of America*. Ann Arbor: University of Michigan Press, 2006.

———. *Higher Ground: Stevie Wonder, Aretha Franklin, Curtis Mayfield and the Rise & Fall of American Soul*. New York: Crown, 2004.

Wexler, Jerry, with David Ritz. *Rhythm and the Blues*. New York: Knopf, 1993.

Whisnant, David E. *All That Is Native and Fine: The Politics of Culture in an American Region*. Chapel Hill: University of North Carolina Press, 1983.

Whiteis, David. *Southern Soul-Blues*. Music in American Life. Urbana: University of Illinois Press, 2013.

Wilkinson, Christopher. "Hot and Sweet: Big Band Music in Black West Virginia before the Swing Era." *American Music* 21, no. 2 (Summer 2003): 159–79.

Willman, Chris. "'Only in America' Could Obama Borrow the GOP's Favorite Brooks & Dunn Song." *Entertainment Weekly*, August 29, 2008, http://popwatch .ew.com/2008/08/29/only-in-america/.

———. *Rednecks and Bluenecks: The Politics of Country Music*. New York: New Press, 2005.

Wilson, Pamela. "Mountains of Contradictions: Gender, Class and Region in the Star Image of Dolly Parton." *South Atlantic Quarterly* 94 (Winter 1995): 109–34.

Wiltz, Teresa. "Yee Haw! The Rise of Black Country," April 21, 2009, http://www .theroot.com/views/yee-haw-rise-black-country?page=0%2C0.

Woodard, Komozi. *A Nation within a Nation: Amiri Baraka (LeRoi Jones) and Black Power Politics*. Chapel Hill: University of North Carolina Press, 1999.

Woods, Clyde Adrian. *Development Arrested: Race, Power and the Blues in the Mississippi Delta*. London: Verso, 1998.

Younger, Richard. *Get a Shot of Rhythm and Blues: The Life of Arthur Alexander*. Tuscaloosa: University of Alabama Press, 2000.

Zak, Albin. *I Don't Sound Like Nobody: Remaking Pop in 1950s America*. Ann Arbor: University of Michigan Press, 2010.

Zanes, Warren. *Dusty in Memphis*. 33 1/3 Series. New York: Continuum, 2004.

FILMS

Atlantic Soul. BBC documentary, 2007.

Built for the People. Directed by Sean and Andrea Fine. Documentary Channel, 1999.

History of Rock and Roll: Rock and Roll Explodes. Directed by Andrew Solt. Time/Warner Films, 1995.

Jerry Wexler: Soul Man. BBC documentary, 1999.

Mighty Field of Vision. Directed by Jason Thrasher and Patterson Hood. ATO Records/Play It Again Sam/Destroyer Easter Bunny Productions, 2011, http://drivebytruckers.com/episodes.html.

Muscle Shoals. Directed by Greg "Freddy" Camalier. Magnolia Pictures, 2013.

Respect Yourself: The Stax Records Story. Directed by Robert Gordon. PBS, 2007.

Rock and Roll: "Respect." Directed by David Espar and Robert Levi. PBS, 1995.

Sweet Home Alabama: The Southern Rock Saga. Directed by James Maycock. BBC, 2012.

Twenty Feet from Stardom. Directed by Morgan Neville. Tremolo Productions, 2013.

Index

Calloway, Harrison, 125
Campbell, Little Milton, 206 (n. 32)
Campbell, Mary, 172
Cantwell, David, 72
Capitol Records, 10, 21, 93, 128, 141, 150, 152, 169; Black Power movement and, 103–4, 105–6; FAME Studios and, 106–12, 118, 124, 125
Capricorn Records, 165–66
Carrigan, Jerry, 28
Carter, Clarence, 124, 166, 186, 210 (n. 12)
Carter, Jimmy, 156, 165
Cashbox, 36, 86, 129, 140, 142, 152, 167
"'Cause I Love You" (Rufus and Carla Thomas), 55
CBS Records, 93
Chalmers, Charles, 75
Champion Records, 72
Chapman, Leonard, 145
Charles, Ray, 27, 31, 36, 133, 138, 154, 160, 172, 174, 191
Cher, 70, 113
Chess Records, 22, 27, 113
Chrisman, Gene, 84
Chuck Wagon & the Wheels, 231 (n. 44)
Civil rights movement, 14, 97, 99, 151, 152, 154, 166, 171, 177, 186, 191, 202 (n. 16); R&B/soul and, 21, 82; rock 'n' roll and, 21, 23; country and, 21, 128–29; Memphis sound as metaphor for, 45–46, 66–67, 78–79; Al Bell and, 85–86; Fair Play Committee, 91; and new southern musicians, 155–56, 161; disco and, 178, 181. *See also* Black Power movement; Integration
Clark, Petula, 70
Clark, Roy, 174
Claunch, Quinton, 70
Clayton, Merry, 162
Cliff, Jimmy, 101–2
Cline, Patsy, 25
Club Handy (Memphis), 49
Color blindness: musical crossover and, 36; country music and, 129–31, 137; country-soul triangle as symbol of,

192; New Right and, 224 (n. 5)
"Color Him Father" (Linda Martell), 144
Columbia Records, 74
Combine Music, 160
Confederate imagery, 152, 154, 156, 162–63
Congress of Racial Equality (CORE), 89
Conservatism. *See* New Right
Couch, Tommy, 182
Country music: whiteness and, 1–3, 4, 10–11, 18, 25, 33, 35–36, 38, 39–40, 42, 65, 70, 128–30, 132–33, 136, 138–39, 144–45, 146, 147–48, 149, 154, 159, 161, 166, 180–81, 190, 202 (n. 7); conservatism and, 1–3, 4, 10–11, 23, 127, 128–30, 131–33, 134, 140–42, 147, 149, 153, 159, 161–62, 164–65, 191 (*see also* New Right); integration and, 2–3, 14, 21, 23, 129–30, 135–36, 141, 149, 154, 155–56, 160–62, 190–91; as marker of southern progress, 4, 11, 151, 152–53, 165, 168–69, 178, 179, 180, 189–90, 191 (*see also* New South); early development of, 7, 16–17 (*see also* Hillbilly music); incorporation of black music, 8, 11–12, 18, 25, 35–36, 71–73, 153, 159–60, 163, 167–69, 170, 171–76, 178–81, 188, 190; R&B/soul musicians' interest in, 13, 17–18, 29, 30, 39, 51, 54–55, 133, 146, 172; Nashville and, 13–14, 17–18, 20–21, 24–25, 27, 31, 33–34, 40, 71–73, 129, 131–34, 135–36, 139–40, 148–49, 153, 159, 161, 168–69; radio and, 16–18, 30, 36, 134, 139, 146, 168, 171, 173; black musicians in, 21, 25, 36, 130–31, 133–39, 146, 147–49 (*see also* Pride, Charley); Memphis and, 23–24, 51, 52–53, 55, 62, 66, 70–71, 88, 95, 168, 173–74; Muscle Shoals and, 26–29, 30, 37–38, 101–2, 124, 131–32, 141–44, 168. *See also* Nashville sound; Outlaw country

Fairlanes, 26, 27

Fair Play Committee (FPC), 91–93, 96–97

"Fallen Star, A" (Bobby Denton), 26

Fame Gang, 118–19, 125

FAME Studios, 5, 9, 10, 35, 42, 68, 72,
111, 113, 123, 139, 148, 160, 162, 167,
168, 171, 172, 182, 183, 187; symbol of
interracial collaboration, 13–15, 190;
labor at, 14–15, 32, 34, 112; development of, 27; Arthur Alexander and,
29–33, 37–38, 74; Jimmy Hughes
and, 38–39; reputation as site of
musical crossover, 38–40, 74–75,
123–24; Joe Tex and, 40–41, 126;
Jerry Wexler and, 43, 44–45, 74–78;
Aretha Franklin and, 74–78; Wilson
Pickett and, 75; departure of Muscle
Shoals Rhythm Section, 98, 112;
Capitol Records and, 103–4, 106–9,
111; Candi Staton and, 109–10;
Bobbie Gentry and, 109–11; George
Soule and, 115–17; George Jackson
and, 116–17, 118, 183; and Fame Gang,
118–19; and Osmonds, 118–21; shift
to white artists, 124, 169; decrease
in opportunities for black musicians,
124–25; Terry Nelson and, 141, 143.
See also Hall, Rick; Sherrill, Billy

"Fancy" (Bobbie Gentry), 110

Felts, Narvel, 179

"Fighting Side of Me" (Merle Haggard), 128

Floyd, Eddie, 125

Foley, Red, 25

Folk music, 64, 81, 147, 203 (n. 23)

Ford, Fred, 51, 210 (n. 16)

"Forever" (Little Dippers), 26

Foster, Fred, 228 (n. 23)

Franklin, Aretha, 2, 83, 91, 106, 112, 150,
154, 169; session at FAME Studios,
74–78; as symbol of Black Power, 79,
80, 82, 87

Frat circuit, 28, 47, 182

Fraternity of Record Executives (FORE),
219 (n. 51)

Freeman, Charlie, 60, 80

Friendship ideology, 192

Friskics-Warren, Bill, 150

Fritts, Donnie, 35, 69, 160

From Elvis in Memphis (Elvis Presley),
68

"FTA" ("Fuck the Army") Tour, 147

Gaillard, Frye, 153

"Games People Play" (Joe South), 150

Garland, Phyl, 65, 66, 73

Garnett, Bernard E., 93–94

Gavin, Bill, 94

"Gee Whiz" (Carla Thomas), 55, 58, 61, 87

Gentry, Bobbie, 109–11

George, Nelson, 178, 185

"Get Involved" (George Soule), 116–17,
118, 183

"Get It Up" (Ronnie Milsap), 179

Gibbs, Georgia, 223 (n. 39)

Gilbert, David, 205 (n. 27)

Gillett, Charlie, 78, 155

Gilley's Nightclub (Houston, Tex.), 180

Giovanni, Nikki, 79

"God Bless America (For What?)"
(Swamp Dogg), 148

Goldwax Records, 70

Gordon, Robert, 49, 55, 59, 202 (n. 12),
203 (n. 21), 215 (n. 111), 217 (n. 6)

Gordon, Roscoe, 206 (n. 32)

Gortikov, Stanley, 105

Gospel, 17, 22, 34, 70, 88, 109, 126, 146,
147, 150, 157, 173, 183; influence
on R&B/soul, 38–39, 55, 178, 185;
Memphis sound and, 61, 62; Staple
Singers and, 99, 101, 102

Govenar, Alan, 185

Grammy Awards, 71, 150

Grand Ole Opry, 16, 39, 53, 54, 132, 133,
138, 174, 191

Gray, Dobie, 228 (n. 22)

Greaves, R. B., 113

Green, Al, 176, 177

Greene, Jeanie, 157

Greene, Marlin, 157

"Green Onions" (Booker T. and the MGs), 58–59, 62

Gregory, Mickey, 97

Griffin, Booker, 81, 122–23

Grimes, Howard, 59

Grissim, John, 72–73

Guirado, Peter, 65

Guralnick, Peter, 4–5, 31, 45, 49, 82, 84, 191

Haggard, Merle, 3, 128–29, 130, 132, 138, 142, 161, 171, 179, 227 (n. 18)

Hall, Joe, 62, 74

Hall, Linda, 38

Hall, Rick, 8, 9, 13, 15, 20, 39, 70, 110, 111, 116, 141, 143, 192; development of FAME Studios, 26–28; Arthur Alexander and, 31–34, 37–38; reputation for musical crossover, 37–38, 42–43, 118, 123–24; Jerry Wexler and, 44–45, 74–78; Wilson Pickett and, 75; Aretha Franklin and, 76–78; conflict with studio musicians, 78, 112; Capitol Records and, 103–4, 106–9, 111; Muscle Shoals sound and, 106–7, 111, 112, 123–24; Osmonds and, 118–21; inspiration for other studio owners, 165, 182. *See also* FAME Studios

Hall, Willie, 97

Hamilton, Marybeth, 204 (n. 5), 210 (n. 25), 230 (n. 30)

Handy, W. C., 22

"Harper Valley PTA" (Jeannie C. Riley), 139–40, 142, 144

Harris, Ray, 74

Hawkins, Roger, 101–2

Hayes, Isaac, 84, 87–88, 89, 95, 177, 212 (n. 57)

Hazziez, Yusuf. *See* Tex, Joe

Hebb, Bobby, 72

The Help (Kathryn Stockett), 159

"He Made a Woman Outta Me" (Bobbie Gentry/Bettye Lavette), 111

Hemphill, Paul, 132, 140

Hentoff, Nat, 174

Hilburn, Robert, 161

Hill, Z. Z., 169, 183–84, 186

Hillbilly music, 7, 16, 18, 20, 25, 51, 135, 145, 204 (n. 5). *See also* Country music

Hinton, Eddie, 69, 102, 115

Hip-hop, 186–87, 189, 190

Hi Records, 62–63, 68, 70, 74, 173, 191

Hirshey, Gerri, 178

Hirt, Al, 73

"Hold What You've Got" (Joe Tex), 40–41, 43, 126

Hood, David, 102, 113, 114

Hood, Patterson, 222 (n. 25)

Hoskyns, Barney, 5, 178

Houston, Tex. *See* Southern rock

Howard, Jan, 132

Hues Corporation, 179

Hughes, Jimmy, 38–39

Hunter, Mark, 180

Hustle & Flow (2005), 232 (n. 1)

"I Ain't Got No Business Doin' Business Today" (George Jones), 179

"I Believe the South Is Gonna Rise Again" (Tanya Tucker), 227 (n. 3)

"I Can't Wait Any Longer" (Bill Anderson), 167–69, 178

"I'd Rather Be an Old Man's Sweetheart (than a Young Man's Fool)" (Candi Staton), 109, 111, 183

"If Loving You Is Wrong (I Don't Want to Be Right)" (Luther Ingram/Barbara Mandrell), 174

"If You're Not Back in Love by Monday" (Merle Haggard/Millie Jackson), 138

"If You're Ready (Come Go with Me)" (Staple Singers), 101

"I Gotcha" (Joe Tex), 126

"I'll Take You There" (Staple Singers), 101–2, 113

"I'm A White Boy" (Merle Haggard), 128–29

"I Never Loved a Man (the Way I Love

You)" (Aretha Franklin), 76, 79

Ingram, Luther, 97, 98, 174

Integration, 162, 190, 192; country-soul triangle as symbol of, 3, 14, 45, 190, 192; Memphis sound as metaphor for, 3, 45–47, 61, 65–67, 73–74, 78–79, 84–86, 89, 92, 94–95, 97, 103; rock 'n' roll and, 23–24; of musical genre, 23–24, 36, 40, 42, 63–64, 121, 144, 150, 155, 157, 159–60, 162; of musicians, 25, 35, 40, 49–51, 60–61, 120–21, 156, 160–61, 162; at FAME Studios, 39, 40, 41, 74–75, 120–21; at Stax Records, 52–53, 56–58, 60–61, 94–95, 101; AFM and, 60; NATRA and, 90; Black Power movement and, 92, 100–101; Staple Singers and, 99–101; at Muscle Shoals Sound Studio, 100–102, 114–16; Muscle Shoals sound as metaphor for, 106–7, 109, 110, 117, 125–26; Charley Pride and, 134, 136, 161; "The School Bus" and backlash, 140–41; Willie Nelson and, 161

International Musician, 72, 135

"In the Midnight Hour" (Wilson Pickett), 213 (n. 69)

Introspect (Joe South), 150

"Irma Jackson" (Merle Haggard), 129

"Is a Bluebird Blue?" (Conway Twitty), 28, 35

Isbell, Jason, 222 (n. 19)

"I Wanna Fall in Love" (Dolly Parton), 179

Jackson, Al, Jr., 57–58, 59, 84, 100

Jackson, George, 111, 116, 118, 125, 183, 184

Jackson, Jesse, 88–89, 91, 170

Jackson, Michael, 121–22

Jackson, Millie, 17, 117, 125, 138, 176, 177, 231 (n. 41)

Jackson, Wayne, 50, 51, 53, 56

Jackson 5, 118, 121, 124

James, Mark, 70

Jarrett, Ted, 21, 210 (n. 16), 226 (n. 68)

Jazz, 17, 22, 88, 185, 204 (n. 5), 212 (n. 58), 229 (n. 9); Nashville sound and, 25, 72, 139, 153, 172; Memphis sound and, 51, 55, 59, 62; Charlie Rich and, 172–74

Jennings, Waylon, 159, 162, 171

Jim Crow. *See* Segregation

Johnson, David, 148

Johnson, Dexter, 26

Johnson, Jaimoe, 228 (n. 33)

Johnson, Jimmy, 77, 78, 84, 89, 112, 114

Joiner, James: and Spar Publishing, 26; and Tune Records, 26

Jones, Booker T., 58–59, 86, 100, 159, 220 (n. 60)

Jones, George, 159, 172, 179, 187–88, 206 (n. 47)

Jones, Lee, 84, 223 (n. 54)

Jones, Roben, 70, 77, 203 (n. 21)

Jones, Thomas, 184

Joplin, Janis, 67

Jukeboxes, 17–18, 20, 35 142, 145

Just a Lil' Bit Country (Millie Jackson), 138, 231 (n. 41).

Karenga, Maulana, 232 (n. 62)

Keisker, Marion, 205 (n. 29)

Kemp, Mark, 153–54

Kenton, Stan, 173

Killen, Buddy, 32, 44, 72; early career, 25–26; relationship with Joe Tex, 39–43, 126–27, 167–68; disco and, 167, 178–79

King, Albert, 73

King, B. B., 233 (n. 5)

King, Coretta Scott, 91

King, Martin Luther King, Jr., 86, 89; assassination, 4, 65, 66, 82, 83–85, 87, 89, 97, 118, 121, 125

King, Stephen A., 231 (n. 59)

King, Wayne, 165

King Curtis, 77

King Records, 205 (n. 15), 205 (n. 22)

Kingsley, James, 111

Muscle Shoals Rhythm Section, 118, 177; relationship with Al Bell, 83, 98–99, 100–102; departure from FAME Studios, 99, 112; Staple Singers and, 100–102; Atlantic Records and, 112–13; confusion over racial identity, 112–15. *See also* Muscle Shoals Sound Studio

Muscle Shoals sound: erasure of black involvement in, 8, 107, 117–18, 124–25, 155, 166; racial contradiction, 10; relationship to Memphis sound, 10; Rick Hall and, 106–7, 111, 112, 123–24; as symbol of integration, 106–7, 111, 113, 121, 125–26, 154, 156; Black Power and, 106–7, 125–26; as vehicle for white redemption, 107; disco and, 176, 183

Muscle Shoals Sound Studio, 5, 10, 112–17, 143, 159, 168; Stax Records and, 98, 100–101, 104; Atlantic Records and, 112–13; decline in black sessions, 124–25, 169; Willie Nelson and, 159, 161: Southern rock and, 161, 162: disco and, 177, 183–84. *See also* Muscle Shoals Rhythm Section

Musical color line, 7, 9, 14, 15, 20, 23

Musicians' union. *See* American Federation of Musicians

"Mustang Sally" (Wilson Pickett), 75

My Lai incident, 130, 141

Nashville, Tenn., 2–3, 7, 9, 10–11, 16, 68, 93–94, 190; country music and,14, 20–21, 24–26, 72–73, 129–31, 132–37, 139–41, 144, 146, 148–49, 153–54, 159–61, 167–69, 171–73, 174, 176, 178–81, 187–88 (*see also* Outlaw country); recording industry in, 14, 20–21, 24–26, 32, 33–34, 35–37, 44–45, 71–73, 129–31, 133–37, 139–41, 144, 148–49, 153–54, 164, 167–69, 173, 174, 176, 178–81, 187–88; R&B/soul music and, 18–20, 25, 33–34, 35–37, 40, 72, 126, 140, 144, 153–54, 159–60,

167–69, 171–73, 174, 176, 178–81, 187–88; Memphis and, 21, 24–25, 45, 71, 96, 173–74; segregation in, 21, 149, 226 (n. 68); Muscle Shoals, Ala., and, 25–27, 28–29, 31, 33–34, 37–38, 39–41, 72, 130–31, 141–42, 144, 161, 168, 172–73. *See also* Country-soul triangle; Nashville sound

Nashville sound, 32, 33, 139, 161, 168; development of, 24–25; black music and, 25, 133, 172, 176, 178; as symbol of cultural change, 36, 129, 181; relationship to Memphis sound, 55, 71-72; Outlaw country and, 153, 159. *See also* Countrypolitan

National Academy of Recording Arts & Sciences (NARAS), 71, 95, 139

National Association for the Advancement of Colored People (NAACP), 89, 92, 97

National Association of Television and Radio Announcers (NATRA), 90, 99, 103, 118, 123, 125, 126, 146, 156; Miami convention (1968), 91–93; Stax Records and, 94, 96–97; Capitol Records and, 105–6

National Association of Working Women ("9 to 5"), 231 (n. 39)

Nation of Islam, 126

Neal, Mark Anthony, 82, 202 (n. 6)

Nelly, 190

Nelson, Terry, 141–43

Nelson, Willie, 8, 152, 188, 228 (n. 21); symbol of New South, 153; Jimmy Carter and, 156; black music and, 159; perceived opposition to mainstream country, 160; Charley Pride and, 161–62; civil rights movement and, 161

New Deal, 204 (n. 4). *See also* Rural electrification

Newman, Floyd, 56

New Right: country music and, 10–11, 127, 128–29, 131–32, 140–42, 149, 156; white backlash and, 129, 132,

triangle and, 15–18; as early professional opportunity for musicians,
16–17, 21, 23, 25, 38, 48, 55, 85–86,
139, 149; musical influence on triangle artists, 16–17, 31, 51, 55, 58,
116, 146, 173; race and, 16–17, 35, 116,
121–22, 133, 134, 136, 145; promotion
of recordings at stations, 34, 56, 182;
as site of black activism, 90–94. *See
also* Grand Ole Opry; WDIA; WLAC
R&B/soul music, 3; relationship to
country music, 1–2, 4, 5, 16–17,
25, 28–29, 33, 36–38, 39–41, 53,
70–73, 95, 129–30, 133, 136, 137–38,
144–45, 147–49, 159–60, 167–69,
171–74, 176, 187–88, 190–91; blackness and, 1–4, 15, 16, 18, 21, 23–24,
28, 30–31, 38, 40, 42, 56, 64–65, 69,
70, 76–77, 79, 80–83, 87–88, 93–94,
99, 100–102, 106–7, 109, 113–14,
116–17, 121–23, 129–30, 136, 137–38,
144–45, 154–55, 160, 176–78, 184–85;
Muscle Shoals and, 13, 14, 15, 26–27,
29–30, 38–41, 74–78, 98–102, 103–4,
105–27, 176–77 (*see also* Muscle Shoals
sound); development of, 16, 18, 43,
44; on radio, 17, 18–20, 25, 90–92,
93–94, 105–6, 121; Nashville and,
18–21, 25, 33–34, 71–73, 93–94, 95,
139, 144, 148, 167–69, 171–73, 174, 176
(*see also* Nashville sound); segregation and, 20–21, 23, 28, 35–36, 42,
47–50, 60–61; Memphis and, 21–23,
45–71, 79, 80, 83–90, 93–99, 103–4,
176–77 (*see also* Memphis sound);
white musicians and, 22–23, 25–29,
48–50, 55–56, 60–61, 65, 67, 68–69,
76–77, 80, 91–92, 96–97, 101–2, 106–7,
109–10, 111–17, 118–19, 120–26, 153,
154, 156–57, 159–60, 165–66, 171–74;
Black Power movement and, 80–83,
88–95, 99, 100–104, 105–7, 114, 121,
123–24, 125–27, 155, 177; as symbol of
tradition, 169–70, 181, 182–85, 186 (*see
also* Malaco Records). *See also* Disco

R&B World, 138
Randolph, Boots, 27
Randy's Record Shop. *See* Wood, Randy
Reagan, Ronald, 11, 166, 169, 171, 186
Record World, 85
Redding, Otis, 61, 87, 91, 115, 143, 165
Redding, Zelma, 143
"Redneck" (Joe South/Swamp Dogg),
150
Reggae, 101–2
Reinert, Al, 161
Reid, Jan, 153, 157, 161
"Respect Yourself" (Staple Singers), 101
Reverse Great Migration, 171, 185
Rhodes, Hari, 122
Rhythm, Country and Blues (various
artists), 190
Rich, Charlie, 173–74, 176
Richards, Keith, 113
Richbourg, John "John R.," 19–20, 28,
72, 90, 228 (n. 23)
Richie, Lionel, 190
Riley, Billy Lee, 57, 58
Riley, Jeannie C., 139–40
"Ring My Bell" (Anita Ward), 182
Ritter, Tex, 132, 225 (n. 35)
Robinson, Jackie, 136
Robinson, Zandria F., 232 (n. 64)
Rockabilly, 23, 25, 28, 53, 57, 173
Rock music. *See* Rock 'n' roll
Rock 'n' roll, 27, 34, 73, 88, 92, 150,
152, 170, 203 (n. 18), 203 (n. 23),
204 (n. 4), 212 (n. 58); as cultural
symbol, 14, 23–25, 35, 71, 145, 170,
184, 190; artists in Muscle Shoals,
113, 124; swamp music and, 157–58.
See also Rockabilly; Southern rock
Rodgers, Jimmie, 190
Rodgers, Nile, 180
Rolling Stone, 65, 72, 153, 155
Rolling Stones, 107, 113, 124
Roosevelt, Franklin D., 15
Rossington, Gary, 228 (n. 37)
Royal Spades, 49–51, 53, 55. *See also*
Mar-Keys

industry and, 164–65; Houston, Tex., and, 165, 180

"South's Gonna Do It Again" (Charlie Daniels), 152, 162

"South's Gonna Rattle Again" (Hank Williams Jr.), 152

South's Greatest Hits (various artists), 165–66

Sovine, Red, 133

Spar Publishing, 26, 32

Springfield, Dusty, 69–70, 115, 158

SSS International Records, 140, 144

Stafford, Tom: FAME Studios and, 26–27; Arthur Alexander and, 31–32, 34, 208 (n. 91)

Stampley, Joe, 173

Staple Singers, 3, 115, 126, 143, 154, 169, 177, 187; Al Bell and, 98–99; civil rights movement and, 99; Booker T. and the MGs and, 99–100; at Muscle Shoals Sound, 101–2; as symbol of musical blackness, 113–14

Staples, Mavis, 101–2, 113–14, 222 (n. 25)

Staples, Pervis, 99

Staples, Roebuck "Pops," 102, 150

Staton, Candi, 109, 111, 183

Stax Fax, 85, 94–95, 99

Stax Museum of American Soul Music (Memphis), 232 (n. 2)

Stax Music Academy (Memphis), 232 (n. 4)

Stax Records, 5, 51, 68, 73, 80, 111, 123, 155, 156, 157, 159, 170, 174, 176, 186, 192, 203 (n. 21); Black Power movement and, 9–10, 83, 87–90, 93–103; Jerry Wexler and, 44–45, 61, 74–75; as symbol of integration, 45, 57, 60–61, 66, 84–85, 94–96, 99, 103, 190–91; Memphis sound and, 52, 57–58, 61–62, 64, 66–67, 87–89, 94–95, 103; development of, 52–56; racial tensions at, 56, 59–60, 75, 89, 96–97; aftermath of King assassination and, 83–85; Al Bell and, 86–90, 93–103, 113, 185; Nashville and, 95;

Muscle Shoals and, 98–102, 106, 113, 125

"Steal Away" (Jimmy Hughes), 38–39

Steinberg, Lewie, 56, 57, 58, 59–60, 66, 74

Steinberg, Luther (Lou Sergeant), 57

Stephenson, Wolf, 182

Steptoe, Tyina, 180

Stevens, Ray, 139

Stewart, Jim, 55, 56, 57, 58, 68; country music and, 53, 70; Memphis sound and, 62, 64, 66–67, 85, 94–95

Stewart, Rod, 113, 124

Stimeling, Travis, 162

Student Nonviolent Coordinating Committee (SNCC), 89

Studio 54 (New York, N.Y.), 179

Sugarland, 233 (n. 5)

Sun Records, 45, 47, 53, 54, 55, 57, 173, 192; development of country-soul triangle and, 22; racial appropriation and, 22–24, 65, 135; integration and, 23–24, 191. *See also* Phillips, Sam

"Suspicious Minds" (Elvis Presley), 214 (n. 93)

Swamp Dogg. *See* Williams, Jerry

Swamp music, 11, 151; country music and, 153, 160; as symbol of New South, 153–54, 156–57, 163, 191; racial politics of, 154–56, 157–59, 166

"Sweet and Innocent" (Fairlanes), 27

"Sweet Home Alabama" (Lynyrd Skynyrd), 162–63

"Sweet Inspiration" (Sweet Inspirations), 214 (n. 93)

Sweet Inspirations, 84

Sylvia, 179

"Take a Letter Maria" (R. B. Greaves), 113

Talley, Bob, 59, 64

Taylor, Johnnie, 186, 224 (n. 2)

Tea Party, 190

Teen Town Singers, 55

Tejano music, 162

Tennessee Valley Authority (TVA), 15–16,

country music and, 146, 147–49; and
politics, 147, 149; Muscle Shoals and,
148; Joe South and, 149–50
"Willie and Laura Mae Jones" (Tony Joe
White/Dusty Springfield), 157–59
Wilson, Julian, 141
WLAC (Nashville), 18–20, 21, 27, 28, 34,
48, 72, 90, 102, 116, 148
WLOW (Portsmouth, Va.), 146
Womack, Bobby, 68, 125, 138, 176, 177
"Woman Left Lonely" (Charlie Rich), 174
Wonder, Stevie, 174, 191
Wood, Bobby, 47, 58, 68
Wood, Randy, 19–20, 33. *See also* Dot
Records
Woodard, Dino, 91, 93, 96–97, 100
Woods, Clyde Adrian, 185
Wright, Andrew, 124–25

Wynette, Tammy, 171

Yelawolf, 190
Yorke, Bob, 105
"You Better Move On" (Arthur
Alexander), 26, 39, 42, 72, 123;
as metaphor for country-soul
triangle, 13–15; recording of, 32–33;
marketing of, 34–35; symbol of
musical crossover, 36; effect on
FAME Studios, 37–38
"You Better Move On" (George Jones and
Johnny Paycheck), 187–88
Young, Reggie, 61, 62, 206 (n. 44)
Younger, Richard, 14, 28, 33, 36
"You Said a Bad Word" (Joe Tex), 126

ZZ Top, 165